QUIET,
PLEASE

QUIET,
PLEASE

Dispatches from a Public Librarian

BY SCOTT DOUGLAS

DA CAPO PRESS
A MEMBER OF THE PERSEUS BOOKS GROUP

Designed by Linda Harper
Set in 12.5 point Granjon by The Perseus Books Group

Library of Congress Cataloging-in-Publication Data

Douglas, Scott, 1978–
Quiet, please : dispatches from a public librarian / by Scott Douglas.
   p. cm.
  ISBN 978-0-7867-2091-0 (alk. paper)
  1. Douglas, Scott, 1978- 2. Public librarians—California—Biography. 3. Public libraries— California—Anecdotes. I. Title.
Z720.D68A3 2008
020.92—dc22
[B]

                                                                                          2007041309

Published by Da Capo Press
A Member of the Perseus Books Group
www.dacapopress.com

Da Capo Press books are available at special discounts for bulk purchases in the U.S. by corporations, institutions, and other organizations. For more information, please contact the Special Markets Department at the Perseus Books Group, 2300 Chestnut Street, Suite 200, Philadelphia, PA 19103 or call (800) 255-1514 or e-mail special.markets@perseusbooks.com.

10 9 8 7 6 5 4 3 2 1

This book is dedicated to Mom and Dad.

Chapter 372.6	Being the Chapter
-LIBR-	in Which Our Hero Discovers
Librarians	He Wants to Be a Librarian
Can't Read:	

"You catch a guy on a computer jacking off, just get a librarian—don't try and handle it yourself." That was the first thing Faren, the library manager, said to me on my first day of work.[1]

I was a library page.

Library page is the lowest place you can be on the library totem pole. Besides putting books back on the shelf, the library page is also responsible for doing the jobs that nobody else feels like doing, which include, but are not limited to, cleaning up vomit, washing the windows, scraping gum off the tables, moving furniture, and keeping a watchful eye out for male patrons who are jacking off on the computer. Being a library page also means you are stupid until you can prove otherwise.

---

1. Faren was short, soft-spoken, and had a peaceful disposition. The words didn't exactly fit her.

"So tell me why you want to work here?" This was the next thing Faren said to me. She asked the same question of all the new employees as a way of showing politeness. She didn't care about my answer, but I didn't know this,[2] so I told her with great passion how I loved books and was even studying literature in college—I told her all of this while she checked her e-mail. When I finished my monologue, she yawned and then asked, "Do you know how to cut paper?"

I looked at her, confused. "Paper?"

She nodded. "We have a bundle of fliers that need to be cut in two—you'd have to use the paper cutter. Do you think you'd be able to do that?"

I got nervous. I imagined that I had said something wrong, and she had marked me out as an idiot. But it wasn't that at all. Like I said, a page is stupid until proven otherwise, and apparently I hadn't proven otherwise. I wanted to assure her that I really *was* smart, but instead I just nodded and assured her I knew how to use a paper cutter.

"Great!" Faren said, adding as I walked out the door of her office, "And make sure you don't cut off any of your fingers. I hate filling out incident reports for stuff like that—it's so time-consuming."

❧

A form of pornography is what lured me to the library. To be more precise, a stripper lured me to the library. It's not as kinky as it sounds. I was young, in college, and in need of a new job, but not actively seeking one. I was looking for the sports section when

---

2. Library pages came and went quite frequently, so nobody got too attached for several weeks.

the classified section fell to the ground and conveniently opened to the job listings. As I bent down to pick up the section, a large-busted, scantily clad woman looked back up at me. I was morally outraged and violated by the ad, and felt I owed it to the poor woman to at least find out what she was advertising. It was a local strip bar looking for new strippers, and they were using the large-busted, scantily clad woman to entice applicants. Seeing no other pictures to be morally outraged and violated by, I went to put the classified section down. But then another job ad caught my eye. It said, in bold letters:

DO YOU LIKE BOOKS?

I liked books. I kept reading. The ad was for a library page in the City of Anaheim. It was dry and simply written—it basically said, "Come shelve books." Most people probably passed the ad off as too boring, but to me it sounded like a literary haven. I applied, was hired, and thus began my library career.

I was sent to a small branch library built in the sixties. It sat next to a park, off all the main streets of the city. It was hidden, and everyone seemed to like it that way. The furniture was as old as the library itself. The carpet was stained. The paint on the walls was faded. There was the smell of old books, a smell that has a way of making all libraries seem the same. Some say that smell is asbestos. It was a run-down little library, but no one seemed to notice.

Those who came into the building made it seem like their secret little library. It had been there for nearly fifty years, and most of the city's residents had never heard of it, let alone been inside. Its parking lot was small, but no one cared, because most patrons walked. People didn't go there for research—that task was left to the city's larger library three miles away. They went there for books that would help them escape.

Over 20 countries share the number-one rank for literacy, with 99.9 percent of their country being able to read. Niger and Burkina Faso take the bottom two literacy positions, with less than 15 percent of their citizens being able to read. The combined population of both these countries is 27 million, which means there are 23 million people who can't read.

It doesn't take a genius to figure out that the better you can read, the better you're going to do in life. But there are statistics to back this as well. Studies from the National Assessment of Adult Literacy (NAAL) put a scale on literacy. A person who reads poorly will make about $18,000 a year, while a person who reads at the highest level will make over $40,000 a year. So basically this means you will make $20,000 more if you prefer to read Tolstoy over Grisham.

The United States spends millions every year to come up with stats like the ones above, which, if they're lucky, will take up a ten-second spot on the evening news. While this money could go to things like literacy programs, we all know it won't because Americans are suckers for lists and statistics. To find out more useless statistics on literacy, visit the NAAL's Web site at http://nces.ed .gov/NAAL.

---

3. This is a commercial society; we can't take anything without a commercial break. So periodically I will fill this book with short pointless interludes to fill your mind with nonsense. It is my hope that such breaks will distract you from the contents of this book, if only for a moment, so you can regroup and return to the pages with a fresh sense of interest.

I didn't want to be known as "the page who might cut his fingers off if you don't watch him carefully," so by my second day of work I had set out to prove myself to my new library coworkers. I wanted to give them insight into just how well-read I was, which, in turn, would make them deem me worthy of working in such a literary place or, at the very least, make me appear smart enough not to cut my fingers off on the paper cutter.

I chose my weapon carefully: a tattered and carefully marked-up paperback copy of *The Crying of Lot 49*.[4] At precisely 12:14 (a time I had observed that most librarians took their lunches), I entered the staff room and bravely pulled my paperback novel to my face and began to read. The room was empty, but I knew that someone surely would join me before my fifteen-minute break ended.

As it happened, a librarian entered not even two minutes later. Her name was Edith. She was a short, pale-faced woman with thick black glasses and a mole the size of a dime on the left side of her chin. She appeared to be at least fifty, but I later learned she was only thirty-six.

She looked at my book oddly and asked, "What's that in your hand?"

I set the book down and proudly said, *"The Crying of Lot 49."*

---

4. Coincidentally, a first edition of this book can be found at the library where I worked. If you bought this from a used book dealer, it would set you back well over $100.00; if, however, you checked it out at the library and then said it went missing, you would only have to pay $10.00. The book was purchased in 1966 when the price of the book was about $5.00, and since the library doesn't account for inflation the price has stayed the same. Why $10.00? There's a $5.00 processing fee. Keep in mind, however, that this is a library copy with mold, crusty pages, and a funky smell. Which, as it happens, some people are really into.

Edith studied the cover curiously and then asked, confused, "You're reading it?"[5]

I took her confusion as intrigue—intrigue that someone my age would read such a challenging book for pleasure. I believed in that moment that she was already marking me in her head as someone of intellect who would definitely go places in the library world. I sat up straight, adjusted my glasses, and looked down at the book as I thoughtfully explained.

"Pynchon writes like a dream[6]—his words, his ideas—they're so absurd, and yet equally real—symbolic, no doubt, of the pathos of man."

I had formed my words perfectly in my mind, and I knew they must have deeply impressed her, maybe even moved her. Then I looked up from the book. She wasn't staring at me impressed; she wasn't staring at me at all.

She was looking in the refrigerator door behind me. "Is that ham and cheese sandwich yours?" she asked me.

"No."

"It's been in the refrigerator for two days now. No one's claiming it, and I don't have a lunch. If anyone asks where it went, tell them it was probably someone on the cleaning crew."[7]

---

5. There are actually a number of things you can do with a book besides read it, and I've witnessed librarians doing several, including, but not limited to, setting it under a table leg to make the table more straight, cutting out the images on the cover to use for the storytime craft, pulling out the pages and crumbling them up to use as shipping protection in a box, taking note of how handsome or ugly an author photograph looks and sharing their thoughts with anyone around them, and attaching it to the bottom of their shoes and seeing who can slide the furthest on a tile surface.

6. A dream I've never really wanted to be a part of.

7. Our cleaning crew, as I later learned, was, historically, blamed for everything—missing books, staplers, tape, and once, even a piece of carpet. The crew did not speak English and probably never knew half of the things they had been blamed for.

I wasn't sure what to think as I watched her get the sandwich. How could I not have impressed her? I convinced myself that she was just being stubborn. I was only a library page—a peon in the library field. To someone as high up on the library chain of command as a librarian, the page was only someone who shelved books, not someone who had ideas, and surely not someone who read Pynchon. I convinced myself as she returned to the table with her sandwich that I would just have to work a little bit harder at proving I was someone worthy of indulging in literary conversation with. "I've read everything Pynchon's written at least once, but this book is my favorite."[8]

With her mouth full of food, Edith asked, "Is Pingkong a new writer?"

I tried not to show surprise. She was messing with me—she had to be messing with me. She had to know who Pynchon was. I decided it was best just to play her game. "He's been writing books since way before I was born."

She studied my face and seemed to be sizing up how old I was. Then she announced proudly, "I'm not much of a reader—don't have time for it."

"And you're a librarian?" The question came out as insulting, but I didn't mean it that way.

"What's that supposed to mean?" she asked. Before I answered, she took the book from my hand and looked carefully at the front cover. She handed it back and then asked a question that still echoes in the back of my mind. "I've heard the name before—isn't he the guy that's going out with Julia Roberts?"

"I don't think so."

8. This is a lie. I had in fact read only *The Crying of Lot 49*.

"I'm pretty sure he is," she said, and then she added, "I loved Julia in *Hook*. Did you see that movie?"

Sure, I've been known to watch a romantic comedy or two, but I couldn't let her know that. In fact, I had even seen and enjoyed *Hook*, as well as almost every other movie Julia Roberts has starred in. I had come into the break room to create the persona of a page who was sort of smart and even knew how to operate a paper cutter. I just didn't believe I could pass this off by saying, "Julia's great, and speaking of *Hook*, did you know Roberts actually had an assistant whose sole responsibility was making sure her feet were clean? Yes, I know, it's geeky that I know this fact. But it says so right in the credits—check it out." So instead I said, "I'm not much of a Julia Roberts fan."

Edith's face suddenly became red and the tone of her voice hostile as she asked, "How can you say that? Julia's one of the most talented actresses that ever lived. Have you even seen *Pretty Woman*?"

I nodded and then added, "I just prefer foreign films, is all." This actually is not true, but it seemed like the smart thing to say.

"Like movies from other countries or something?"

I nodded.

"Oh." She took another bite from her sandwich, and explained, "I know this guy who was all into this British movie, and he was always trying to get me to watch them. It was something with a snake in the title—like Mighty Python. One day I finally agreed to watch it, and I hated it—I hate any movie with subtitles."

Before I could reply, Gina, another librarian, entered the room, and Edith explained pointing at me, "He's never seen *Hook*."

The way she pointed her finger made me wish I had just said that Julia Roberts was a great actress.

"You've never seen *Hook*?" Gina asked, like it was the oddest thing she had ever heard. "Julia Roberts played Tinker Bell in it—she was absolutely amazing. Of course she's amazing in anything she's in."

"Like *Pretty Woman*?" Edith suggested excitedly.

"Oh, my gosh. That last scene where Richard pulls up in the limo to carry her away was like one of the most beautiful scenes in the history of all cinema."

As they both proceeded to go into loud giggling and to reminisce of the career of Julia Roberts, I made the assumption that they had each never seen *The Seventh Seal*. I was tempted to spoil their *Pretty Woman* fantasy by telling them about the early version of the script, which had Roberts addicted to cocaine and taking the whoring job with Richard Gere in part because she wanted to go to Disneyland but didn't have any money on account of her addiction. The movie ends, in this version, with Roberts and her hooker friend on a bus heading to Disneyland. Richard Gere also tosses Roberts out of his car in this version. (I am not joking about any of this.) I decided not to tell them this because (A) it didn't seem like an intelligent thing to know, and (B) it would probably seem odd that I know such freakish facts about an actress I had just said I didn't really like. So instead, I finished my break in the bathroom, where I pretended what had just happened was just part of some cruel and strange library hazing ritual.

I returned to shelving after my bathroom moment and spent the next hour convincing myself that the librarians in the break room were just poseurs—that they could not have actually graduated from an accredited graduate school and come away with Julia Roberts as a conversational topic. They had to have gone to some Internet school where people had only to log in to be eligible for a degree—and if they were too stupid to log in then they had someone log in for them, in which case the fact that they were associated with a person smart enough to log into the computer made them eligible for the degree.

As I shelved my truck of books, I felt like someone was staring at me. I turned, and saw a large black-and-white photo of the city's first children's librarian, the woman the library was named after. I had noticed the photo before, but had not paid attention to it. I stared at her eyes and her face, and I wondered what she had been like. She looked like someone who had read me stories when I came to the library as a child—someone who knew, and had read, every kids' book the library owned. She looked like everything a librarian should be.

When I returned to shelving, Edith was sitting quietly at her desk studying a copy of *Pride and Prejudice* that had just arrived at the library the day before.

"I love that book," I said.

"I couldn't get past the first sentence. It has really pretty illustrations though." She held up one of the drawings proudly so I could see.

Later in the day, I saw a patron go up to Edith as she displayed the new copy of *Pride and Prejudice* and say, "Can I check that out? I hear they're going to make a new movie out of it."

Edith handed her the book and said, "You can be the very first person to check it out."

The patron studied the cover and then looked up at Edith and asked curiously, "Have you read it?

"Oh, sure—Jane Austen is a wonderful writer."

"I've never read her, but I like anything by the Brontë sisters.[9] They write like her, right?"

Edith nodded. I wondered if she even knew who the Brontë sisters were.

The woman smiled and quickly went off to check out the book. Edith continued to shelve new books with a certain look of satisfaction on her face. I continued to shelve. That was that. I had gathered the facts and now knew the truth: the librarian of my youth was gone, and Edith[10] had replaced her.

I was in denial at first. I believed Edith to be an isolated case. I would find comfort by staring at the Dewey Decimal numbers and thinking to myself, *Poor ol' Melvil Dewey would be rolling in his grave if he knew about Edith.* This helped until I learned that Dewey himself was sort of an elitist racist dick. He was a brilliant dick, no doubt.[11] One would hope that it was librarians fighting for civil liberties, but Dewey ardently approved of segregation and opposed women's rights.

What I quickly learned was the dark truth about librarians: they simply did not find the time to read. For many, working with books for so long had made them uninterested in having anything to do with them outside of work.

---

9. All three sisters died way too young. Emily died of tuberculosis, which she caught from being out in the cold at her brother's funeral; Ann also died of tuberculosis; some believe Charlotte's death was caused by excessive vomiting during her first pregnancy; their father lived longer than his wife and all of his six kids. (Not one of his kids lived past the age of forty.)

10. I am told I should change identifying characteristics about characters who might seem to be portrayed a bit negatively, so as not to receive a lawsuit. That said, Edith had "Dukakis for President" tattooed to her forehead.

11. He began working on one of the most widely known classification systems (the Dewey Decimal System) at the age of twenty-three and started a journal (*Library Journal*) and cofounded a professional organization (the American Library Association) at the age of twenty-five.

Libraries for me had always been a place of knowledge, a place to see people who had spent their entire lives reading books and were eager to share their knowledge and love with you, a place I went to discover new ideas. Working at the library had shattered my vision of the library. And yet I stayed.

The longer I found myself within the confines of what I once had believed was a storehouse of knowledge and information the more I saw that the information was still there—it had just changed forms. For many years I had a vision in my head of that old reference librarian who used to sit behind a desk reading a book. She had been there when I was a kid; she knew everything, including which book was just right for me. I began to see, however, that this librarian of my youth was probably no different from Edith. To people who didn't know Edith—who just came to the library to ask her where a book was—Edith was this magical creature who knew all things and could do no wrong.

Edith didn't like to read in her free time, but she was a great children's librarian; she read to kids on a regular basis, and when she did they listened to each line of the book with eyes that begged to hear what came next. I saw in her something that I had never really thought about: it takes more to be a librarian than a love of books. Libraries were the place where people of diverse backgrounds and cultures could come together for the common pursuit of discovering something new. Librarians were the people who helped them find this discovery. Librarians weren't dumb or foolish people. Many librarians simply don't read. My world had for so long been about books and writing and anything remotely literary. The library—the place in my life that was full of books— began to teach me that books weren't everything.

I soon began to pay less attention to librarians and everything they weren't and more attention to the library patrons that visited each day. They were businessmen and women looking for books to get them ahead; they were mothers who didn't know how to read or speak English who were bringing their children in to get books because they knew that literacy could bring them a better life than they ever had; they were widowers who wanted to find books that would help them pass the time. They all had one thing in common: they wanted to learn—and they fascinated me. I began to see that librarians would change, technologies would change, even patrons would change, but the role of the library as the gateway to something greater would always stay the same.

As the years until I graduated with my literature degree became months, I began to have serious concerns about my future. I would soon have a degree in literature and I had no idea where to go with it. I began to wonder if the library was where my destiny lay.

Chapter 004.16	Being How,
-GATE-	for Better or Worse,
The Day of the	the Computer Changed
Gateway:	the Library Once and for All
	(and Why the Perverts Now
	Will Never Go Away)

I didn't think much about it when I walked to the staff entrance of the library and saw a large truck by the loading dock. I surely didn't think that the contents of the truck would, for better or worse, change the way libraries do business.

When I came into the library, I saw the twelve Gateway PCs sitting in their boxes by the reference desk. Art, an older librarian who was in charge of the library while Faren was on vacation, was standing near the boxes, looking quite confused.

"So now what?" Art asked the delivery guy.

The man smiled and said, "Now you solve the digital divide."

Art watched him leave and then turned to me. "So what do you know about computers?"

I shrugged. "I have one at home."

"You think you could put them out on the tables and get them set up?"

"Maybe you should wait until Faren gets back," Edith said. "There might be some kind of mistake."

"She won't be back for a week. I'll take the blame if something goes wrong." He turned to me. "Make sure nothing goes wrong, okay?"

I nodded and took to the task immediately. As I did so, the librarians and clerks all gathered round, as if I was unraveling something magical. Every now and again someone would say, "Careful now—you don't want to break it."

I looked at their curious stares and swelled with a sense of power. Each of them was much older than me, and yet here I was, a "know-nothing" page who suddenly had the keys to the future.

"They make the library look very modern," Edith said as I booted up the first of the PCs.

"We don't need them, if you ask me," Brenda, one of the library clerks, said. "Libraries are for books."

"Times change," Art said, and then stood in front of one of the computers. Everyone stood behind him. He moved the mouse slowly and stared at the cursor moving on the screen. I suddenly became unimportant and was pushed aside. I had hooked up the computers and now I was just a library page again.

"The man said to double click to open a program," Edith reminded Art.

Art nodded and clicked on top of an icon twice. "Look at that—that's our library!" He said, and then laughed as the Internet browser opened with the library's home page.

"You better be careful," Edith warned. "You don't want to break it."

Art nodded and stood, slowly backing away from the computer. "We'll fiddle around with it some more a little later."

As everyone started to walk away, Art put his hand on my shoulder and said quietly, "Wait. We men need to band together. Sometimes I feel all these women are conspiring. Don't you think?"

I shrugged.

"You *have* to see," Art insisted. "They plan all the time. Haven't you ever walked by a group of them and they get all quiet?"

"I guess."

"That's them planning. They have a stronghold over this profession, and we have to stick together."

"Okay."

"You don't believe me."

I laughed.

"This isn't a joke." He looked toward the front of the desk where two women hovered over the circulation desk. "Look around. There are fifteen people that work here and only three are men—and three is a high number!" He paused. "I want you to show me how to use these things—we can take back the library! They've been the heroes of this place for too long. It's time to evolve!"

I had had many conversations with Art during breaks. He was a nice man. He had worked for the library for over twenty years, and was full of interesting stories. I never realized how crazy he was until that moment. But I still liked him. Insanity, when used right, can be a true virtue.

~

There are two important periods in the evolution of the public library. The first was between 1883 and 1929, when over 1,600 libraries were built thanks to funding from Andrew Carnegie. His contributions mark the real beginnings of public libraries.

Before then, public libraries were stuffy research facilities that big cities liked to brag about to other big cities. It was the elitist version of "my penis is bigger than yours." If you lived in a small town, you were out of luck. No one saw any reason to give farmers and factory workers books.

When asked why he put so much effort into building public libraries, Carnegie would always tell the story of Colonel James Anderson, who, once a week, would open his personal library up to the boys of his neighborhood. Carnegie saw libraries as egalitarian institutions. He wanted everyone to have the same opportunity he did.

But Carnegie didn't just hand the money over to libraries. Instead, he considered himself a business partner with the city, giving a library to any town with at least one thousand people. The town would then be required to provide a site for the library and would be responsible for taxing themselves for 10 percent of Carnegie's gift. This tax would fund new books, maintain the library, and pay library staff. Carnegie's main concern was that once the library was built it would be supported for years to come. It was important to him that he wasn't seen as the "patron saint" of the library. As part of his guidelines he actually forbade them from hanging his portrait.

Large cities had a hard time accepting Carnegie's gifts. They balked at the idea of allowing just anyone into their libraries. Many of them used to close before five, just so factory workers wouldn't be able to visit when they got off work. By accepting Carnegie's gift, libraries could no longer keep "undesirables" out. Smaller cities stood to gain the most from Carnegie's generosity. Libraries were often built in the center of things, usually near a train station. They became a badge of pride, a way to show visitors that in *this* town people valued learning and books.

Patrons came and went that day, the Day of the Gateways, mostly ignoring the new computers. Some would comment—"Look at that"—or brag about the person they knew who was "an absolute computer whiz," but no one dared to ask if they could try. There was a great community need for the computers, but it would take months for the public to realize we had them.

Doris, a library regular, came in later that day to get her weekly dose of mystery novels. She claimed she had read every one that the library owned—twice. This sounds pretty incredible, but it's surprisingly not that rare. There were a few patrons who claimed to be making their way through the library's entire collection. One woman came in every week, same day, same time, and was going through the fiction in alphabetical order. (She was up to the letter *J*.)

Doris stared at the computer until Art walked up behind her.

"Come to check your e-mail, Mrs. McDonald?" Art said with a weak laugh.

"Heavens, no! When did these arrive, anyhow?"

I covertly listened to the conversation while pretending to sort books.

"Just arrived today."

"Never thought I'd see the day when computers were in the library." Doris looked at the computer screen closely. "My grandson, Gregory, he has one. He's a genius when it comes to them—he even says he has a home page that you can see from anywhere in the world. Whatever that means."[1]

---

1. Her grandson came into the library with her months later and he nearly got thrown out for looking at his home page. Turns out it was pornographic. Art was there that day and handled the situation pretty tastefully by making sure Doris didn't discover what the boy was doing. Her grandson never came to the library again.

"They're going to send all of us librarians to some sort of work-shop to teach us how to use them."

"Well, maybe you can show me. My Gregory's always telling me, 'Grandma, when are you going to get the Internet so I can e-mail stuff to you?' And I always say, 'Gregory, you can talk on the phone with me if you want to talk.' But I don't know—I guess it's the future, and I'm going to have to learn. If I don't die pretty soon."

"I'd be happy to show you how," Edith said coming up from behind, "just as soon as I figure it out."

Art looked angry, but he said nothing.

~

Some 100-odd years after Carnegie's largess, Bill Gates would follow in his footsteps and give birth to the second most impor-tant period in the evolution of public libraries. Gates, being ever so generous, decided that it was high time to give libraries computers. His generosity probably had more to do with long-term investment. By having computers in libraries, people who had never used them suddenly saw what all the fuss was about. It was similar to a strategy he used on college students. At the time we got the computers, students could buy Microsoft prod-ucts for dirt cheap. We're talking less than twenty bucks for the entire Office Suite, which sold in the store for well over $200. Why? Because when students got out into the working world, they would then naturally buy Microsoft products for their company.

Gates used the same strategy in rural areas that had never even heard of the Internet. He approached libraries and asked them how desperate they were for computers. The more desperate, the more computers.

~

The next day, while Art was at the reference desk, a teenager with a pierced nose came to the desk to ask if he could use a computer. Art didn't really like teenagers too much—especially teenagers with piercings—but, nonetheless, he smiled courteously and went over the policy for using the computer.[2]

After politely listening to Art ramble for just over a minute, the teen asked, "What's the computers' connection speed?"

"Connection speed?"

"Is it T1?"

Art shrugged and looked over at me. I nodded, and Art said, "That sounds right."

"All I have is dial-up at home. Can I use one?"

"Just sign your name."

The teen sat at a computer and began clicking, scrolling, and typing. Art watched, trying to make sense of things, but it was no use. The teen was in a zone that the librarian just couldn't understand.

A woman pretended to look for books on the donation table, but I knew she was covertly spying on the boy. Everyone in the library was spying, wanting to understand.

Another woman came to the desk shortly after the teen got on the computer. "I'm applying for a job and need to make a resumé," she said. "Can these computers do that?"

"I don't know," Art admitted. "I suppose they could. They're pretty fancy."

---

2. There were policies for pretty much everything in the building, from inappropriate uses of the water fountain to the priority of which books should be shelved first. The computer policy had been adopted a month before the library received the computers. It was laminated, carefully placed at the reference desk, and clearly outlined appropriate use of the Internet. Each day a patron came into the library to use the Internet, they were asked to read the policy and sign their name on a sheet of paper. They signed their name, but never read the policy.

"They have Word?"

"Word?"

"The computers. Do they have Word on them?"

"I'm not sure what you mean."

The teenager, who was listening, turned in his chair and said, "Yeah, they got it, lady."

Art smiled at the teen.

"It's real simple to create a resumé," the boy said. "Want me to show you?"

"That would be real nice," she said.

The next day, the boy brought a friend. He, too, was in "the zone." And the next day that boy returned with another friend.

Soon, all day long the computers were filled with people. Most of the librarians couldn't make sense of what these patrons did. They just watched and quietly imagined that they, too, were in the zone. But they weren't. They weren't in the zone.

One night, while Edith was closing the library, she caught two thirteen-year-old boys looking at pornography. "Tell me your phone numbers—I'm going to call your parents." She was shaking. I knew the boys could be trouble and quickly went to stand next to Edith to show support.

"Not our parents!" One of the boys laughed.

"You need to learn when to shut your piehole, old hag!" the other joined in.

They both stood and ran quickly from the computer to the door. At the exit door they both yelled "Bitch!" and held up their middle fingers.

Edith crossed her arms and watched the boys sadly. She looked at the library clerk, who seemed embarrassed. Edith stared quietly at the computer screen. Finally, she turned off the monitor. She was mostly quiet for the rest of the night.

The next morning, Edith sat in the staff lounge drinking coffee with Art, as had always been their morning library ritual. Art read the paper. Edith read a paperback mystery. I sat quietly on the couch—they didn't like it when I talked.

"I'm transferring," Edith said as she took a sip of coffee.

Art looked up from the paper. "Say it again?"

"I'm transferring."

"Transferring?"

Edith nodded.

"Really?"

She nodded.

"I didn't even know you were considering it."

"Times are changing, Art."

He nodded and said, "It wasn't because of last night, was it?"

"How'd you hear?" Edith asked.

Art looked at me and I looked down.

"Every day it's something new," Edith admitted. "I just can't keep up with it all. I've actually been thinking about it for quite some time. I feel like I'm not helping this library anymore. Things are too different."

"Of course you're still helping, Edith—no one knows more about children's books than you do. And the kids who come in here on class visits adore you."

Edith shook her head. "I just think it's time."

"The computers won't go away. You'll transfer and then in another few months that library will get one, too."

She nodded. "That's a few more months away. But it's not just that. You know how this library has changed. There are so many more people now. I just feel so overwhelmed sometimes."

Art nodded. I didn't know how it had been before, but I had heard from several that it had been pretty dead until Faren became manager. "We'll certainly miss you here."

Edith nodded and sadly looked down.

FOR SHELVING

Henry Adams declared in *The Education of Henry Adams* that Dynamo was one of the greatest achievements of mankind; he believed history would put it up there with the discoveries of Galileo and Columbus, and then he went a step further and declared it to be basically as great as God creating the world.

Most readers are probably wondering two things. One, was he right? And two, what the in the name of Bea Arthur is a dynamo? If you have to ask the second question, you have already answered the first.

A dynamo is basically a generator that can turn kinetic energy to electrical energy. It was not so much the dynamo that was important as the industrial revolution that followed it. For thousands of years revolutions had been man-made; then, for the first time, revolutions were created by machines. While the dynamo cannot be consider the sole force in all this, it certainly gave way to a chain reaction of new technologies such as the Internet. So, in that regard, Adams was right.

When he saw the dynamo, he saw the birth of God in some respects. Who would have thought then that he was right—that technology would essentially become man's God, the thing we put our hope in? We don't pray that God will put an end to cancer, we hope that science will find a cure; we don't believe that God will come and put an end to

(Continues)

(Continued)

the world, we believe that science will ultimately put an end to us;
and we don't believe in an eternal afterlife, we believe that if science
keeps advancing it will help us live longer.

I can't look at the computers in any library without thinking of
Adams and the dynamo and how true it is that we have evolved just
as Adams predicted we would. The dynamo has not only taken over
our homes and churches, it's taken over our libraries as well.

A single tear left Edith's eye as her very last class left the children's room. She had read to thousands of kids over the years.

A small staff party was thrown in her honor in the staff lounge, and everyone told stories of the past. The laughter broke up when two patrons began fighting about the public computers. It was a fight between two women. One yelled at the other for supposedly watching as she typed. (This was a problem that happened quite frequently. I never did understand it. I always tell people that it's a *public* library and everything on the computer is *public*. That means if you don't want people to know your credit card number, you'd better not put it on the screen. People always look at me confused when I say this and then go ahead and do it anyway. There were never any serious hacks into the library's computers, although, once, someone uploaded a bunch of pornographic pictures and was able to switch the book covers shown on the library's catalog with naked women. That was a clever prank.)

Michael was a lot like me. We both grew up in Anaheim and graduated from high school about the same year. We both were in college. And we both cited *Saved by the Bell* as instrumental in our teen years. The difference? He was hired as a part-time computer

clerk and I was a page. He had less than half the computer knowledge than I, but I wasn't bitter. (I was, in fact, bitter.)

Michael wasn't officially hired as Edith's replacement, but it
seemed that way, as Edith's position went unfilled. It was the
library administration's decision to hire staff who were more
computer savvy and pay them less than librarians. I was not even
told about the job opening, but, like I said, I wasn't bitter.

For over a month I fell behind shelving books because I had to
train Michael to use the computer. Apparently he had gotten a little carried away on his interview. He knew enough to keep his
job, but that was about it.

It wasn't fair, but that's life.

One afternoon, after helping several patrons on the computer, I
passed Art, who quietly mumbled, "Not fair, eh?"

I turned and looked at him curiously. "What's that?"

"Getting paid less than him, when you seem more qualified."

I shrugged but said nothing.

"You were just hired as a page—wouldn't have been right to
give you a better job when you were so new." He smiled to himself and said, "That's city politics for you."

I wasn't sure why Art was telling me this; it didn't exactly
make me feel any better. I started to leave, but before I could Art
stopped me again.

"How long before you graduate from college?"

"About a year and a half, I guess."

"And then?"

"What do you mean?"

"What will you do when you're finished?"

"Maybe get my MFA in writing or something."

"Well if that doesn't quite pan out, maybe you should give
library school a chance. We sure could use a few librarians with

computer knowledge." He paused, and smiled. "And male ones on top of that."

"I'll think about it."

Art nodded. "Do you think you know all there is about computers?"

"Not everything, but I know quite a bit."

He nodded. "Tell me what you know about libraries."

"What do you mean?"

"I mean just that. What do you know about them?"

I shrugged. "I know that you go there to get books. I don't get what you mean."

"Ever think of a world without libraries? Ever imagine why a community needs them?"

I shrugged. I hadn't really thought about that.

Art went on. "You have a lot to teach me about computers, but I have twenty years of libraries to teach you. I think we should work together, and one day maybe, just maybe, you can walk in these shoes."

"My feet are pretty big. You sure they'd fit into those shoes?"

Art smiled and then looked at the twelve computers in front of him. I followed his stare. The longer I looked at them the more I had a vision of what the library was turning into—a digital fortress where people used computers as primary sources, and books only if they couldn't find what they needed. I saw the future of libraries and saw where I belonged.

When I left that night, Art had dropped a flyer in my box. It was for a state grant to send city workers to get their master's in library science. They would pay for everything, and I didn't have to commit to anything. They were that desperate for librarians from my generation.

I graduated from school later that year, applied for the grant, and qualified. Soon I would embark to San Jose State, where I would supposedly become a librarian. Maybe I didn't have what it would take; maybe I wouldn't even *want* to be a librarian. But, as of that moment, I didn't really care. The tuition was free and it allowed me to put off my life choices for just a bit longer.

Chapter 355.0097	Being How I Prepared
-BOOT—	for My Pending Career
Boot Camp:	

I had interviewed for exactly four jobs in my life. I got all of them. I could have looked at this as a pro—seen the glass half full, if you will. But I don't think like that.[1] Not only was this my first professional interview,[2] it could also make or break me. Being the type of person who sees the glass as half empty, I was pretty sure it would break me.

Some of the librarians had coached me on what things I would be asked during the interview. Only one person, Brenda, the clerk, told me I didn't stand a chance. "You can't go from page to library technician without being a clerk—you got to do the steps."

---

1. I'm sort of bitter that way.

2. That is, for which I had to wear a tie.

"Never know."

Everything the librarians had coached me to do fell away when I walked into the room and saw the stone-cold looks of the interviewers. Not only was I certain this interview would break me, I didn't even see the glass anymore. It had simply vanished along with any hope of being a librarian. All I could see was Brenda laughing and saying proudly, "I told you so."

I recognized only one of the librarians. Her name was Dan.[3] Apparently her real name was Danielle and, back in the day, she had been dainty and graceful. But then she became a librarian and all the grace went away. One day she was getting a book and had her back turned. Someone approached her and mistook her for a man. Someone suggested calling her Dan after that as a cruel joke, but for whatever reason she wasn't offended. The name stuck and that's what she is called to this very day.

I looked around the room as I took my seat. It was intimidating in its simplicity. There were eight chairs, but only two were taken. The smell was like new office furniture. Blueprints for a new library hung on the wall. Nothing about it reminded me of a library. Except the interviewers. They were distinctively librarian—large-framed glasses, granny hairdos, and uptight frowns.[4] I half expected them to interview in library whispers and shush me if I answered too loudly. Instead their voices were booming and a little obnoxious.

Their first questions were simple and generic and were about why I wanted to work for the library and what I liked to read. These questions made me comfortable and confident. They made me drop

---

3. Yes, *her* name was Dan.

4. The stereotypes about librarians are largely true.

my guard. When my guard was completely dropped the real questions started. Questions about supervision and working with others; questions about improving literacy throughout the city; even questions about good old Melvil Dewey and his shelving system. Nothing about the questions seemed relevant to the position.[5]

I answered well (I thought). But the interviewers' faces made me wonder otherwise. Their faces looked angry. Their faces made me nervous.

Then, when my nerves were at a breaking point, they asked what different groups liked to read. I said the first thing that came to my mind: "Old people like mysteries." Dan looked really ticked. The other librarian had a smirk on her face. Then I remembered: Dan loved mysteries. Every year she hosted a large mystery gala and made it common knowledge to everyone that she liked mysteries more than anyone else did. It very well could be true that old people, for the most part, did read mysteries, but the fact that I admitted it was not something to brag about knowing in an interview.

That was the last question.[6] That was my last answer.[7]

I walked out certain that I would not get the job, that I would soon start library school without actually having a library job and would have to spend the next several months trying to find a way to pay for grad school while combing the want ads for any job to pay the bills.

Brenda meant something different to everyone on the library staff, and that meaningful something was never anything good. To

---

5. I soon learned that none of the questions had anything to do with the job.

6. Actually, the last question was whether I was handicapped.

7. Actually, the last answer was "no," but this is more dramatic.

some she was the person who told them they looked like a slob, commented about their weight gain,[8] or asked if someone's son was mentally challenged; to most she was the person who tried to boss them around. To me she had always just been a sad person who was always putting herself down and trying to pull others down with her because she didn't want to be alone in her self-loathing. She wasn't the kind of person anyone would wish dead, but she wouldn't be missed if she was pushed off a tall building.

When I got back to the library following the interview, Brenda asked politely, "So how'd the interview go?"

Her question seemed innocent enough but I knew Brenda always spoke with a double-edged sword, and I was always carefully guarded. I played it cool and just shrugged. "Could have been better, but we'll see."

"I'm sure you'll get it," she said, then looked down sadly. Then came the part where she would put herself down and try to pull someone down with her. "You'll get it and think you're better than me for it."

"Stop, Brenda! You know I never would do that."

"That's how it always is." She paused. Her lips appeared to snarl, and her tone seemed kind of satanic when she spoke again. "Don't think you'll be able to boss me around, though."

"Well, I promise you I won't," I said. I liked Brenda because she was paranoid; everyone was always out to get her and she complained about everything anyone did.[9]

"I'm sure you won't," Brenda said and then threw a book at my foot and walked away.

---

8. She was, in fact, three times the size of a normal woman.

9. I also liked her because she got in trouble for e-mailing the director of all the libraries a dirty joke.

"Looks like you just had a Brenda moment," Andy, a page, said, pushing a cart of books by me.

"Did she just throw a book at me?"

"I'm sure you had it coming."

FOR SHELVING

Boot camps aren't bad things; history is full of a great many follies that could have been avoided had people been properly trained.

In the late eighteenth century, the Austrian army wasn't exactly anything to brag about. Commanders were chosen by connections and officers often didn't speak the same language as their troops. In short, the army was a complete and utter joke. It probably wasn't a good time to be at war with Turkey, but, alas, they were.

On September 17, 1788, a group of Imperial Hussars[10] were sent across the Timisul River to stop the Turks from crossing. When the hussars got across the river they found a wagonload of gypsies who were more than happy to entertain them with liquor.

Infantry arrived a little later in the night. The hussars had no intention of sharing their booze and chased away the infantry. The infantry was, understandably, upset, so they came up with a scheme to get back at the hussars. They would pretend to be Turkish soldiers in order to scare the hussars away, but this only caused panic, confusion, and stupidity.

Everyone began fighting everyone. In darkness, shots were fired randomly at whomever each believed to be their enemies; those who weren't hit by bullets were trampled by the horses, which had been spooked by all the sounds of shooting.

---

10. Fancy word for a type of cavalry.

Their enemies, the Turks, did arrive two days later and found a big surprise—some 10,000 dead and wounded soldiers. Needless to say, the Turks won the battle without even trying—literally.

Somehow, in spite of insulting one of the interviewers, I got the job. I was on my way to a library career. I would be a library technician.[11] But getting the job really meant nothing. It didn't actually mean I was prepared to sit at that sacred post called the reference desk.[12]

In actuality, my idea of a librarian was Sylvia Marpole, Goofy's girlfriend from *An Extremely Goofy Movie*. She was reserved at work, but an animal after hours. I knew enough librarians to know how false this stereotype was, but I still liked to pretend. As much as the career interested me, I couldn't shake the feeling that I had made a mistake, that I would forever be sucked into the vacuum of the mundane and hate my job forever. It was hard not to wonder if I had chosen the job out of true love or convenience. Was I picking this job merely because that was all I knew?

I decided it was time to learn a thing or two about my chosen profession. As it turned out, I had a lot of catching up to do, as the history behind libraries is massive and dates back thousands of years. The books that I devoured became my boot camp for library school and libraries in general.

You really don't have to look further than the Old Testament to see how serious early civilizations were about recording and

---

11. The technical name for the person who does everything a librarian does, but gets paid less, on account of not actually having a master's degree.

12. Actually, it was called the information desk at my branch, because people don't know what reference means anymore.

storing facts about their people, but traces of people keeping track of their civilizations go back as far as the invention of writing. The precursors to libraries dated as far back as the earliest civilizations. In ancient Mesopotamia, clay tablets noted how many animals, baskets, and ideas were found in the community; much like the epic inventories found in the Old Testament, the ancient libraries were nothing more than catalogs of the society. As the library evolved, it slowly progressed into something more. The ancient Chinese, for example, would use a form of library to keep a record of what blessings they had asked of the gods.

It took hundreds of years for libraries to take on the form of cultural institutions of learning. At one point, having a library meant you really had made it in the world—you were the coolest cat on the block. The trouble with having your own personal library was where did you find material for it? You couldn't exactly go to the local Barnes & Noble and buy up whatever your heart desired. Kings solved this problem by going to war with other countries, stealing that culture's tablets, and putting them in their personal libraries.

And you think librarians today are little brats, with their fines and threats of taking you to collections over a two-dollar fee for returning a book late?[13] Early libraries were much worse. One of the first warnings found inside a book included the following:

He who breaks this tablet or puts it in water or rubs it until you cannot recognize it [and] cannot make it be understood, may Ashur, Sin, Shamash, Adad and Ishtar, Bel, Nergal, Ishtar of Nineveh, Ishtar of Arbela, Ishtar of Bit Kidmurri, the gods of heaven and earth and the gods of Assyria, may all these curse him with a curse

---

13. Libraries do not usually waste the time to take someone to collections unless the fine is greater than $20.

which cannot be relieved, terrible and merciless, as long as he lives, may they let his name, his seed, be carried off from the land, may they put his flesh in a dog's mouth [*Libraries in the Ancient World*, Lionel Casson, Yale University Press, 2002, p. 14].

The best part about such nasty notations was who the words were coming from. Often the librarians were priests and monks. I would pay good money to have a priest say the above phrase to me!

So what happened to all these early tablet-filled libraries? Civilization happened. The libraries, for the most part, ceased to exist when the empires that built them fell.

The next step in the evolution of the library occurred during the Greek empire. One shortcoming of previous libraries was that people didn't really know how to read. The Greeks built one of the first empires that cherished learning and the arts. As the Greek library began to flourish, a new trade was developed: bookselling. Just as merchants were trading goods at the ports, sellers began to sell books, which helped diversify collections.

All this gave way to the first great library: The Library of Alexandria.[14] This library, unlike many of the past, was public and open to anyone with fitting qualifications. It was the civilization's equivalent of a think tank; the RAND Corporation would eat their heart out if they saw the people who were members of this library: the most noted writers, poets, scientists, and scholars of their time. In return for being tutors to the ruler's children, they were given membership to the library, a good paycheck, food and lodging, and a tax exemption. In short, this civilization treated the brains of the society well, and the library was basically used as leverage to lure even more smart people to the city.

---

14. Founded approximately 300 BC.

Like other libraries of the past, the library of Alexandria some-times played dirty to get books for its shelves. Buyers were sent out with enormous amounts of money and the sole purpose of buying books. What they couldn't buy, steal, or barter for, they would copy. The policy of the library was to acquire everything.

What happened to this great library? That's a debate that's never been resolved. Some say fire, others war. In actuality, the library probably wasn't destroyed so much as it was simply neg-lected and forgotten; over time, it simply deteriorated.

After the great library of Alexandria, most libraries were held by private citizens. In the Roman Empire, the largest libraries belonged to producers of plays, who collected copies of plays for future use.

One of the final evolutionary developments of libraries, in later centuries, came about because of Christianity. Libraries of the Greek and Roman worlds were largely secular. During the birth of Chris-tianity, monasteries realized that the only way to do critical research was to build their own libraries. Thus, works by Basil, Eusebius, Augustine, and Jerome exist today largely because of the churches.

What would follow after these libraries would be the academic and public libraries that we know today.

～

Not long into my history of the library binge, I caught Anne, the librarian who was taking the place of Edith temporarily, sitting quietly at her desk meditating on a bookmark.

"Hey," I said brightly, "did you know kings used to go to war with other nations just so they could improve their personal library collection?"

Anne sighed and looked up at me, irritated. "I'm really busy right now, and I don't really care about what some king did to a library thousands of years ago. Who cares? Honestly?"

"Sorry."

"I know you're all motivated because you're starting school and it's exciting, but I just don't have time for it."

I nodded and watched as Anne continued to stare at her bookmark.

I thought about what Anne said for a long time. "Who cares?" Why should I care? It was really pretty simple. Why are libraries important? Because those buildings of long ago are what shaped the buildings of today. Without them I would be out of a job. Too often the things we cherish most are lost not because we don't find them pretty or useful anymore but because we simply forget why we cared in the first place.

To be great at something, you must look to the great ones of the past and improve on the ideas and techniques that they started. I was motivated to do better—to improve on the ideas of others. In short, I was ready for library school.

Chapter 973.931	Welcome to
-WELC—	Your New Career
9/11:	

Not long after I had been accepted to library school, I began working as a library technician. My first day of work was the week of September 11, 2001. I started my morning eating breakfast as I watched smoke coming from the two World Trade Center towers and listened to reporters saying the buildings might fall. I drank coffee as I watched people jump to their deaths from the burning towers. I listened to radio hosts describe the towers falling to the ground as I washed my hair. And finally, I heard for the first time a news reporter say "Our lives will never be the same" as I walked out the door to start my new job.

As I drove to work, I knew that terrorists had staged similar attacks in other parts of the country. I could see Disneyland in the distance[1] and wondered why they had left California out of their plan.[2]

The reporter had said the country would forever be changed, but I didn't consider this on that day. I spent the next eight hours answering the same two questions, "Are you open?" and "Can I use the Internet?" I watched the people come into the library going on about their lives. They still checked their e-mail. They still checked out their best sellers. And they still came in to do their homework. Maybe they just didn't want to deal with it, and maybe they didn't know how they were supposed to deal with it. How much they were affected by the attacks depended on which news station they watched and how long they watched it.

Faren was at meetings most of the day, which meant Anne was in charge. She told me to be conscious of everyone and made me read twenty pages of emergency procedures. Anne went by the book, which didn't really fit the library. As I read through the pages, and believed, like everyone else, that something catastrophic would happen any moment, a shadow appeared over me. I turned and saw Brenda staring down at me. She stood in such a way in front of my chair that I could not stand—she wanted me to look up at her.

"Let's get one thing straight right here and now," Brenda said, looking down on me. "You're a rookie. You may think you're high and mighty because you're going to grad school, but people

---

1. Disneyland is about two or three miles away, close enough to see the nightly fireworks and help the occasional confused tourists who are trying to find their way to the park.

2. Of course no one admitted it then because it would have been insensitive, but I did learn months later that many had this thought on their mind. It wasn't like we were jealous, but there was this deeply subconscious emotion of wanting to feel closer to the attacks and not being able to because we didn't have an attack close to our own home.

turn to me in times like this. I know how to handle things. I know the things to look for."

I should have just smiled and nodded, but I was young, immature, and didn't know any better.[3] I said, "So if people turn to you in times like these—if you're so good at dealing with problems—then why are you a clerk? You've been here longer than almost anyone else. How come you never got a promotion?"[4]

"How quickly you turn against me," Brenda said. "You'd think you'd have a little more respect in light of everything that's happened today. I'm really emotional right now. My sister's son lives there—he might be dead."[5]

~

When people talk about the cultural artifacts either destroyed or stolen during WWI and WWII, they will most likely cite paintings and sometimes churches. A frequently forgotten, but certainly important, part of what was lost was libraries.

In World World War I, Germans entered Belgium, a neutral country. All was well until August 25, 1914, when a couple of German soldiers were killed in the town of Louvain. The military decided the town needed to be punished for their deed. German soldiers executed 200 townspeople, then burned down historic buildings within the downtown area. One of the buildings was the library at the Catholic University of Louvain. Over 200,000 volumes were destroyed. It really upset a bunch of people and at the end of the war plans to restore it were included in the Versailles

---

3. I was also distracted by the alarming amount of nose hair growing out of Brenda's nose.

4. I am aware that I was being a dick.

5. As it turned out, her sister's son had lived in New York but he had moved three years prior to this, and he had never lived anywhere near the city; he lived just outside of Buffalo. But she, like so many others, wanted to have a connection to that day.

Peace Treaty. In 1928 the library opened its doors once more, only to be destroyed by German artillery in 1940. At the end of World War II it was rebuilt for the second time in less than twenty years.

Beginning with the invasion of Poland in 1939, Nazis sought not only to kill off Jews but to erase them from people's memory. One way this was done, as is the practice in all cases of "ethnic cleansing," was to destroy books and private collections. One of the most significant losses was the 1944 destruction of the National Library in Warsaw; over 600,000 volumes were destroyed. By the end of the war some 15,000,000 of the 22,500,000 volumes contained in Polish libraries had been lost.

Nazis became so gung ho about wiping all traces of Jews from the face of the earth that they formed a specialized squad to destroy synagogues, schools, and libraries. Many of these libraries contained rare books that were not available anywhere else in the world.

Not all was lost. At the end of the war many cultural artifacts and books that had been raided were recovered. The Jewish Cultural Reconstruction, Inc., was created to help collect and organize what was salvageable.

Class visits[6] were a regular thing at the library, four to six classes a day. The library was surrounded by two elementary schools within walking distance, neither of which had very good libraries, so they took advantage of ours.

A week after 9/11, a tall black man entered the library and loudly announced, "You have a bomb coming."

6. Class visits are when the little kids (prekindergarten to sixth grade) come to the library to hear a story, get a tour of the library, and find books to check out.

Most of the people in the library jumped; Brenda literally dived under the circulation desk.[7] I saw the class coming in behind the man, and knew what he was talking about. His comment didn't faze me. He apologized and said he shouldn't have said bomb. I agreed. For months there were certain things that you could not say or do. Everyone was edgy, and everything was suspect.

We received memos on what to do in case of an attack on the city, memos on proper emergency procedures, and memos about how to tell if a package possibly contained deadly chemicals, and we had to sign each memo signifying that we had read and understood it. There were several such memos the first six months, a few the next six months, and none in the years to follow. It seemed ironic that the city did everything to make sure we were all prepared after the attacks. Who strikes when people are prepared? I'm sure most people have forgotten those memos by now.

~

On Saturdays I frequently worked with Art. I liked Art because, on top of being slightly crazy, he wasn't afraid to be politically incorrect, even while he was working. One day I asked him what he did in the Korean War, and he said bluntly, "I killed people." And, as it turned out, he was serious. That's exactly what he did.[8]

---

7. The circulation desk is shaped in such a way that there really is little space for ducking, but she found a way to hang her head partially in one of the cabinets under the desk. Coincidentally, the reference desk does have a fair amount of ducking room, which might say something about who the library values. This is California—earthquake capital of the country—why not design the circulation desk with a little better ducking room? Maybe one day a clerk will sue because a book fell on her head during an earthquake when she had no place to take cover.

8. That is not, however, all he did. He had all kinds of cool war stories. Most of the time he helped on the mortar fire, so he probably never saw the person he killed, but he made no joke about being responsible for it.

During the months leading up to the Iraq War (part 2), he'd talk at great length[9] about why he believed the president wanted to go to war with Iraq. He showed me articles and told me about shows he'd seen and books he'd read. He questioned the president's intentions, and I admired him. So many people were consumed with the media. They trusted the information they received because they didn't want to take the time to question it. Art took the time to question the media, to look for other viewpoints.

I had started attending library school during this time, and I began to wonder why the teachers weren't preaching the same messages as Art.[10] I didn't think the school needed to get political and have faculty implement viewpoints, but I thought it was important to study the way media, both online and on TV, had radically changed the way people sought information. How can librarians teach others how to think critically and objectively when they themselves are not doing it?

Art never went to library school. I'm pretty sure all he had was an AA degree. He began working in libraries part-time after he retired from his first job. But Art taught me that, as librarians, we are responsible for teaching people how to seek information—and how to filter out fact from point of view. He taught me to look beyond people's degrees, and look instead at people's experience. Art had experience. He was one of the best librarians I ever knew.

~

9. Saturdays were slow, and talking was about the only thing we could do to pass the time. I honestly don't know why two of us were in the building together—it seemed like a waste of money—but I never complained, because I enjoyed the stories and the pay (about $17.50 per hour at the time).

10. Actually I sort of know why: schools are infatuated with being politically correct; everyone is so fearful of offending people who might in turn sue for having their rights violated that we've violated several other freedoms in the process.

You can make the case that some extremist Muslims have followed in the Nazis' footsteps, destroying libraries and trying to wipe out culture. Ironically, though, Islam is a very literate religion. It was an illiterate Mohammed who first encouraged his followers to copy the Koran, and thus made Islam a religion that values learning and books. Followers built libraries at a pretty rapid rate; by the end of the eighth century, the Abbasid dynasty had made Baghdad one of the world's premiere places for learning. Sadly, the Taliban did much to destroy history and culture throughout the 1990s.

In 1998, Taliban soldiers destroyed the library of Hakim Nasser Khosrow Balkhi Cultural Center in Kabul, Afghanistan. The soldiers must have been in a hurry, because they didn't even bother opening the doors. Instead, they got their rocket launchers and fired away at the main entrance. When they had finished their rocket job they entered the library and tossed any remaining books into the river. Not a single book survived the attack. The library contained over 50,000 volumes; many were rare manuscripts from the tenth century. Apparently the Taliban was angry because it contained Persian writings they didn't agree with; there was a different interpretation of Islam by the Persian minority. During this same period the Taliban had a death list out for several librarians in the region.

The Taliban did have the heart to leave the National Library of Afghanistan standing, but not for the sake of the books inside. They didn't believe people needed books, so those books were burned as fuel or used as food wrappers.

One of the Taliban's most disturbing acts of cultural destruction was that of the Buddhas of Bamiyan, two massive statues of Buddha carved into the side of a mountain in Afghanistan, probably dating back to the fifth or sixth century. The Taliban believed anything that did not represent their view of Islam was idol worship. They TNT'd the statues in 2001.

As with many of the libraries, there is currently an effort being made to rebuild the Buddhas and all that was culturally lost.

~

I remember reading a story about how Osama bin Laden might not have even been involved in the 9/11 attacks. I told this story to one of my friends who was gung ho for the president. He called it liberal propaganda. Maybe it was liberal propaganda—whatever that is—but I read several similar articles and they had interesting facts. I told some liberal friends about the story and they had a similar reaction: "Osama's gotta be the man."

I began realizing that people needed someone to blame for the attacks. You don't do something that tragic to America and get away with it. Americans need justice. If there is no one to blame, then you find someone to blame. We need that peace.

September 11 began to show me as a librarian how people sought their information. It showed me how media controlled peoples' lives—and how, strangely, people wanted to be controlled yet didn't want to know they were being controlled. I had read about this; I had even watched a movie, *Wag the Dog*,[11] about it. All of this was suddenly made real by 9/11.

~

After a few weeks of watching reporters say the country was in mourning, I went to lunch with a friend and asked, "How long

---

11. I thought this was a great film when I watched it, but I can't remember much about it now. Maybe it wasn't so great after all. Fun fact: the 1-800 number shown in the movie was (800) 555-0199. This same exchange is used almost universally in movies because it is the only number the phone company allows to be used by media.

until we forget?" My friend was the patriotic type who also can be pretty blind. The guy literally decides who he will vote for in coming elections based on who has the most convincing television ads. He was also the kind of guy who bought all the 9/11 memorabilia he could get his hands on because he believed he would make a lot of money off it in ten years—and the kind of guy who looked suspiciously at any Middle Easterner who walked down the street.

"Forget about what?" he asked with his mouth full of pizza.

"About the towers," I explained. "How long until people don't remember what 9/11 means?"

"How could anyone forget?"

I looked down at my pizza; my friend had picked the place for lunch because he had seen a commercial on TV advertising free bread sticks.[12] I looked at the words on his shirt—"God Bless America." He ordered it from a Christian organization he had seen on TV. I looked around the restaurant and saw so many others just like my friend. I looked up at my friend sadly and asked, "Do you remember what happened in Oklahoma City in 1995?"

My friend looked at me, confused, and shook his head.

"How about Timothy McVeigh? Does that name ring a bell?"

He shrugged and said, "Wasn't he in a movie last summer or something?"

I shook my head. "He was executed for taking part in blowing up the Oklahoma City federal building."

---

12. I don't really like bread sticks, but I'm always excited when I get handed a free sample while waiting for the pizza.

My friend continued looking confused. "I don't remember that."

I nodded. Of course he didn't—the media didn't talk about that one anymore. Yes, the towers were more glamorized and even stylized on the media, but what made them more lasting? I knew my friend could tell me what happened at Pearl Harbor, but I doubted he could tell me how it changed the country.[13] How many people were like him? How many people were devastated by Columbine in 1999 and even the first World Trade Center attack in 1993, but had now long since forgotten?[14]

Later that week, after I had just returned to class from a lunch break, someone ran in to say the United States was bombing Afghanistan. There was excitement in the room. We were finally getting back at those terrorists. I looked at the expressions of those in the room—the same ones who would go on to oppose the war in Iraq—and I wondered if this was one of the ways the world had changed: it turned even liberal librarians into patriots who were excited to hear news that Afghans would die that day, because now we had some payback, whatever that meant.

---

13. I wasn't even certain he could tell me where Pearl Harbor was.

14. I remember seeing one documentary that showed the towers falling to classical music; all the style in the shots made it seem more like a movie than real life. Maybe that says something about how we sometimes see real events more as fiction than real life. The media have a tendency to make tragic events slightly more tragic and less real because they know that people will become more emotionally attached. The art of manipulation isn't just a human trait anymore, it's an actual job; people sit in little rooms and have meetings about the best way to get people sucked into a story. The weird part was, because the tragedies had been fed to us more like movies than real events, they weren't as lasting. We got over them as soon as the media stopped talking about them. It was that easy. We had rage when we heard about Elián González and Terri Schiavo, but mere days after it we didn't even question what became of the story. How could we be so emotionally involved in a story and then not wonder at all about it when it was taken away? Easy. It was not real. It was presented almost artistically to manipulate our feelings, but, because those feelings were not real (only manipulated), when it was gone we didn't care.

Reading about conspiracy theories (such as the ones that centered around 9/11) is, more often than not, more interesting than reading actual facts, especially when the people who created the theories become so passionate about them that they start believing they're true.

We've all heard the theories that we didn't really land on the moon (O.J. Simpson even starred in a movie about it), and, if there is truth to polls, as many as 10 percent of all Americans believe the entire thing was staged. What of the theory? It's one thing to actually say you don't believe it was real, but it's another to actually have a foundation to the accusations. So what do these doubters say of what they believe to be one of the biggest hoaxes of all time?

Skeptics wonder why no stars could be seen in any of the moon photos, and why the astronauts have admittedly agreed that they don't remember seeing any. They will also point out that the flag placed on the moon appears to be blowing in the wind, which makes sense, except there's no such thing as wind on the moon. And how exactly did the astronauts get past the earth's radiation belt without dying of radiation poisoning? And when they did get past it, how did they bring film back that wasn't fogged by radiation? There are far more claims than this—some scientific-sounding and others quite absurd.

Scientists have shot down all of these theories and more. Then again, many of these scientists also worked for NASA, which made over 20 billion dollars off the moon landing.

Motel kids are something in every big city. It's hard for them not to break your heart. They're the ones who never seem to have clean faces, whose clothes are always faded, dirty, and often ripped, who ask for spare change because they lost their money when in reality they had no money at all.

Late one night two of these kids were stranded in front of the library waiting for a ride. They were both under ten—too young to stay outside the library by themselves after nine. So another coworker and I stayed outside the library with them.

Thirty minutes after closing their ride finally came. "Get in the car!" a man screamed before the car was even stopped.

"Hi, my name's Scott. I work for the library. I just wanted to make sure you are aware of the library's policy regarding not picking up your child." I handed him the form.

"My kids are fine. They are by themselves all the time."

"This neighborhood really isn't the safest place for a kid to wait for a ride."

"You telling me how to raise my kids?"

"I'm just making you aware of the library's policy—we have the authority to call the police."

"Get in the car." Before they had shut the door, he had already started pulling away.

As the tires squealed, I saw one reason why communities needed libraries—to help kids with parents like that. Art had told me quite some time ago that there was more to a library than books. I believed him, but I never really understood him until I started doing more than just shelving books.

~

I went to New York ten months after the towers fell. I of course went to Ground Zero; I had to see that image that had been so lasting on my TV set. I watched as people took family photos in front of the destruction, as people bargained with vendors for the best prices on memorabilia, as children played games with each other, and as parents tried to force their children to look at the site and remember it. Then I watched as people in suits walked quickly down the street doing their best not to look at the site. Some seemed to be avoiding the tourism, others looked at it shamefully. These were the people that I studied the most. They had been there that day. They had heard the sounds, they had cried, they had been terrorized. While I was eating breakfast and drinking coffee, they were wondering if they were going to live to see tomorrow. I finally saw the people whose lives had truly been changed, who would indeed never forget that day or hour. I looked at their eyes and it was like they were telling me to go away—this was their moment, this was their pain, and I didn't know anything about it. They were right. In spite of everything the media told me, it was their moment, and no image I was fed on TV could change this fact.

My library career began on the day the world changed. What did that mean? Not much.

As months turned into years, the paranoia that began that day went away. The orange terror alerts became less worrisome until they, too, simply went away completely. The country is safe again, until the news tells us differently. It's a new dawn for the way we are seeking and are fed our information. For better, for worse, things will never be the same.

Maybe the date was important to librarians, but I didn't see it. What it taught me was that it really wasn't librarians who protected information. Rather, it was society. No one is going to stop destroying an important relic because a librarian says not to. In the end, it's not destroyed because people have sense enough to know the relic is important enough to preserve. When the Catholic University of Louvain library was destroyed in WWI, it was a community that expressed outrage and saw to its rebuilding; when it was destroyed again in WWII, it was again a community, and not a librarian, who got it rebuilt. When the Taliban decided to destroy the Hakim Nasser Khosrow Balkhi Cultural Center, no librarian could stop it, but now a community is trying to rebuild it. Throughout history[15] there have been similar stories of communities coming together to rebuild.

There's something deep in the heart of every person that wants to protect culture. The only thing about my pending career that changed because of 9/11 was that I began to see it was the community, not the librarian, that was important to the library. Librarians were only as important as the community they inspired. If I was going to continue with this career, my job wouldn't be to protect information, it would be to bring members of the community together and inspire them to appreciate everything a library stands for.

---

15. I don't mean to make Nazis and terrorists the only monsters in a campaign to destroy culture. For as long as people have had buildings to store information, people have destroyed them. Other recent examples of libraries that have been destroyed because of war can be found in Bosnia, Croatia, Colombia, and El Salvador—just to name a few.

Chapter 378.1616 -DMAN— The Man Who Went Up the Mountain a Library Page and Came Down a Librarian:	Being the Part Where Our Hero Discovers Library School Is Pretty Much the Most Absurd Thing Librarians Ever Invented and His Faculty Advisor Is Kind of a Dick

When I tell people I went to library school, the most common reaction is either "You're joking, right?" or "They have schools for librarians? Do they teach you how to properly sssh people?"

But it's true. There are schools for librarians—and the idea's not as ridiculous as it often sounds.

I like to imagine that library school was started because of some sort of silly bar bet where a guy got really plastered and told his buddy that he could convince people that librarians needed to be trained in the art of librarianship. Sadly, this is not the case; its roots are a bit more academic.

Some 150 years ago people got it in their heads that having an accredited degree makes you seem more professional: lawyers were going to school, dentists were going to school, teachers were going to school—everyone was going to school.

So a bunch of men (women would have been there, but librarians were too sexist then) got together and said, "If people are going to take us seriously, then we need to have degrees. And a professional organization would be nice too." Up until this point, most librarians were scholars in other fields (like science and history). So they started the American Librarian Association (ALA) and started tossing out ideas for how to start a library school.

Columbia University[1] was the first school to offer a library science program, and they chose Melvil Dewey (of Dewey Decimal System fame) as the head of the first program; he was fired shortly after the program's launch for admitting women into the program. (His reasons for this were actually quite sexist.)[2]

~

A lot had changed since library schools first started some 150 years ago, a fact I did not realize when I took a seat near the back of the classroom at my graduate orientation.

The first person to speak was the director of the library science program. Her name was Virginia. She was a bitch, a fact that I wrote in the orientation worksheet that had been passed out at the door. I've heard all about Virginia from people who've been through the program,[3] and everyone was in agreement. There are,

---

1. I tried to visit the library at Columbia University, but a security guard stopped me because I wasn't a student in New York.

2. Dewey's rationale for admitting women was that he thought they would be perfect as subordinates to the male faculty who used the library for research.

3. A funny footnote to how foolish school administration can be: I was first processed as an engineering student by mistake. I don't have the best luck getting things processed at schools. Twice, as an undergrad, I was mistakenly given a D instead of an A. The first time it was no big deal, but the second time it could not be fixed in time to qualify me for a $10,000 scholarship . . . oh, well.

of course, other stories about her—there are other stories about most of the library school faculty. For Virginia, the stories are usually about how she'd rather appease faculty than students, or how her office door is always open but she is never in her office.

At first, I was like all the other sixty-plus people who had come to the orientation with pens drawn and notebooks out, ready to write down as much insight as our hands could keep up with. I quickly discovered there was really nothing wise being said. Virginia rambled quite extensively about how challenging graduate school would be, about how many of us would either drop out or flunk out before the year's end, about how taking more than one class would prove too stressful, about how we should expect to spend four years in the two-year program, and, finally, about how cutting-edge the program was.

The next person who spoke was Professor Howlin. He was a cocky, boastful goof who used big words to prove points. Nothing he said made any sense, but I liked him because he had sweaty armpits, which were fun to draw in my notebook in lieu of real notes. It turns out Howlin was the former head director of a large library in Seattle. Apparently, he had bitter feelings about leaving. I'm pretty sure leaving wasn't his choice. His armpits sweated more whenever he said *Seattle*. He also turned out to be the only faculty member who mentioned actually ever having had real experience working in a library.

Four other faculty members spoke, and then the final instructor came to the front of the class. She said her name was Professor Dickman, a name I quickly recognized because, according to my letter of acceptance, she was my faculty advisor. I wrote in my notebook, "Dick—faculty advisor."

Dickman talked about the importance of catalogers and then proceeded to explain the cataloging system she invented for her own library collection at home. She laughed a lot as she talked about her system, but no one in the room laughed back, except for the man next to me who was watching *There's Something About Mary*[4] on his laptop.

Virginia gave concluding remarks about how excited she was already about the incoming class of students and then she told us to go home. Her concluding remarks were encouraging, completely opposite from the first spiel of nonsense she rambled on about.

I looked down at my notes before I left and reread, "She's a bitch." And that pretty much summed up everything I got out of my orientation.

~

The next day I returned to work and felt a little more librarian-like. I had, after all, begun my formal training to be a librarian. As I walked past Anne's desk, I stopped and said, "So, yesterday I had my library school orientation."

Anne was looking at an e-mail greeting card; when I spoke, she didn't turn. "You should go tell Cindy about the experience. She went to San Jose State, you know?"

I looked at the reference desk several feet away, where Cindy was placing newspaper on her chair. "What's she doing?"

Anne turned for the first time, and looked at her. She shrugged, then turned back around. "That's her new thing—she puts newspaper down before she sits down."

"Why?"

"She says the chair is infested with small insects that bite at her skin, and the newspaper blocks them somehow."[5]

---

4. Fun fact about this movie: The scene where Ben Stiller is arrested at a rest stop for allegedly engaging in homosexual activities was actually based on a rest stop sex raid in South Carolina.

5. Turns out the chair really did have bugs—fleas, to be precise. Weeks later we found out that a library page who prided himself on taking showers only every other week (because he believed in conserving water) had been using the chair in the morning to process books at the desk before we opened the library to the public. Cindy was the only one who didn't have flea bites.

"Oh. So where did you go to school?"

"UCLA."

"Oh, yeah? I hear that's where you go if you want to work at an academic library."

"No—that's where you go if you just want to go to work and not ask questions. San Jose is for gossips. UCLA is for professionals."

I left Anne and let her read her online greeting card.

~

My first real graduate class was a library management course taught by Professor Howlin, who, as it turned out, was even more bitter about that whole Seattle thing than he let on at the orientation; he also didn't sweat quite as much, so he either had switched deodorants or was using a thicker shirt. Whatever the case, Howlin turned out to be a pretty good teacher. True, he was boastful, cocky, and a bit of a jerk, but he had been an actual librarian and had the battle wounds to prove it.

I think I also liked Professor Howlin because he didn't have a Ph.D. He wasn't trying to publish his lectures,[6] he was just trying to teach. Howlin, as I quickly discovered, also gave papers As if you cited his name in the work.[7]

In the other two classes I took that semester, I wasn't so lucky. The teachers were no doubt intelligent and everything one would

---

6. He was, however, trying to publish articles, as he proudly made known on his home page, where he showcased his published and unpublished work. I wondered, however, how many he actually wrote. It is common practice for a teacher to have a graduate student write a paper and then get co-credit for the work. Graduate students are willing to disgracefully do this, because it's sort of a catch–22—if you want to go to post-grad school you really need the publications, but it's hard to get them without being a teacher.

7. He actually commented in the margin whenever he saw his name. Other students didn't believe me, but one or two tested my theory and were equally rewarded with As.

expect from graduate school, but their classes didn't seem to carry any application I'd be able to use in the profession.

The first class, a cataloging class with Dr. Dickman (my faculty advisor), had the class writing out definitions of cataloging terms[8] I'm not even sure are used in libraries. I've never used them, anyway, and it made me feel like I was in fifth grade.

One day, for fun, she brought into class photographs she had taken on a recent trip to Thailand, and then had us create a database to catalog them based on various aspects of things in the photo. No one had fun doing this, but Dr. Dickman didn't seem to notice (or perhaps care), because she had us do three similar assignments during the semester: one with photographs of cats she had owned but that had since passed on, one with a collection of men's rings, and one with photographs of photographs. When the class moaned about the assignments, she'd only laugh and say in a loud, freakish voice (strangely enough, all library teachers spoke loudly—I'd always imagine they'd be quiet, like librarians), "I know you really like them." And the weird part was, I really think she thought we were enjoying them.

Most students had had enough of Dr. Dickman by the first day. The class began with forty-three; by week one it was down to twenty-seven; by week two, twenty-two; and by the end of the year, thirteen. On the last day of class, Dickman did her first role call of

---

8. Examples of meaningless cataloging terms: *Analytics*—bibliographic records that describe parts of a bigger item; *Colophon*—needless thing at the end of an item giving information about one or more of the following: title, author, publisher, printer, date of publication; *Enumeration*—numbering, as in serial volume and issue numbering; *MARC*—Machine-Readable Cataloging, a term that covered many different formats in many countries; *Preliminaries*—the title page or any pages preceding the title page along with the cover; *Retrospective Conversion*—converting bibliographic information from card to computerized records.

the year. She realized for the first time just how many people had left and said happily, "Why, that's more than last year!"

The other teacher went by Dr. L (he had a last name, but thought it sounded cooler as just *L*). He taught a class on school media libraries and wrote the self-published book for the class. He told us during nearly every class that he wrote the book. Every time, he'd open by talking about how he spoke at conferences worldwide and was a leading expert in his field. He also told the class several times that he was a Catholic.[9]

I never wanted to be a school librarian, but I took the class anyway, mainly because it was offered on the weekend and I heard he graded 85 percent on attendance (meaning you got a B guaranteed just for showing up).

On the last day of Dr. L's class, he pulled me aside as I walked though the door and said quietly, so other students wouldn't hear, "Son, I believe you're in the wrong class."

I stared at him, confused, and wondered why it had taken him all semester to tell me this. Finally, I asked, a little hurt, "Why?"

"Well, it appears our classrooms have been switched—the business class is now meeting next door."

"But I'm not in the business class."

"What class are you in?" Dr. L asked, confused himself.

"I've been in your class all semester."

~

My first class of the second semester was a course on interface design and functionality; I was prepared for another semester of rhetoric and theories. I was not prepared for Professor Vu.

---

9. He also told us several times that it went against his principles to teach class on a Saturday, but he believed God would forgive him for this. I think he expected us to say that we agreed and that all would be well with his soul. Nobody told him this.

Everything about Professor Vu was a bit odd. He was Asian, but his name was Lenny; he frequently wore yellow socks and black jeans; his hair was always combed with a crooked part; his glasses were the wrong fit, and he would spend much of his lecture time pushing them back up; more than once he had missed a button and buttoned his shirt wrong; and he always seemed a bit lost. The first six weeks of the semester he would walk into the classroom a little late and then ask confusedly if he was in the right class.

Professor Vu's quirkiness ended at his appearance: his lectures were inspiring, his mind was brilliant, and his love of libraries made every student walk a little prouder.

"This class," he said insightfully on the first day, "is about defi-nition. You are the historians. It will be your job to define our past. It will be your job to tell the world everything the past twenty years of technology—of the Internet and computers—has done for society. You get to define what the past twenty years meant. Who's up for the challenge?"

I've never seen people so eager to raise their hands. It wasn't completely what he said, it was how he said it. He made each of us believe.

Professor Vu smiled and nodded. "Well, then, we have our work cut out."

I walked out of his class that day feeling like I belonged; it was the first time I felt like graduate school was making me something.

On most days Professor Vu would enter and leave the class in a hurry. The second month of school he stopped by my desk as he made his way for the door and asked, "So did you catch that Lakers game?"

I looked around; I didn't understand why he would ask me this. I thought for sure he was talking to someone else. When I saw no one I shook my head.

"It was a great game!" He paused and studied me. "You're sort of tall—you must like the game."

I shrugged. "It's okay." I wondered if he was trying to bond.

"When I was a boy in China I wanted to play basketball. My father forbade me, but I secretly played after school. When I came to the states to go to college, I picked UCLA because it was close to where the Lakers played. I had it all planned out. I'd tell my dad I was going to college but I'd secretly get a job playing basketball for the Lakers. Then I'd make all kinds of money and my dad would be proud of me and he'd forgive me. You know what happened?"

"What?" I imagined it had to be a joke. Professor Vu was barely five feet and couldn't even hold a pencil, let alone a basketball.

His face became sad. "They wouldn't even give me a shot."

"Oh—that's too bad."

He nodded. "I could've been a superstar like Shaq or Kobe." He paused. "But this is better because I get to make a difference here."

I nodded.

He put his hand on my shoulder. "You made the right choice, too. There are enough Shaqs and Kobes in the world." He smiled as he reflected. "The right choice indeed." And then he walked off, disoriented.

FOR SHELVING

The U.S. Census Bureau Web site (www.census.gov) is a fun place to go when you need useless facts to cure your boredom. The census discovered many things about school in 2000. Among the highlights:

Students are paying 75 percent more ($9,326) to go to public colleges than they did in 1990, and 84 percent more ($27,711) if they are going to a private school. It's no wonder that only 27 percent of all adults over twenty-five have BAs. But if that seems like a lot, consider the fact that New York pays more than $10,000 each year to send one kid to first grade.

Going to college does have its payoff in the long run. The lifetime income of someone with a Ph.D. is $3.4 million; $2.5 million with an MA; $2.1 million with a BA. Considering the lifetime income of someone with only a high school diploma is about $1 million less than someone with a BA, it's worth it to spend a little bit of cash for education.

You will need extra cash, considering families spent more than $5 billion in 2000 just for back-to-school clothes.

My second semester I also began making friends.[10]

I felt out of place my first semester. I was twenty-three in a school of thirty-five- to forty-year-olds who all seemed to be in the midst of a midlife crisis and in dire need of a career change. There were former screenwriters who finally gave up on their dreams, bored schoolteachers who no longer liked kids, and mothers whose children had grown and left them with nothing else to do. Over half of them came with no prior library experience (except for a few volunteers here and there). I had worked in libraries five years and felt like a seasoned pro.

During lunch one day in my first semester, I joined two women who had signed up for school together. I asked what they wanted to do after they finished graduate school, and they said in unison, "Become library pages." They were willing to invest at least six years of schooling to make minimum wage shelving

---

10. That sentence makes me sound like such a dork. Please don't hold it against me until you read just a little bit more.

books.[11] I almost began to laugh until I realized they were serious. When I told them that perhaps they were aiming too low and that I had become a page with hardly any knowledge of libraries, they became intrigued. They began asking me questions like I was an expert. And they took notes.[12]

During my second semester, I finally began to meet people closer to my own age and with similar job experience. Together we learned that the friends you make in school are more important than the education you receive. Connections are everything in the library world.

One friend I met at school, Steve, became my writing buddy because he wanted to be a writer, too.[13] We also talked about indie music and foreign films.[14]

Theories were needed. It wouldn't be grad school without them. But sometimes you needed a little break from the scholarly world, and that's where Steve came in. Our conversations would usually go something like this:

"Best movie librarian of all time?"

---

11. Note the requirements for library page usually go something like this (please note that graduate school is not mentioned): processing and preparing library materials for public use; retrieving and checking in library materials; moving, sorting, and shelving library materials in boxes, bins, and on book trucks; maintaining library materials in correct shelf order; and preparing rooms for library programs and community meetings (source: City of Anaheim library page job description).

12. I observed one day that the amount of notes a person takes is usually determined by the person's age. Younger people took fewer notes than older people. During a typical lecture I usually wrote down three or four things, and at least two of those things involved when the lunch break would be and when the bathroom break would be.

13. Steve was also like me in that he did everything he could to take classes that had nothing to do with library school. He even became a DJ for the school's Internet radio, which, I'm pretty sure, he got graduate credit for.

14. Strangely enough, I have used our discussions more at work than any theories learned in class. People don't come to public libraries, or any library, for that matter, for theories— they come for facts. Because of our discussions, I know quite a bit about facts.

"That's a pretty small list—Parker Posey in *Party Girl* or Noah Wylie in *The Librarian*. Both movies were crap if you ask me."

"You're not thinking hard enough! How 'bout Sylvia Marpole?!"

"Who?"

"Goofy's love interest in *An Extremely Goofy Movie*."

"I guess she was pretty hot."

"Oh, they get hotter—much hotter! Marian Paroo in *The Music Man,* played by the enchanting Shirley Jones."

"I think you're a little *too* into it."

"And one must not forget Lynn Wells in *Major League,* played by the talented Rene Russo!"

"I can't believe you seriously know their names!"

"Maybe if you cared a little more about your profession."

"How does knowing the name of a librarian Shirley Jones played in a movie over forty years ago make me not serious about my profession?! And seriously—*Major League*?! Does anyone over the age of twelve watch that movie?"

"Hold your tongue!"

The talk was nonsense, but nonsense was exactly what both of us needed.

It's a cruel world, and unless you're blessed with some talent people will pay money to see, your friends are the only people who will get you where you need to go.

The oddest thing about many of my new friends was how many I never met in person, not even to this day. We lived miles apart from one another, and talked only online.[15] By my second semester, half of

---

15. Once, when I was leaving a class that actually met in a physical setting, I walked past a guy I'm pretty sure I talked to quite frequently online. We both gave each other a curious glance and kept on walking.

my classes were either partially or entirely online. By my second year, I never set foot on campus except to pick up books or do research.[16]

Aside from the obvious underwear factor, online classes are great because they make not-learning easy. Before online classes, not-learning was a challenge. You had to make sure the teacher wasn't looking before playing FreeCell. For online classes, this wasn't even an issue.[17]

Oddly enough, though, online learning actually proved more powerful at times than classroom learning. Students I had seen in class who were afraid to speak were suddenly participating frequently in message boards. And while the students who frequently rambled about pointless topics were still there, rambling mindless thoughts cyberly, their thoughts could be avoided easily.

Online classes proved to be far more about interaction than about theories, and the model of learning actually worked. Could I have learned the same thing by working a few more years in a library? Most likely, but now I didn't have to.

❧

Halfway through graduate school, a new librarian was finally hired to fill the gap Edith had left, and Anne was transferred to a new library. The new librarian's name was Pam. She was loud, bossy, and emotionally unstable. She had also gone to graduate school at UCLA.

---

16. The truth was, I was spending more time in the library studying than probably just about any student in the program; I just wasn't studying library-related material. I was studying religious movements in Southern India; I was studying the way Shakespeare used personification in his plays; I was studying musical acts of the 1960s and 1970s. I was studying everything that looked interesting.

17. It wasn't like I was a slacker. I just learned that I wasn't going to get anything from the degree except a job, so I figured why bother? I was working in a library and knew how useless the information was.

"I hear you're in San Jose's MLIS program?" Pam said the first day that I met her.

I nodded.

"I went to UCLA," she proudly said with her mouth full of food. "San Jose prepares fine librarians, but I'm going to be a library manager. I needed better training than a state school."[18]

"Okay." I wanted to say *you're actually wrong* and then point out that she had crumbs all over her mouth, but, at least for now, Pam was my superior and it was best if I did not press the issue.

"I went to San Jose," Cindy, who was at the kitchen sink washing her hands, said bitterly. "I hated that school."

"Why's that?"

"The teachers are complete idiots! They'd fail me for the most ridiculous things! It took me almost five years to finish."

Cindy was the first person I met who had actually failed something in library school. The classes were hard, but, for the most part, you did the work and you got a passing grade. I liked Cindy, but the longer I worked with her and listened to her stories, the more I saw she was utterly insane!

"How many classes have you failed?" Cindy asked as she vigorously washed her hands.

"Um—well, none, actually, but I'm only halfway through," I said.

Cindy left us, and Pam quietly laughed and said, "Guess we know the reason why she can't find full-time work."

Yeah, I wanted to say, *but we still don't know the reason why you've been a librarian for ten years and not a manager, if UCLA indeed makes you prepared for such things.*

⌒

---

18. I'm not into statistics, but, in actuality, I was pretty sure that SJSU had produced more library managers than UCLA.

The vast majority of library school students ended the program by writing two thesis papers of no more than twenty pages each in length. It was a ridiculous thing to ask students. Writing a paper wouldn't make us any more prepared for the real world, but I wrote them because I knew this was what I needed to do to graduate.

My papers were on two separate topics: the first on digital reference, and the second on what role librarians needed to play in solving the informational divide. The first topic I rushed through. It was sloppy, but it answered the question. The second question I was actually excited about. This was something I might just be able to use when I graduated. I had believed throughout graduate school that librarians needed to offer patrons more in regard to computers.[19]

I set out to write the paper with fury and passion. I wasn't just going to answer the question, I was going to write a work of art that would motivate librarians to get off their butts and give their patrons what they needed. I wrote about what types of computer classes librarians should offer to patrons; I wrote about what programs to offer; I wrote about how to get grants; I wrote about how to do programming. When I finished, I looked at the paper and I wanted to cry. It was beautiful. It was genius. And, according to the faculty member who read it, it failed.

The papers were graded pass or fail. If it failed, you had to write on another topic the next semester. If that one failed, then you flunked out of the program. The faculty would not comment to you directly on why your paper failed. They would only give you a one-sentence answer on a letterhead sheet of paper. The reason for failure that they gave me made no sense; it said, "Libraries don't do, librarians do." I asked my advisor what it

---

19. I still do.

meant; she said the program prohibited her to tell me. In library terms that means, "Oh, well for you—better luck next time."

One thing I did learn was how the papers were graded. A bunch of teachers sat in a room and read them. One teacher decided if it would pass or fail. If it passed that was it. If it failed, the paper was passed on to another teacher to make sure that teacher didn't have a bias. It seemed fair until I learned that some teachers fail over half the papers read, and other teachers pass all of them. It was all about luck. And if a teacher failed your paper, the second reader never disagreed because this could start an argument between teachers.

Lucky for me, the paper I didn't even make an effort on *did* pass, so the next semester I'd have to write only one paper. The new topic was how terrorists in Southeast Asia operate.[20] This paper would have absolutely nothing to do with libraries, but I didn't care. I just wanted to get out of the program. I wrote the paper with no passion. I answered the question. I passed. I was through with library school.

Before I turned in my final papers, the director, aka the Bitch, asked graduating students to tell her what they learned from the program. I was honest and maybe I went wrong here. I wrote passionately about how the program could improve, about how they needed to stop this whole "graduating by writing term papers" and instead require students to get actual library experience through practicums[21] and internships.[22] I wrote how they needed to offer more about actual library-related situations. I wrote about how they

---

20. I kid you not—the paper that would determine if I had what it took to graduate with a degree in library science was about terrorism. It was like a math student having to pass a class by playing Bach on the piano.

21. Basically, a practicum is a fancy way of saying internship; there's just a little bit more writing and coursework involved.

22. I did a practicum over the summer of my first year at Biola University. It gave me real experience working in an academic environment, and I have since recommended that anyone who is in library school should do a practicum as well.

needed to combine cataloging into a general class about libraries because, yeah, it's an important subject for librarians to understand, but hardly any librarians catalog anymore, and those who do can just as easily learn it at work. I wrote about how they needed to demand that librarians be experts on the computer because obtaining information through the computer would be the future of libraries, and students were leaving unprepared. My letter was over a page in length and, I felt, worthy of praise. The Bitch never responded. The Bitch didn't care. She didn't ask the question because she wanted to know what we thought; she asked it because she had to. Her door was always open, but she was never there.

After I finished school, I was made a full-fledged librarian. Other librarians treated me differently. It was like now I was finally equal. I hated that. I wanted to be equal because of the things I was doing or could do for the library, not because I could now attach MLIS to the end of my name.

I stuck with the program largely because I did not have to pay for it; I mastered theories of library management, interface design, and collection management; I wrote my senior thesis papers; I met all the requirements and was awarded my degree. Yet I didn't feel any more like a librarian than I did when I'd entered the program. I knew the subject well, but knowing about something doesn't *make* you something. I was about to enter the library workforce still unsure of what I was supposed to do with my life.

Not long after I finished school, I went back to the library science department office to drop off some papers. I noticed an orientation going on. I stood in the door frame and watched for a few minutes. The speech was the same; the students were different. They were young, some younger than me. I saw hope in their eyes; it was the same hope that I had once had. My hope wasn't gone. I just wasn't as certain about my choice anymore. For a mo-ment I wondered if I had wasted two years of my life for a degree I would never use.

"How 'bout them Lakers?" a voice said behind me.

I turned and saw a beaming Professor Vu. I smiled. "Yeah how 'bout them?"

"You're finished with school, then?"

"Yeah."

He nodded and extended his hand to shake.

"In school we defined the past. Now it's your turn," he said, shaking my hand. "Go define the future. Take everything you learned from me and every other teacher and add to it."

Chapter 641.5 -POPC- How to Make Popcorn, and Other Things I Didn't Learn in Library School:	Being the Reasons Why I Love This Job and Why I Think I Just Might Quit

I don't know who decided the library should give out free popcorn on Saturdays. I just know we did—and it came with no warning.

One morning, I came into the library innocently enough and nearly stumbled over the popcorn machine. In retrospect, I don't know how I didn't see it. It was large, red, and had the word *Popcorn* printed in a bold yellow font. Taped to the outside was a lengthy note from the manager with my name at the top; it contained detailed instructions on proper usages and cleaning. At the bottom, the note said, in all capital letters, PLEASE DON'T BURN YOURSELF.

Next to the machine sat a large barrel of kernels, an army-sized container of oil, and enough butter-flavored salt to give an entire elementary school a heart attack.

Just as I began to read the instructions, Andy, the part-time page and quite possibly the bitterest person who has ever lived, arrived for work.[1] His head, as usual, was directed at the ground, yet he immediately noticed the popcorn machine. He sighed and asked, "Are we hosting a carnival?"

I shrugged. "So you know how to use one of these things?"

"What?" came his sarcastic reply. "They didn't teach you that in library school?" (Andy said "What, they didn't teach you that in library school?" to almost every question I asked him, from "Do you know if that book is checked in?" to "Is anyone in the bathroom?")

"I'm only in my first semester. They only teach popcorn making to second-year students."

"You've been in school for over five years, and the best job you could find has you making popcorn. How's that make you feel?"

"You're fifty years old, living in a trailer park, making minimum wage. How's that make you feel?"

"At least I'm not living with my parents."

"Why don't you go shelve books now?"

"Why don't you go kill yourself before you end up like me?"[2] He laughed as he walked away. He was almost to the staff lounge when he turned and added, "And try not to burn yourself today, okay?"

I was left by myself to make sense of the note, which, as it happened, was quite simple to understand.

---

1. Andy, at age fifty, is also one of the oldest pages in the city. He has been working at the library for over ten years and lives in a trailer he bought with money from a work-related injury. Despite his constant bitterness and depression, I like Andy, and we have become friends.

2. This is actually how many of our conversations end.

After giving the machine a practice run in the back of the library, I pushed the popcorn cart to the main floor of the library just in time for the conclusion of the Saturday story time.

Patrons surfaced from all corners of the library to stare at this wonder of a popcorn vessel, and children ran to the cart when they saw me tape a handwritten note to the top of the machine that read "Free Popcorn!"

"It's free?" The first boy to the machine asked as I started popping the kernels.

I nodded, turned to Kate, the storyteller that Saturday, who had just finished, and asked, "Does any of this seem unorthodox?"

"Look how happy they are!" Kate said, pointing at the waiting children, who had already formed a straight line in front of the cart.

I looked down at them. They were happy, but that didn't justify this: popcorn in a library. What was next? Vending machines? Snack bars?

The role of the public library, as all my instructors at library school would happily agree, was to provide the community with information. Nothing about a popcorn machine had anything to do with information. Every rule of the library institution had been broken. Children had run in the library and even shouted in excitement when they saw the machine. What was worse, their fingers, freshly saturated with greasy oil from eating popcorn, went on to touch and leave marks on books.

When the day was over, I looked at the library and saw popcorn everywhere. The cleaning crew would clean it after we left, but that wasn't the point.

Kate came up behind me and stared in equal disbelief at the scene, but then she smiled and said, "We made a lot of kids happy."

"But at what cost?" I pointed out. "Those kids are going to grow up with complete disrespect for the library if we carry on with this."

Kate was quiet for a moment, and then asked, "Do you know how many of those kids will leave the library today, and that bag of popcorn will be their biggest meal of the day?"

I continued to look at the mess, trying hard to ignore that question. I did not, in fact, know how many kids would go home like that, and neither did she. But we both knew the neighborhood. We both knew how many kids came from households that didn't have a lot of food to put on the table. We both knew that indeed a lot of kids would go home and that bag of popcorn would be their biggest meal, but I tried hard not to think about that.

Michael, the computer clerk, arrived at work later in the afternoon after the popcorn machine had been put away. It took him less than five minutes to say, "*My*[3] keyboards are disgusting! Why are they so greasy?"

Kate and I smiled at each other but said nothing.

"They passed out popcorn all morning long!" Brenda said.

"Popcorn! In a library?"

"That's what I said," Brenda replied. She had, in fact, said it all morning. She had said it to me, to Kate, to the page, and to every person who checked out books. When Brenda was unhappy, everyone knew it. And when she found someone to be unhappy with, she formed a bond and tried to make that person even angrier. "Doesn't it just make you sick? All the work you'll have to do to clean those keyboards. Doesn't seem worth it."

Michael looked at the greasy keyboards and thought for a moment, then finally acknowledged, "No it doesn't, but I bet it made a bunch of kids happy. I can't argue for having to work. That's my job, right?"

Brenda didn't answer.

~

---

3. He was very possessive about his computers.

The following Monday, I had written an entire thesis in my mind of things I would say to the manager about my opposition to that popcorn machine. I hated everything about the machine, from the way it smelled to the way it sounded when it popped the kernels.

Pam was sitting with me at the desk. She had her opinion, too—she had shared it with me all morning long. "We have to stand together," she explained to me at the desk, "for the sake of the library. Faren is going to run this beautiful building to the ground."

I stared at a piece of mold that had formed on the wall and thought about the beautiful building, but I said nothing to Pam.

"So how'd it go with the popcorn on Saturday?" Faren asked brightly as she passed us at the reference desk on the way to her office.

My fists tightened at the thought of that awful machine, and I was about to spew out the first bad thing that came to my head. I looked over at Pam, who nodded her head in approval of the disgust she knew I was feeling. Then I saw Kate walk up behind Faren. She stared at me, and what she had said on Saturday haunted me; this time I couldn't ignore it. As hard as it was for me to admit it, the city was turning into a miniature Calcutta,[4] and if that popcorn gave those kids enough pleasure to keep them happy for the rest of the day, who was I to deny them?

I turned away from Pam. I didn't want to see her reaction to what I was about to say. "Oh, it went great!" I finally replied.

"Glad to hear it. We're going to start doing it every Saturday!"

---

4. Okay, so the city isn't that bad, and certainly it isn't that smelly, but it isn't pretty either. Actually, half of the city is quite nice, but it always seemed odd to me that not a single manager or high-ranking library person lived in the city. For the most part, families have food (though not a lot, and it just wasn't the same amount of food that flowed from my refrigerator) and shelter (though there is an ever increasing number of motel kids coming into the library).

"Great!" I said, pretending to be happy.

"I don't think that's such a great idea," Pam said. "It's not really promoting what the library is about."

Faren looked at Pam with concern and asked with interest, "What is the library about, Pam?"

"Books, for one."

Faren nodded. "Books, for one, is right!" Faren said brightly. "But more important than books is community! Libraries are about community! And community loves popcorn!"

"Not everyone."

"Nonsense. I think you're just afraid of working the popcorn machine. We'll have you trained on it in no time—it's a piece of cake."

Faren was gone before Pam could argue.

~

In ancient Rome, one of the most common places to find a library was the bathhouse. So, in all honesty, I can't say it's unorthodox to have popcorn among the stacks, because there is no such thing as orthodox when dealing with a library. It's a representation of community, changing from one generation to the next to meet the needs of that community.

But I still didn't like the idea.

~

The next Saturday, there were rat droppings by the popcorn machine, and marks where a rat had unsuccessfully tried to tear the box of kernels. I ignored the droppings and prepared the machine for use.

As I ate my lunch that day, I saw the rat. I named him Fred. He was bigger than I had suspected from the size of the droppings; he was also pretty bold. I had never seen a rat so bravely come into a room with a human. And it wasn't the first time I'd seen a rodent inside the library.[5]

I stared at Fred, and he stared right back. He waited for me to move, and when I didn't he went for a bag of popcorn I had set next to the machine. He proceeded to eat it right in front of me. When he finished, he tilted his head and stared. I think he was wondering why I didn't smash him with the broom. I had given him his last supper, and I'm sure he knew that's what was supposed to happen next.

But killing rats wasn't in my job description.[6] I let him go.

On Monday, Faren did her managerial duty and called facility maintenance[7] to have the rat disposed of. The rat catcher arrived just after I returned from lunch. His name was Bork, at least that's what his badge said (although I can't imagine what kind of parent would name a child Bork). He smelled a little like garbage, was missing his front tooth, and was wearing a cap with the city's logo that didn't appear to have been washed in decades.

"I hear ya all have yours selves a's rat problem." He said to me. Faren had told me to handle Bork because she's scared of rats and didn't want to know anything about the traps.

I nodded.

---

5. At least three times I have witnessed a pigeon fly into the library, smash into the window (not being able to see there was a window), and stun itself. I've also seen a librarian pick up a stunned bird with her bare hands and take it back outside.

6. Neither was making popcorn.

7. Facility maintenance is in charge of doing everything librarians don't know how to do, want to do, or need to do. This includes, but is not limited to, disposing of rats, putting locks on bathrooms, replacing light bulbs, installing signs, replacing windows, and pointing out things that need replacing but that the library doesn't have the funding to fix (such as leaking roofs, structural damage caused by earthquakes, torn carpeting, etc.).

"Anybody see it?"

I nodded again. "Last Saturday I saw it in the break room."

He looked at me eagerly. "No kidding? 'Bout how big would you say it was?"

I shrugged. "Maybe five or six inches."

"Oh, that's nothing. I've caught them at the Convention Center that were the size of a large dog. They got them some fat sons of bitches of rats there, I'll tell you what. They feed off all the food left over from conventions."

"That's pretty impressive."

Bork nodded. "And they're messy to clean up. When the trap goes down on them, their guts go all over the place. But the things are so fat, sometimes the trap only hurts them a bit and they get away and I have to follow their trail of blood to find them and finish the job with a stick."

"So where are you going to put the trap?" I said, trying to change the subject.

Bork pointed toward the back of the library in the closet where the money safe was kept. "You ever seen a dead one?"

I nodded.

"Rats are nothing," Bork continued to explain as we headed towards the closet. "I went out to the Angel Stadium with a guy once to catch a possum and the thing popped out of nowhere and bit the guy's nuts. It just kind of hung there on them acting like it was dead, and I had to smack it several times with a bat to knock it off. Guy retired not long after that." Bork gave a wicked little laugh as he thought back on the moment.

He looked over at me to see how shocked I was, and then admitted, "That there is nothing, though. We have a run-in of some sorts with snakes every other week when we have to do work down at the Santa Ana River. I hate them little bastards. That's about the only thing I just can't handle. Whenever I get a call about a snake, I tell'em to send someone else in. I make up a story about how my brother had his eyeball plucked out by a snake while he was sleeping when he was a kid and it just brings back too many bad memories. That always does the trick." He paused, and then asked me suspiciously, "You don't have any snakes here, do you?"

"I don't think so."

"'Cause I hate them sons of bitches. I kid you not, you're on your own if I see one."

"Good to know."

"Little bastards—I hate them."

"Well I think you're safe. Should I show you the closet?"

He nodded.

When we got to the closet, Bork quickly set the trap and explained, "Now you make sure and tell everyone 'bout this here trap, and to be careful not to step on it. I know a guy who stepped on it with work boots and it still nearly tore his toe right off."

I nodded, "I'll make sure and tell everyone—wouldn't want that to happen."

"And if you hear it go off, you'll have to come back and make sure it killed him good and dead. If it didn't, just smack it a few times with a broom—that should do the trick." Bork turned and looked at a book sitting on the processing counter. "Or maybe you can just drop a dictionary on it; that would flatten it out. Just make sure it's a heavy one."

I nodded again and really wished Bork would leave.

"Call me when you've got it dead, and I'll come and get it."

Before I replied, he left the library whistling "It's a Small World after All."

The history of popcorn is quite complex. Popcorn is one of the oldest snacks around, as traces of it date back thousands of years. Columbus wrote about Indians wearing popcorn on their clothing. During archeology digs in New Mexico in 1948 scientists found ears of popcorn that dated back over 1,500 years.

While a few Americans did enjoy the treat,[8] it wasn't until the first popcorn carts were invented in the late 1800s that popcorn really took off with Americans. The carts began appearing on street corners across the nation.

The popcorn industry saw its biggest boom from 1920 to 1940 due to two major factors: the Depression and the war. Popcorn is cheap, which made it one of the few snacks Americans could buy during the Depression. During World War II, when most of the sugar was being rationed and sent to the soldiers, popcorn became one of the snacks of choice for most Americans.

While popcorn may not be as popular today as it was sixty years ago, it's still big business. How big? If you get fifty one-liter bottles of soda, empty them out, and fill them with popcorn, that's about how much the average American eats each year. Assuming you don't saturate it with butter and salt, popcorn is also one of the healthiest snacks you can eat.

8. Even eating it as cereal for breakfast in colonial times.

For the next two days, I heard Fred periodically running above the lights overhead. I didn't understand why he didn't try to get the food from the trap. I made up a story that he was one of those smart rats I had seen in cartoons, that somehow he would out-smart us all. He was a disgusting little creature, but I felt for him and quietly rooted for him.

My feelings for the rat, however sincere they were, were completely isolated. No one else felt the way I did for him.

"This is insane! Completely insane!" Pam complained as she ate lunch in the back with Brenda and me. "Listen to that!"

"I hate it," Brenda replied. "I don't feel safe in here. I told my husband just last night that I was certain I'd get rabies. And don't think I won't sue when I do."[9]

"What lesson are we teaching the children?" Pam asked.

"No lesson at all," Brenda replied. Up to this point, Brenda did not know of Pam's displeasure. Now that she did she seemed eager to form an alliance. "We should start a protest."

"A protest?"

"A protest! Write a letter saying the following staff members disagree with this."

"You think it would work?"

"She'd have to listen if we all complained." Brenda studied Pam for a moment, thinking of a way to convince her to join her side. When the thought came, it flew from her mouth quickly and with little grace: "You're in a powerful position, Pam. She may not listen to me because I'm a clerk, but she'd have to listen to you."

Power. That single word is enough to make a foolish person take action. Pam leaned back in her chair and thought about the suggestion. As she did, I heard the trap go off. It was way in the

---

9. Brenda was always saying she was going to sue for something or other; she told me once that she believed a person could make a living doing nothing but suing for frivolous things, and was researching how to do it so she could retire from the library.

back of the library, but the snapping sound was loud enough for everyone to hear.

Andy came quickly from the bookshelves, excited. "Was that the trap?!"

I ignored him and slowly made my way to the back of the library where I saw Fred lying dead in the trap. He seemed longer than I had remembered and a little fatter.

"Maybe we should feed it to the kids on Saturday. We could burn him up, and then mix his ashes with the hot oil," Andy suggested.

"Do me a favor—don't tell that to Faren. It might give her an idea." I looked at Fred's dead body and began to feel guilty. He came to the library because we started offering patrons popcorn. If the food had not come, Fred would have stayed away.

"So what do you do with a dead rat?" Andy asked. "He's too big to flush him down the toilet."

"Facility maintenance will take care of him."

"What, they don't teach you how to clean up dead rats in library school?"

"Aren't you supposed to be shelving books?"

"You want a moment alone or something?" Andy laughed, and added dryly, "You're not going to molest it or something, are you?"

I ignored Andy and continued to stare at Fred, who had given his life because he had been tempted by the bait of the trap.

We opened a snack bar about the same time I began to accept the fact that popcorn was there to stay. Apparently I had sounded too eager about the success of the Saturday snack fest, and Faren wanted to extend the effort to include more than just popcorn. Her new campaign included individually wrapped bags of cookies, potato chips, and pretty much every other snack that contained abnormal amounts of sugar and fat. To wash it down we would start selling soda.

To cover our tracks and to make sure there was a greater reason for this new campaign than making children fat, a price tag was stuck on the snacks. Anyone who complained about food being sold in a library was promptly told, "Due to the city's shrinking budget, the library is selling food as a fund-raiser to buy new books."

As a joke, I put a bunch of titles on diabetes next to the food. Faren who did not see the humor, quickly took them down and asked, "Do you have a problem with selling food?"

"No, but it would be nice to have at least a few healthy snacks."

She ignored the suggestion and returned to her office.

Kids soon began coming to the library like it was the corner 7-11. Some would complain about Costco having better prices, but most were just happy to have something to eat while they waited for their parents to pick them up.[10] I heard one kid say to his parent on his cell phone, "I already ate at the library, so I won't be home for dinner."

Brenda and Pam's alliance ended at just the two of them. Pam wrote a petition, but she could find no one but Brenda to sign it. In the end, the two of them went to Faren's office and expressed their concerns. Faren listened and ultimately said the good out-weighed the bad. The popcorn and food would stay.

They weren't happy; there was tension for several weeks, but they both knew they could do nothing. Ultimately, Pam could only say, "Things will be different when I'm manager."

∾

---

10. Libraries are a popular meeting place for young children who have no one waiting for them at home. Some arrive at three every day and don't leave until their parents pick them up at eight. They clock more hours in the building than most of the staff.

Everyone on the library staff knew popcorn was a bad idea except Faren. From the moment I saw it, I knew people would line up to vocalize their complaints, and Pam would be the first person who would talk to them. But a funny thing happened: no one complained. A few people would give it odd looks and acted like they were going to say something, but then you offered them a free bag and they'd smile, take it, and go away.

It was, granted, a pretty ridiculous notion, but it made people happy. It made everyone happy but the elderly.

"I can't believe you're giving popcorn out in the library," one elderly woman said when she came into the library and saw the sign.

"It's to promote our summer reading program."

"Well, I don't like any program that trashes up books with greasy little fingers. It's just appalling."

"We've been doing this for quite a long time and we've never had a problem with that."

"Oh, no? Look at this floor. There's popcorn everywhere!"

"We have a cleaning crew that cleans it up daily. It comes right up."

"Well, when I was a girl, you know what we got for reading a book?"

I nodded.

"Knowledge. Reading was a privilege. No one had to cram my mouth with popcorn to get me to read."

"Well, times have changed—some kids need the incentive to read."

"Well, then, they don't deserve books."

Is any kid undeserving of a book? I wanted to question, but decided not to. There was nothing I could say to win her over.

"Clifford," she said looking at her husband, "tell him how disgusting this is."

Her husband nodded and looked around the library absent-mindedly. He sort of looked like he wanted a bag himself, but he was afraid to state this fact to his enraged wife.[11]

"I'll be bringing this up with the city librarian. I am just not happy seeing this in a library, of all places."

She had a point. It was completely unlike libraries, but that was sort of the point. You have to change to grow.

～

Yeah, selling food and giving out popcorn went against library theory, and it was unorthodox. Yeah, some books were destroyed because of food. Yeah, some kids didn't really need the extra sugar. But the kids were hungry.

It took a bit of popcorn and a library snack bar to make me realize that being a librarian was about more than just giving people information. It was about serving a community. And if the community is hungry for more than just knowledge, then maybe it's about time to open a snack bar.

The food had taught me the true meaning of the word progressive. I liked the word—usually. There are consequences of every extreme measure; the consequence of being a progressive library was losing Art. He didn't go right away; he went slowly—just sort of faded away. One week he began getting half his hours at another branch, and then slowly he started getting all his hours there. As hard as it was for me to see him go, sometimes that kind of change needed to happen.

---

11. The loudest elderly women always had the quietest elderly husbands.

Chapter 808.543	Being the Chapter in Which
-STOR-	I Explain How to Make
Storytime:	Kids Laugh by Farting,
	and Other Observations
	on Children

There are three general rules about storytelling: rule one, it's an art that not every librarian is cut out for; rule two, all storytellers think they are gods of this sacred art, even the ones that suck at it; and rule three, if you're ever in danger of putting an entire class to sleep because the story that you're reading is boring, tell a fart joke. Or, if you don't know any fart jokes, make a fart noise.

I knew these three rules well, but I never thought much about them for three logical reasons: first, I am a guy, and guy librarians don't need to worry about these things since we very rarely get called upon to read stories; second, it was a known fact in the library that kids kind of didn't like me, and when kids don't like you, then you're not the best choice for storyteller; third, and most logically, Faren, the manager and person in charge of scheduling for storytelling had told me, "Don't worry, you'll never have to read a story."

Then one day my web of preconceived notions came crumbling down when Faren cornered me at the reference desk and said brightly, "How would you like to read to a class tomorrow?"

When I didn't answer right away, Faren added, "We're really desperate. I've asked everyone."

"So I'm your last choice?"

She nodded.

"What if I say no?"

"Then I guess there'd be a lot of unhappy children."

"If I read a story there'd be even more unhappy children."

"You'd do wonderful!" she cheerfully said. "I'll even pick the stories for you—and I promise you'll never have to do it again. Just one class."

I looked at the carpet and mumbled, "Just one class?"

"Great!" Faren said, taking my answer as an agreement. "I'll get the stories for you by this afternoon. You'll have all day to practice."

Most people have some sort of childhood memory about the library. Maybe it is of the crabby librarian who told you not to run or talk loudly. Hopefully, it is of the kind librarian who read you books and made you want to read on your own. In either case, the idea of letting kids in the library is still a pretty young idea (only some 150 years old). The first places that really tried to encourage kids to read were churches. In the 1850s many churches got it in their heads that offering kids the opportunity to read would be great outreach; it was also during this time that books for kids became more popular.

While some librarians strongly preached that public libraries could not continue to claim to be educational while barring children from using them, many librarians dragged their feet and fought bitterly to keep bookshelves closed off to kids. One strong critic of letting kids in the library was Melvil Dewey; for all the genius that he was, he really could be a major dick.[1] Like many librarians, Dewey feared that kids would destroy the books.

There were many reasons why children were eventually let into the libraries, but one of the biggest reasons was that times had simply changed. Mothers were working jobs and kids were causing trouble on the street. So progressive reformers eventually were able to convince libraries to open their doors.

Opening doors gave women a place to become librarians. They were often hired to give a motherly feel to the library and to make kids feel more welcome. They were also meant to serve as the mother kids did not always have at home.

One thing male librarians rejoiced at was the fact that they could save money by hiring women; at the time, women who did the same job as men at the library earned less.

❧

During my tenure as a library page, I tried to stay away from the children's area of the library for three reasons. First, the books had small spines, which made it more difficult to read the call number, and hence more difficult to shelve. Second, the books were often returned sticky, smelly, and disgusting in every way. Third, the children's room was a vast open area, and I preferred to shelve in areas of the library where I would not be easily caught reading while I was supposed to be working.

Nonetheless, I had on numerous occasions shelved in the children's area and had thus become quite aware of the children's books that were popular. When Faren came to me later in the day, as she had promised, with two books I was quite familiar with:

---

1. I normally don't mention the "dick" factor when I tell kids visiting on class visits about his numbering system—I don't think they'd understand.

the first, *More Spaghetti, I Say,* and the second, *If You Give a Moose a Muffin.* The problem was, as much as I could say with confidence that I, in fact, knew *of* the books, the same could not be said of what I knew about their contents, which was nothing.

I had in fact never read a single children's book in all the years I had worked for the library.[2] Even as a child, the only children's picture book I had any recollection of reading was *Green Eggs and Ham.*[3]

Because I only remembered reading *Green Eggs and Ham,* I had falsely assumed that the cardinal rule for all picture books was quite simple: it had to rhyme. It was fortunate for me that the two books that Faren had chosen for me did, for the most part, rhyme. Granted they were no Dr. Seuss, but they were nonetheless charming, funny, and easy to read—essential ingredients for a novice storyteller.

So, with books in hand, I began to delve into their contents, reading the stories aloud in my mind and laughing childishly at some of the more humorous passages. By the end of the work day, I had memorized key passages from the books and had become confident that my knowledge of the stories' contents would

---

2. Years earlier I had worked as an after-school child care substitute and read a story to about ten kids; I was never asked to do it again. And once, I babysat a six-year-old who asked me to stop reading so he wouldn't have bad dreams.

3. The only reason I had a memory of this book was because when I was a child my grandma got the bold idea that perhaps she should have something at her house for grandchildren to do in the rare event that they visited; so she bought *Green Eggs and Ham* and put the copy under the coffee table in her living room. As it happened, we visited her house quite frequently, and my brother and I would always fight for who got to read the book. The person without a book in hand would have the unfortunate consequence of having to listen to Grandma recollect stories of her younger, more curious, days—which, in retrospect, was actually quite interesting (except to a young mind that would rather be outside doing something stupid).

somehow compensate for the fact that I really had no idea of how to do a public reading to a group of little kids.

"Glad I'm not you," Andy bitterly said as I read through one of the dozens of books I had picked out as potentials.

"I'm glad I'm not *you*."

Andy shrugged. "At least at the end of the day I won't go home with the image of fifty little kids laughing at what a fool I was."

"No. You'll just go home to your cat and stroke its back pretending it's a woman because that's the best you'll ever have—a cat."

"Well, at least I have a cat. That's more than you have."

"Let me read!"

"Like reading it's really going to make you better," Andy said, laughing to himself as he walked away.

∽

Every now and then I'd hear loud noises coming from the story-telling room of the library. That was about as close as I came to actually knowing what to do during a class visit, which is to say I knew nothing.

So when the class of twenty second-graders arrived and made their way excitedly into the storytelling room, I really didn't know what I was supposed to do next. I knew I was, at some point, supposed to read them a story, but what I didn't know was how I was supposed to lead into it.

I looked at their eager and anxious eyes, and they looked back. Some appeared to be disappointed that I would be the one telling them a story. I didn't blame them.

"So how is everyone doing today?" I forced out. I didn't care how they were doing and it probably showed. I just wanted to get it over with so I'd never have to do it again.

"Are you going to read us a story?" a red-haired boy asked.

"If you're good." I paused. "If you're not, I'm going to have to put you in the library dungeon." This, I quickly learned, was not the best thing to say. Their eyes grew wider in fear.

A girl in the front row raised her hand and then fearfully asked, when I nodded at her to speak, "Where's the normal story reader?"

"She had to go to the doctor."

"She's sick?"

"That's usually why you go to the doctor," I sarcastically replied. I learned by this reply why sarcasm doesn't go well with small children. The girl looked like she might cry. All the children kind of looked like this. The teacher in the back of the room appeared offended. I looked down at the picture book on my lap and then back up at the fearful class. "How 'bout a story?"

They nodded yes, and I began to read the text without looking up.

"That's not how you do it," the red-haired boy said confidently.

"What do you mean?"

"You're supposed to hold the book out so we can see it, too."

I sighed and rolled my eyes, then held the book so they could see it as well.

Then a funny thing happened: they laughed. Their laugh made me laugh. The more they laughed the more I laughed. The more I laughed the more I got into the story.

When I had finished reading the first story, the kids clapped and told me to read it again. One boy said, "You're silly!"

I spent quite some time helping people learn how to use the computer and showing them how to find books, but I had never felt more valuable than in that moment. I learned that doing something as simple as reading a story could leave a positive imprint on a kid's life.

I read the next story with even more energy and enthusiasm. I even exaggerated passages, improvised lines, and asked silly questions about the story. I was, granted, not great, but I felt happy. And so did the kids.

"The kids looked like they really liked you," Brenda said after she checked the class out.

I nodded proudly.

"It's because you're a guy, it's not because you're good. It's just because you're different."

"Thanks."

"That wasn't a compliment."

"I know."

"I don't know why you even agreed to do it—you didn't have to. It's not your job. You're not a children's librarian. You should have just said no. Then maybe they'd get us some help out here."

I shrugged. "I had fun doing it."

"Well, it's that kind of attitude that makes Faren think it's okay to make us do things not in our job description."

"It's a small library, Brenda. Sometimes you have to do things that aren't in your job description. That's just how it works."

FOR SHELVING

The children's literature genre is a relatively new concept. It's difficult to say when exactly it began, because it really depends on the definition of what is classified as a children's book. If the definition is a book that kids read, then the history is quite old, because 1,000 years ago some kids were reading philosophy books; up until the eighteenth century the only books written exclusively for kids were of an instructional nature.

(Continues)

(Continued)

Most scholars would agree that the book that started the genre was *A Little Pretty Pocket-Book* by John Newbery (perhaps that's why the Newbery Medal is named after him), which was published in 1744. It was a simple little book that contained rhymes for each letter of the alphabet; to market the book, it came with a ball for boys or a pincushion for girls. Before this there were other books for kids (such as John Bunyan's *A Book for Boys and Girls*), but Newbery's book was the first to strike a balance between amusement and instruction, which would become an essential ingredient in most forthcoming books in the genre.

While the genre did blossom and see the publication of such classic collections as those by the Brothers Grimm, it wasn't until over 100 years after Newbery's book that the classic books kids read today began appearing (like *Little Women* [1868], *Treasure Island* [1883], *Alice's Adventures in Wonderland* [1865], *The Wizard of Oz* [1900]). The reason was twofold: one, novels themselves were still a relatively new concept (and just as difficult to define—*Don Quixote* [1605] is as good a work as any to pinpoint as the first novel) and two, many authors felt that writing books for kids would be wasting their talents.

Picture books quietly sat in the shadows of children's books during most of the early history of children's literature; the reason is the high cost it would have taken to reproduce and print illustrations. As the process of lithography advanced, more and more picture books were produced. The first notable picture book was *Millions of Cats* (1928) by Wanda Gag. Prior to this, picture books were usually seen only in the libraries of upper-class families.

Faren appeared to be avoiding me when she returned from her managers' meeting later in the day. When we took our lunch at the same time and met awkwardly in the staff lounge, she had no choice but to ask, as I bit down on my sandwich,[4] "Oh, I completely forgot to ask. How'd it go with the class today?"

I knew she had not forgotten to ask; she just didn't want to ask, because she feared my reply. But I went along with her. "It went well. The class really responded to the stories."

"Really?" She questioned doubtfully.

I nodded.

"Well, I told you that you'd be able to handle it."

"And now I'll never have to do it again?"

"Never again," Faren confidently assured me.

I looked down at my sandwich, disappointed. "I wouldn't mind if I had to fill in again sometime."

"Serious?"[5]

I nodded. "It was actually kind of fun."

She looked at me curiously. "Well, there is another group of kids coming in. I was going to take it, but I have a lot of paperwork. So you want to take it?"

"Sure, I can do that," I said enthusiastically.

~

Every library has a troupe of storyteller stars, who each say they are the best storyteller of them all. Myself excluded,[6] there were three storytelling stars at my library. There was Pam, who struggled with

---

4. People are statistically less likely to yell, curse, or otherwise be rude with their mouths full. Faren was aware of this—she had studied management in college.

5. She sounded like a gossipy teenage girl whenever she got excited.

6. I don't consider myself a storyteller, since I'm basically nothing more than the best of what's left and don't do near the amount of storytelling that the storytelling stars do. (In fact, I hardly do it at all anymore.)

words when she read stories[7] and yet still believed she was the greatest storyteller of them all. Next there was Sarah, a goth-looking woman who always wore dark clothing and colored her hair differently each week. She didn't have kids and didn't want to,[8] but she really enjoyed reading to kids. Finally, there was Melissa, who wanted to be an actress but somehow got stuck working in libraries.

The three stars walked taller than the rest of the library staff. Kids knew their names and often drew them pictures. The star storytellers also got to go to the fun workshops,[9] while other library staff went to the boring ones.[10] A part of all the library staff envied them because they were heroes in the eyes of children, and who doesn't like that?[11]

⁓

I didn't become a regular storyteller figure. I became the storyteller to the rejects—the classes no one else liked reading to—which was fine by me. These classes taught me two very important lessons about life: one, if you can read to the classes that no one else likes and still have kids walking away happy, then you're really prepared for anything life throws at you; two, if I ever have kids, I'm going to be extra picky about finding out about their teachers before I let them be in the class. Some of the classes I read to had some pretty bad teachers, teachers that really made me question

---

7. She had to sound out many three-plus syllable words like "tenderly."

8. I found it odd that almost none of the storytellers had kids, or were married, for that matter. I have since discovered that a pretty high percentage of storytellers don't have kids, and don't want to ever have them.

9. Like "Dynamic Storytelling" and "The Art of Puppetry."

10. Like "Dealing with the Angry Patron Who Wants to Go Fisticuffs on You" or "CPR Training."

11. As it turns out, many librarians don't want to be heroes in a child's eyes, because children demand too much attention and too much of their time.

how restrictive the state of California is when issuing licenses to teach. One such teacher was Ms. Von.

Ms. Von was new to the teaching profession. She became a teacher because her mom was a teacher and her mom told her she should do the same. I was always curious about why Ms. Von had lived so long without committing suicide. She had low self-esteem and complained to me more than once, in front of the class, about how worthless she felt.

The first time I met Ms. Von and her class of third-graders, I was caught a little off guard. I met the class, as I always did, at the front door of the library. When all the children were in the library, something seemed off. I looked around at the children and realized what it was: there was no teacher.

"Did you come by yourselves?" I asked, confused.

"Ms. Von is in the parking lot talking to some guy," a girl said, and then pointed to a young Asian woman in the parking lot flirting with a man who looked slightly homeless and drunk.

"Does she know him?"

The girl shrugged.

"Well, would you mind going to her and telling her that the librarian is waiting for her?"

She nodded and ran to the parking lot as I waited impatiently with the rest of the class at the front of the library. The girl tugged at Ms. Von's leg, explained what I had said, and then pointed at the library. Ms. Von looked at me with disgust and then walked to the library.

"You know," I explained when she reached the entrance, "I'm not certified to be alone with a class."[12]

---

12. Many teachers have made the assumption that since librarians read to kids we therefore also have a license to teach. Some librarians do, but the majority do not.

"I could see them," Ms. Von explained hostilely. "You could have started without me."

I nodded. "Well, I'm actually more comfortable when the teacher is present, if it's okay with you."

Before she could reply, I turned and led the class into the story-telling room. Ms. Von had not followed. She went to the computer terminals to check her e-mail. I left the class alone in the story-telling room, and once more repeated my previous point.

"Ms. Von, maybe I wasn't clear—I don't have teaching credentials." I added more intensely, "It's against the law for me to be alone in that room with the class. You have to stay in the room with them."

She nodded understandingly. "I'm coming."

She didn't come. I stood beside her and waited for her to stand. When she finally did, she headed for the magazine racks.

"The storytelling room is this way, Ms. Von," I explained, pointing.

"I know where it is—I've been here before. I'm just going to get a magazine, so I have something to read."

"The class is waiting," I pointed out.

"I'll be there in a minute. You can start without me."

When I finally started, the class had been in the library for nearly ten minutes. Throughout the story, Ms. Von would laugh loudly at things she read in her magazine. And then she'd yell at her class when they laughed at something in the story.

No other teacher was as bad as Ms. Von but plenty were just as rude. They would take cell phone calls, yawn loudly, or wander aimlessly around the room. When two classes came together, the result was often quite disastrous on the rudeness scale. While I read, many teachers would carry on casual conversations with each other while simultaneously telling the kids to be quiet and listen to the story.

In the same way that I learned to loathe some teachers, I began to have extreme admiration for others. My favorite class was a group of twelve developmentally challenged students and Mrs. Warren, their teacher. I was nervous at the thought of reading to developmentally challenged students. I was sure they were nice and all, but I had never been close to kids who were developmentally challenged. I wasn't sure what to expect and didn't really know what to do with them. As it turns out, you do the same thing with them as you would with any other kid.

As I nervously looked around the class during our first meeting, I saw a boy rocking back and forth, staring aimlessly at the carpet, a girl rubbing her fingers on the carpet and then licking her fingers to see what the carpet tasted like, a boy who wouldn't take his finger out of his ears, a girl who kept slapping the boy next to her, and several others who just looked confused.

I immediately told myself to just read quickly and get out of there. But when I started reading, they did something that was most unusual: they listened. When I finished, they told me without being asked what they liked most about the story, why they thought the illustrations were interesting, and that they saw a dead cat. Except for that dead cat comment, they seemed smarter than any of the other classes I read to. They connected to the stories like no other kids I'd read to and they had the ability to engross themselves in the story to the point that it was almost as if they were in the story.

Mrs. Warren's class of kids was different from other children their age, but that wasn't a bad thing. It takes all kinds of kids to make the world go round, but some, as was the case in Mrs. Warren's class, were much more wonderful than others.

Usually the thing I liked most about reading was the kids, but sometimes it was the teachers. One teacher I liked more than others: Mrs. Greene. Mrs. Greene was an elderly teacher who spoke with a southern accent. I first saw her class of third-graders running through the park. I figured this was just a class doing PE. They were not. As it turned out, they were making their way to the library for their story.

"We're ready for our story!" Mrs. Greene said, out of breath as she walked into the classroom.

I laughed at the sight of the out-of-breath teacher, who had to be over seventy years old, way past the age of retirement. "Next time, you really don't have to run. I won't mind if you're a little late."

"That's not why we're running, darling," she explained. "We were running because we didn't have time to fit PE in today."

I laughed again and led the class into the storytelling room. When I finished the story, Mrs. Greene announced to the class, "I go to church on Sunday because I believe in Jesus. He's my personal savior."

The story I had read was called *Tuesday* and I think Mrs. Greene had mistaken the name for Sunday. At least, that was the only reason I could think of.

After her class had selected their books and left, I laughed as I watched them begin their jog back to school. *You don't see teachers like that anymore*, I thought to myself.

～

One day my world was knocked out of alignment when my manager asked me to read a book to a class visiting the library. Most people would consider this a rewarding task. I considered it punishment for making kids cry. I never quite mastered the art of storytelling like some librarians, but the more I did it the more I felt like I was making a difference in the lives of a few kids. Maybe I didn't know what I wanted to do for the rest of my life, but reading to kids gave me a bit of rest while I figured things out.

Chapter 658	Being the Part Where
-SHUT-	Our Hero Explains Why
Sit Here,	Committees Are Almost
Shut Up:	as Useless as Library School,
	and Other Reasons Why
	He Just Can't Get
	Enough of Them

Librarians are professionals. No self-respecting professional organization can be professional without forming a committee to prove it. And no professional can be a good professional without going to such committee meetings. It was a rite of passage. Pam, not me, decided I should be professional, and, as such, recommended I go to a meeting to prove it.

I could have been more excited about Pam's decision for me to be professional, and perhaps I would have if the conversation hadn't gone like this: "There's a meeting next week. It's really boring and I don't want to go. So I asked Faren to send you instead." She added with a sarcastic laugh, "I think it'll make you more professional."

I just didn't feel the love.

"Just so you know," Michael told me later that day, "I should be going to that meeting. I never get to go to those things!"

I nodded. "It's not my call."

"That doesn't make it right."

Michael and I hadn't had the best relationship since I became a librarian, not that we had the best relationship before this. But before, he could rely on taking credit for all computer issues because pages didn't do that stuff. Now that I was a librarian, I had a responsibility that had previously been his.

"I'm not trying to take your job. Everyone values you. It's just the meeting is for librarians and you're not to that point professionally yet."

"You were nicer as a page," Michael said. "Now you think you're better then everyone else."

I had a feeling Brenda had been talking to him.

~

The closest thing to an official city meeting I had ever been to was a CPR class put on by the fire department.

I hated that class.

I had to wear a tie because I was going to work afterward. Everyone else at the class was from parks and recreations.[1] They were wearing dirty T-shirts and shorts with grass stains; they looked like they had just come from a not-so-friendly game of football in the park.

During the training video they told crude jokes and whispered they'd better be careful or the suit would tattle on them. I wasn't even wearing a suit. In retrospect, I'm pretty sure any person who tucked in his shirt was considered a suit in their minds.

When it came time to perform mouth-to-mouth on the dummy, all they had to do was look at the thing to get the air to

---

1. The jocks of city employees.

flow. I used all my breath and it barely moved. It didn't help when a guy in the back of the room whispered, "Just pretend it's your boyfriend, sweetheart."

I'm sure when it was over they all went out for beer and talked about their favorite monster truck driver.

When that is what you think of when you think meeting, the thought of it is intimidating, to say the least.

~

The meeting was on computers. It was the committee to decide which software and hardware to buy and implement. I was the branch liaison. It would be my job to voice exactly what my branch needed. For the record, I had no idea.

The meeting was held at the main library in the same room where I was first interviewed to be a library technician. The room made me nervous. It looked like a board room and I had this paranoid vision of librarians yelling at each other from across the table. Hollywood had done bad things to my head.

As I walked down the halls of the upstairs office area, I had flashbacks of that horrible interview. I cringed. My flashback was halted when the director of all the libraries turned the corner and I was face to face with her. I had heard stories about her, and standing there I felt I should bow as if she was royalty.

"Scott!" she said to me, "Are you here for the committee meeting?"

I nodded.

She smiled. "Well, it's so nice to see you here. I'm excited to hear what ideas you have." And then she walked away.

I had met her once at a division meeting over a year ago; it was only briefly. The fact that she knew my name made me feel valued.

I was the first to arrive at the meeting and I used the time to study the meeting agenda. On the agenda:

- Review the minutes from the previous meeting
- Discuss the implementation of new online reference database
- Discuss new computer classes
- Discuss the possibility of a new card catalog
- Discuss the possibility of free wi-fi at all branches
- Decide the time and topics for the next meeting

I planned my attack. I decided what I would say so I would not come out sounding like an idiot.[2]

Robert, an aging, flamboyant librarian who always exhibited some form of pink as an accessory, was the first to arrive at the meeting. I smiled at him. He ignored my smile and announced to the clock he was studying intently, "I got ten minutes—I'm taking a nap." He then went to the chair furthest from the door, closed his eyes, and collapsed his head on the table. Every now and then he'd snore a little.

Pearla[3] arrived next. She was fifty but dressed thirty, had messy brown hair, and walked with a skip in her step. "I'm Pearl!" she brightly announced to me. "You must be Scott?"

"Nice to meet you."

"So you're in library school? What are your plans? You going to get married? Someone said you live with your parents? Is that true? You must save a lot of money that way? Do you think it's weird? I bet a lot of people think it's weird? I'm going to library school next semester—do you think that's a good idea? I have my degree in literature, so that's okay, right?"[4]

---

2. It was, after all, my big chance to score brownie points with important library people (or so I thought).

3. Who went by Pearl.

4. I had talked to her for only a brief moment, and she had spoken only in questions.

I started to answer, but she stopped me. "I ask a lot of questions, huh? People say I do, but I don't know? I'm a writer—did you hear about me from others? About my writings?"

I shook my head.

"I've had several letters to the editor published in the *Orange County Register.* Did you see them?"

"I don't really read the letters section."

"You want me to e-mail them to you?"

"Okay," I said to be polite.

"I write letters about anything—don't you think that's funny? I just like to see my name in print, you know? Every little publication helps, right? Someone told me that they didn't count as publication credit, but I think they do—what do you think?"

"Oh, I try not to think."

"You're being funny, right?"[5]

"I don't know."

"What do you think, Robert?"

Robert didn't wake. "He's so cute, don't you think?"

I shrugged.

Melody,[6] an aging librarian from a small branch, arrived next and Pearl immediately bombarded her with questions and completely ignored me.[7]

As the room filled with others, I passed time by staring blankly at the clock. Occasionally someone would glance at me

---

5. I wanted to see what her letter to the editor looked like just to see if it was just one giant question. Something like this: Shouldn't we put our children first? Isn't that what our role as a parent is? Am I wrong? Does anyone out there think I'm wrong? Then why is it this way? Why?

6. Who went by Mel.

7. Which I was happy about.

or introduce themselves. Fifteen minutes after the meeting was supposed to begin, the meeting began.[8]

The person who headed the committee was Murdock, but everyone called him Murd. I don't know why. Murd got things started by reading off the minutes. As he did, Robert continued to sleep. I wondered if anyone would wake him up, or if this would just be his nap time. I was the only one who even seemed to notice he was sleeping, so I gathered no one was going to wake him up.

When Murd finished he said, "So first order of biz." Murd giggled to himself, apparently amused that he had used the word *biz* in a sentence. He added more seriously, "The director really wants to make a push for more online reference tools. Anyone have input about what they'd like to see?"

Donald, who went by Don,[9] said bitterly, "Murd, I could care less what you do. I just come here 'cause they make me. I retire in six months, so do whatever you want!" Everyone laughed. I failed to see the humor. The thought of a bitter old man who couldn't care less about what the library did because he was retiring was just a little sad. I looked around the room and noticed for the first time that half the people in the room would probably retire in another two years. When computer terms were mentioned, they seemed clueless.

"You're young," Murd said to me. "You must know this stuff real well. What do you think?"

---

8. Apparently the first fifteen minutes at such meetings are designated for socializing. To be fair, they gave the excuse that they were waiting to see if another person was coming before beginning, but I later found out that person hadn't come in over a year.

9. I was beginning to notice everyone in the room abbreviated their name (including Robert who went by Rob), and I wondered how I could have abbreviated mine. I thought I could legally change my name to Scotty but then insist everyone call me Scott.

"Honestly?"

"Of course! You don't ever have to flatter us with half-truths! We're only librarians. Save the butt-kissing for the managers!"

"Well, I think you're talking about spending thousands of dollars to buy something that people won't use. This is generation Google and Yahoo. Maybe the main city library needs to have something like that, but the branches?"

"Do you really think you can use Google for scholarly research?"

I shook my head. "But, realistically, how many people come into a public library for scholarly research? Adults come for books. Students come for homework."

"Yeah, but don't they need online journals for their homework?" Pearl asked.

I shrugged. "In an ideal world, it would be nice for them to be learning how to use it, but like I said, this is generation Yahoo and Google. They won't attempt to do anything halfway academic 'til college. And until teachers make them do otherwise, then we're sort of wasting time."

"Wasting our time?" Don said, irritated.

"Sort of."

"Young man, there are plenty of things teachers aren't teaching their students, but that doesn't mean we shouldn't. We're educators, too."

"Realistically, if we had money for this we would have to get it. If we didn't, then the money would just go to waste. So let's not talk about if we need it. Let's just assume we did," Murd said. "But, honestly, we probably won't have the funding for it anyway. But just to be safe, everyone think about it and come back to the next meeting with a list of every database you'd like to see the library subscribing to if money were no obstacle."[10]

There was no money for anything. The whole point of the meeting was to discuss what the library could do if they had the funding. They did not have the funding. Apparently everyone but me knew they didn't have the funding. Of course they probably would have the funding if they didn't waste all their money sending people like Don and Rob to committee meetings they had no intention of contributing to.

On the way out, Don caught me in the hall. "Didn't mean to give you a hard time in there, Scooter."[11]

"That's okay. You have a good point."

He nodded, "But so do you. I think you're going to do some good things for the city. We need some youngsters in here to shake things up. And don't be afraid to argue back at me. I'm just a bitter old man! What am I going to do?"

"What difference does it make? I don't think we'll have the money to do anything soon."

Don laughed. "Oh, we'll never have the money!"

"That's encouraging."

"Let me ask you something. I'm on the verge of retiring. What the hell am I doing on a committee meeting for technology concerns I don't care about?"

I shrugged.

"Honestly, I just didn't feel like working, and committee meetings are the best excuse to get out of work. And you know how I got on the committee?"

---

10. No one would, in fact, return with such notes, including me.

11. I don't like the nickname Scooter.

"How?"

"I made a bit of noise! We're never going to have the funding, the staff, the goods, or whatever to get anything done! But you can't let that stop you! The city will spend everything on fire and police protection, but they won't give the library a dime if you don't twist their arm."

I didn't speak.

"You're not a page anymore. This is the big leagues. Like it or not, you're a professional now. If you want people to treat you like one, then don't be afraid to act like one."[12]

FOR SHELVING

Everyone has heard of modern corporations like Microsoft and IBM, but what about corporations from earlier? They sort of didn't exist, at least in any major memorable way.

Corporate law in the nineteenth century focused on public interest. To form a new corporation, a company required an act of Congress. (I'm being serious about this. Because corporations were regulated so closely by states, oftentimes an act of legislation would have to happen before the corporation was formed.) Tough regulations were no fun for big business, so many used tricks to avoid them—Rockefeller set up Standard Oil as a trust, and Carnegie set up his steel operation as a limited partnership.

Eventually, states relaxed regulations so companies like Enron and WorldCom could be formed. To this day many states maintain less strict rules on corporations as a way of attracting more businesses.

(Continues)

---

12. I thought about Rob and wondered if Don put him in the ranks of professional.

(Continued)

As a matter of useless trivia, the oldest corporation of the western hemisphere is Harvard College (founded in 1636).

Pam called me to her desk later that day. She told me to sit down, then turned and looked at her computer screen blankly. She continued to stare several seconds and finally said, "Oh, I know what I was going to ask you. How was the meeting?"

I shrugged. "Seemed a little pointless. I mean, we don't have money to do any of the things they want to do, so why bother talking about it?"

"What is it they wanted to do?"

"Mostly we just talked about buying reference databases."

"Oh, gawd! That's so stupid! Did you tell them we don't want them?"

"Well, I said it would be good at the main library, but not so much here."

"Good! The people that come in here are kind of stupid. The high school students that do manage to graduate have the intelligence of a sixth grader."

"The ones I've talked to seem pretty nice. And smart."

She ignored me. "Hey, you're pretty computer smart—do you know how to crop a picture and put it in a report?"

I nodded.

"Excellent!" She turned her computer screen toward me, opened a picture of her son, and said, "Show me how to crop this picture and copy it into Word." She opened the Word document and it said, "Come to Jag's seventh birthday party!"

I thought about what Don said about being a professional; this didn't exactly seem professional and I looked at the screen a little surprised.

"I know what you're thinking. I've been meaning to ask you this for a long time, and now that I finally remembered, I don't have a report for you to demonstrate on. I just want the practice."

I didn't really care what her excuse was. It seemed a bit unprofessional, but she was my boss and I couldn't exactly question her judgment. So I smiled, nodded, and showed her what to do.[13]

When I finished, she asked me, "Now, let me ask you this, what do you think of Terry?"[14]

"She's okay. Doesn't complain. Keeps on task."

"I don't like her. She's too slow. I think she's a little bit retarded."

How do you respond to someone saying, *I think she's a little bit retarded*? I responded like this. "I don't think so. I think she's just learning the ropes. She's a hard worker. I think she'll be fine once she learns her way around."

She nodded yes. She agreed. Then she said, "I'm going to ask Faren to fire her. I don't like her."[15]

～

I finished the day with two voices in my head. One from an elderly librarian telling me to be more professional; and one from a

---

13. To be fair, it took less than five minutes and was kind of on break time.

14. Terry was a page; she had been working for the library for three weeks; she had just graduated high school and this was her first real job.

15. It was not unusual for Pam to make such a request. She believed telling the manager who to fire made her look like she was more capable to be in charge.

librarian who should have been like a mentor—the person I should be learning from—saying someone was retarded.[16]

As much as I loved my job, it was hard not to wonder if I was ready for it. And what exactly did it mean to be professional anyway?

I heard stories from friends who were pursuing careers as actors or musicians; they were struggling and a part of them knew they would never make it, but they were also living and that was commendable. They weren't settling for the first career that came their way just because they were out of college. They were taking the time to live out their dreams.

I felt like libraries somehow were my destiny, but I didn't feel quite ready to experience my destiny just yet. This isn't exactly the thought one wants to wander through their mind when they had just spent a nice chunk of their life trying to master the subject.

16. In all fairness to Pam, she is not as unprofessional as I make her sound in this book; my apologies in advance to anyone who feels they are being misrepresented in this memoir. Kindly note that if you simply bring up the fact with me that you have been misrepresented, I will most surely say that the person you think is you in the book is in fact not you. Things about the characters have been changed for their protection and to bring more humor to the story.

Chapter 795.43	Curious Observations
-HOWT-	and Random Cures
How to Do	for Boredom
Nothing	That Don't Include
and Get Paid:	FreeCell

I start each day telling myself I'm not going to play FreeCell. It should be easy to resist. I hate that game. It's pointless and you accomplish nothing. And yet by the end of each day I have played more than a few hands. That's just what happens. You sit at the desk at the start of the day and it's fine at first, but then no one comes in and you have nothing to do. You check e-mail; you check the news; you do everything you can think of online just to make it look like you're doing something.

You have to look busy—you always have to look busy. If you don't, the powers that be decide that they don't need to schedule so many people, and your hours are cut in half. Whenever a manager would ask me how the previous night went I would always reply, "Busy! Haven't seen it that busy in ages." In reality it was always slow. Sometimes it was so slow that staff were the only people in the building and we'd break out the checkers and play a few games.

Whatever the case, however guilty I felt getting paid to play card games, I'd always go back to them; what else could I do? Really? That was my life, stuck in a community service job where a large part of my job entailed doing absolutely nothing. It sounds nice, but it really isn't. On slow days I look back and wish I was still working any number of my old labor-intensive jobs. At least I was doing something.

Could I complain? I was getting paid over $17.00 an hour to look busy; at least it wasn't minimum wage to ask if they wanted fries with that. Could I really complain?

I could and I did.

I complained to everyone. That's what you do when you have nothing better to do. You act miserable and take it out on others. Soon I decided it wasn't right and I just needed to talk it out.

I asked Cindy, "Why do you want to work here?" I knew she'd give me a motivational talk on libraries' influence in society.

I was wrong.

"What else am I supposed to do?"

I shrugged.

"Don't shrug your shoulders. I'm serious. Where can I go? Do you really think I haven't looked? I have. I've even been on interviews. No one wants me."

"Oh."

"You think this is the worst of my problems, though?"

I shrugged.

"I wish! You think you got problems? Try living with your boyfriend."

I had heard about her boyfriend nearly every day since I began working with her; every day it was either on or off, "I love him" or "I hate him." The only thing I could be certain of was that if she loved him Tuesday she would hate him by Wednesday.

"Why don't you just break up with him? Is it really worth all of this?"

She looked down sadly and nodded. "We're starting counseling next week. It's a new counselor, not that guy we used last month. That guy was a complete joke."[1]

"Who does that?"

"What?"

"Counseling? I mean you're not even married."

"You sound exactly like my last counselor!"

"Maybe he had a point?"

She nodded. "I can't break up with him! I love him."

"Sounds like it."

"I do!"

"What do you love about him? You don't like the way he treats you, you don't like the way his house smells like dog, you fight every time you're together. I mean, yeah, he's a great guy, and maybe even a great friend, but what do you love about him?"

"You wouldn't understand. You don't even have a girlfriend."

"But at least I'm happy."

"I am happy." Before I could say more, she left and washed her hands.[2]

Maybe that's what the degree was for. People like her. Smart people who do nothing else because they weren't developed socially. Maybe that's what a librarian was, someone who lacked social skills. And maybe that's why I was having such a hard time with it.

---

1. That guy had suggested they break up, get independent counseling, and get back together only when, and if, they could help themselves.

2. Several months later they finally did break up because she found out he had been cheating on her—with a man.

Was this going to be me in ten years? Stuck in a job I hated because where else could I go? Dating some girl I couldn't stand just because that's the best I could get? I was confused before. Now I was outright depressed.

I decided maybe I shouldn't put all my confidence in one bitter librarian's decision. I needed two library opinions to sink into complete and utter eternal depression. I needed Art. His hours at the library had been cut, but I still saw him occasionally.

"Art, why do you do it?"

"What?"

"This. This job. Why do you stay?"

He shrugged his shoulders. "Beats saying, 'Welcome to Wal-Mart.'"

"That's it?"

"What do you want me to say? That I like the people? That I just find books exciting?"

"For starters."

He laughed at the notion. "If you ask me, this job can be a pain in an old man's bum."

I didn't speak.

"No job's perfect." He thought and then added, "Are you asking why I do this, or are you asking why you should?"

"Both."

"Well, I think you're asking the wrong question."

"What should I be asking?"

"Any job is like a marriage; love can only take a relationship so far. If you want it to work, then you have to give it a little work. The question isn't what you should do with your life, because you're already doing it; the question you need to start asking yourself is if you're in a marriage worth saving."

I nodded.

"Well? Is this marriage worth saving?"

"Sometimes. Every marriage is rocky at the beginning. I think there are two kinds of people. Those who constantly remind themselves why they got into the marriage to begin with and those who don't bother. The ones that don't bother are the worst off. They're always depressed. You need to make the effort to get what you want."

I nodded.

"Don't rush in or out of anything. Just take the time to find out who you are, and who the library is. See if the two of you are compatible."

"I get it, Art! Enough with the metaphor."

"I haven't even told you about having sex with the library."

"Just keep that fantasy between you and the library, yeah?"

He shrugged. "Your life."

When the library announced it would be hiring a full-time clerk, it was big news. Libraries are staffed with lots of qualified part-time people who desperately want to be full-time because they need the benefits. These positions are hard to come by, and when one does open up people are obviously eager to get it. Two of the many eager people were from my library, and, in the end, neither got the position. One was Rosie, who didn't get the job because her accent was too heavy; the other was Brenda, who didn't get the job because she was a lazy, obnoxious bitch.

In a move marked with controversy, the job ultimately went to Toni, a city employee who had never worked in a library and had only on rare occasions been inside one. As much as people complained that it wasn't fair because so many people from inside the library wanted it, I didn't care—I liked Toni from the start.

How could I not? The first thing she said to me—before I had even been formally introduced—was, "I only took this job because it paid more than my other." It was hard not to like that can-do attitude. Brenda claimed she wasn't bitter. "I'm glad I didn't get it," she told me the day before Toni came. "It's too much work, and I really didn't want it anyway. I only wanted them to offer so I could turn it down."

Brenda, in fact, was bitter. Everything Toni did, she criticized. About the only thing Brenda enjoyed more than criticizing was when Toni actually did make a mistake and she got to point it out and comment behind her back about how slow she was.

I think what I liked most about Toni was how mad she made Brenda. I liked Brenda, but it kind of made my day when she got mad because she was always so immature about it.

FOR SHELVING

Think you have a boring job? There are doctors who actually have done serious research on boredom. Just when we thought it was safe to be bored for the sake of being bored, scientists had to screw it up by saying not only was there a reason but there are different types of boredom. Just to name a few:

PATHOLOGICAL BOREDOM: Occurs when a person is looking for distractions because they are trying to repress something.

ACUTE BOREDOM: The normal boredom that most people have while on long car rides through the desert.

CHRONIC BOREDOM: A person engages in what can be considered a risky behavior just to make things more interesting. Some experts have gone as far as calling this kind of boredom a medical condition.

Research suggests that kids are easily bored not because they actually are but because they do not have the temperament to understand what they are learning. People believe research because it uses fancy words that they don't understand, but when a group of teens senselessly beat to death a homeless man[3] because they were "bored," research begins to fall apart. What other things have people done in the name of boredom? Teens in rural areas used to get bored and go cow tipping. Now? Cow killing. In Tennessee, teens killed over twenty cows because they wanted to see what it was like. In California, men rammed a horse to death.

---

3. True story.

As if my job couldn't get any more mundane, one day the library decided it needed stats. The library would be applying for a state grant and needed stats about the demographics of the library.[4]

When a library decides to do stats, it does them hardcore. It jams the stats so far down people's throats that the people don't even want to come into the building.

It was a simple enough survey. Ask each person who walks into the library where they live and to point it out with a pin on a large map, which would be taken down daily. Sound polite and easy? It was. Until about an hour into it. Pam came out to supervise and

---

4. The city was so keen on getting this grant that it literally spent thousands of dollars on a consultant who would help write it. I saw this man exactly two times. He made me aspire to be a consultant.

said immediately, "You can't let anyone into this building who hasn't answered the survey."[5]

That wasn't so bad the first day; it wasn't so bad the second; by the third day regular patrons were irritated. "I've already answered it! You know where I live!" I felt bad for them. But I had to ask it. I would be scolded if I was caught letting a patron go by.

Patrons were pretty understanding and saw it as a bureaucratic joke. One patron was quite insistent about not stopping. He was obviously homeless and didn't want to tell us where he lived because he didn't live anywhere.

"Did you just let him pass by without him answering?" Pam asked.

I nodded.

"I told you not to do that. Everyone who comes in this building has to answer those questions."

"He was homeless," I quietly said.

To which she loudly answered, "I don't care if he's homeless! We don't discriminate here. *Everyone* answers those questions."

She looked at the man, then at me. Others were staring as well. She had created quite a scene. I didn't move.

She grabbed the clipboard from my hand and said, "I'll show you how it's done." She went to the man and said brightly, "Hello, sir. I noticed you forgot to answer our quick survey."

"I didn't forget nothing. I don't have to take no survey to come in this building. It's a public place and I have a right to be here."

She stood taller. "Sir, there is no need to have attitude."

"Well, there ain't no need to be harassing me like this."

---

5. This was, in fact, true, but no one took it seriously, because it wasn't realistic. But Pam wanted to go by the book to impress administrators.

She nodded. "I do apologize for the inconvenience. If you could just tell me what city you live in."

"I already told you, lady, I don't have to take no survey and I ain't gonna do it."

"Is this going to be a problem?"

"The only problem is your harassing me. I came here to study in peace,[6] not to be harassed by some white woman. I don't see you harassing no white folk."

"Don't accuse me of being racist, sir. Everyone in this building has answered this *very* short survey except you."

"Well, I ain't everyone. If they want to have their rights violated that's their prerogative. I don't have to answer nothing and I'm not going to. I know my rights."

"It's just a simple survey. I don't understand why you can't answer the questions. It's very short, and it helps the library with its statistics. It will help us get a much nicer building."

"Don't think I'm not excited about this building and your project. It's wonderful that you have something to keep you busy. I think you're wasting too much time harassing people and not enough time planning out how you're going to build this new building of yours."

She smiled. "If you could just tell me the city you live in."

"Lady, you need to go away from me now."

"Is that a threat? I can call the police, you know."

"You do what you need to do, but I'm not answering that survey."

She crossed her arms, tucking the clipboard against her chest, and walked back to me. She handed me the clipboard and said, "That man smells so bad. His mouth smelt like crap, like crap

---

6. In fact, he had come there to sleep.

was coming from his mouth every time it opened. Mark him as Santa Ana."[7]

Andy, who had seen the whole thing, laughed to himself and said, "I love this job."

"You ever think about leaving?"

"Absolutely not! I've had several jobs, but this is the best one yet."

"You must have had some pretty bad jobs then, because you seem miserable here!"

"That's just how I am—you know that."

I nodded.

"I used to work for Boeing. That was a high-paying job. I was a janitor, but I did alright and the benefits were as good as they come. They never even noticed when I smoked joints on my breaks!"

"What happened?"

"Cleaning toilets wasn't my thing." He paused and snickered. "They may make airlines, but Boeing boys drop bombs!"

I rolled my eyes. "Too much information."

"Money isn't everything. I don't get paid much here, but I get by. And I'm happy. I don't have stress. I don't go home worrying about anything. If I do something wrong it's no big deal. You can't complain about a job like this."

∽

Ernest was a regular patron who was also homeless. He was more than happy to walk into the library each day and answer our survey. "I live right here," he said cheerfully each day, pointing at the library.

---

7. Pam was usually good with people, but when a patron happened to hit her the wrong way she could handle it quite oddly. The sad part about memories is that we tend to remember the bad more than the good.

Ernest had the kind of life I would live if only my balls were a little bigger. Some fifteen years ago he left his job and bought a van. He had already seen the world during a tour of duty in the Vietnam War; his kids were all grown; he had no wife. All he had was books—he loved to read. Every now and then (for two to three weeks) he'd work some random construction job. He'd live in a motel during these weeks but save most of his money for food he'd need in the coming months. When he wasn't staying at a motel, he'd park in front of a friend's home and sleep. He never asked for handouts and refused to inconvenience anyone.

He was like the library's adopted patron saint. He watched over our cars in the parking lot, told us to call the police when it looked like a drug deal was about to go down in the park, and always had a story to tell.

Some days when I was leaving work, Ernest would be barbecuing steak and he'd offer me some. He had little money, but he was willing to cook me steak because of all the books I would help him find.

Ernest made me like me more.

When I doubted my life it was people like Ernest who made me know that I could go on. Maybe I wasn't always happy with my job, but every time an Ernest came into the building I could work one more week without doubts.

～

Toward the end of the week a poster was put up with the library's design for a new building. This revived the interest in the survey, because at last they could look and point and feel there really was a point to the survey.

Suddenly memories came flooding in about how much the city needed a new library, and the patrons would do whatever it took to help it get built.

It's funny how much a photo can change the way we see the world.

It also made people talk; I hated these people the most. They would come and ask, "So how exactly will these stats be used?"

I would always give the answer "No idea. I'm just taking down the stats—I'm not inputting them." And this would never appease them. They would tell me about how political polling was done, or any number of things that had absolutely nothing to do with the library stats.

～

About the same time I started doubting where my life was headed, Michael started to experience similar doubts. His doubts and behaviors were different from mine. "I just don't feel right," he confided in me one day.

"How so?"

"You just ever feel like—I don't know, I can't describe it. There's just something. I don't know." And then he left.

Maybe I started noticing him acting weird after that because of what he said, or maybe he had actually acted weird all along and I just didn't notice it because he never said anything strange. All I know is, after that, things were different.

The first thirty minutes of his day were spent straightening fliers that were perfectly straight. When I'd tell him someone needed help on a computer, he'd get frustrated and say, "I have to finish straightening." I often caught him for extended periods of time just staring at the desk. I'd ask him what he was staring at and he would simply reply, "Oh, just the dust." Then he'd move his fingertip over the dust, lift it toward me to show me his find, and then stare vacantly at his fingertip.

"You doing okay, Michael?" I asked him more than once.

"Lot on my mind, but I'm fine, I'm fine," is all he would ever say.

"You getting tired of your job—bored I mean?" I'd ask him.

He stared at me for several seconds, and then announced, "I should go straighten."

Maybe I wasn't always satisfied with my job, but at least I wasn't going crazy.

~

Every job needs a tattletale who is willing to forsake her own job duties to tell others what they are doing wrong. Brenda was my library's tattletale. I didn't mind. She liked me. She had told me several times that she did and sometimes I even believed her. But turning me in meant that for just a brief second she felt control over me. She needed this.

After forming an alliance with Pam when the library started passing out popcorn, Brenda believed that she could finally start making a difference in her tattling. They would spend lunches, breaks, and, ultimately, company time discussing who was meeting or not meeting expectations. I would find myself on their hit list every now and then; everyone would. Usually it was because I was caught reading e-mail or playing FreeCell.[8]

When I would get called into Faren's office, I would confess and apologize. I would explain how I had nothing else to do, but that I had indeed been unprofessional. She would say, "Well, maybe I will find you something to do so you're not so bored." I would nod, but knew nothing would come of it, because as much as Faren said it was bad, in the end she didn't really care as long as I got my other work done.[9]

~

8. Brenda and Pam both played FreeCell so seriously that they wrote down the numbers of the games they didn't win and then would continue to play that same game until they won it. They claimed they were doing this only on their breaks, but on more than one occasion I had caught them telling a patron who wanted to check out books to wait while they finished a transaction, when in fact it was FreeCell on their screen.

9. It's not as if I did nothing. I did have real work to do and I took it seriously.

When the week was over and all the stats were collected, the night crew celebrated the only way we knew how. By doing nothing. Nothing on that particular night involved a paper airplane contest.[10] The paper airplane contest was scheduled for 8:02 P.M. There were only three people working that night. It would be just Jonathan—a new library tech—Toni, and me.

Jonathan had started a month ago. He was young, idealistic, in library school, and kind of looked up to me. I wasn't a very good mentor, but I think he liked me because I didn't make him work. He told me he wasn't ready for a career, so the less he had to do at work to remind him that he was in one the better. I respected his wishes and did my best to make sure he never worked. I decided the winner would get to leave a full minute early. Every second counts at the library. Sixty seconds is like receiving a gift from the goddess of all libraries: J. K. Rowling.

Toni looked like she had never made an airplane in her life. Her plane looked like a wad of paper. When she launched the wad into the air, she did so underhanded. It went straight up in the air and then drifted back down. I was a bit disappointed because she had received her BA degree in art, and I would hope the art of paper airplane–making had been a required course.

---

10. My fascination with paper airplanes went as far back as elementary school. Every kid had their schoolyard game they liked to play. Some kids had handball, others tetherball. I had paper airplanes. This lifelong love affair with making paper glide began in third grade. It was innocent then, but it progressed over the years. By fifth grade the paper airplanes my friends and I made would be more technical then your typical play. Multiple sheets of paper would be needed, as would glue, paperclips, and scissors. Ultimately, the final models would need slingshots to launch them into the sky and would take days (sometimes weeks) to build. They would go several feet; we pretended they went for miles. We would have wars trying to knock each other's planes from the sky, or simply see whose could go farthest or do the best stunt work. In the end we had elaborate competitions, which ended in sixth grade when our teacher confiscated our slingshots because a few of us had also used them to shoot rocks at people's heads.

Jonathan's plane looked like the kind of plane an engineer from NASA would create. He folded the paper carefully and made sure there were no errors in his design. It took him ten minutes to finish his creation. I was slightly surprised that it did not include landing gear and lights. He did shoulder rolls to warm up his throwing arm and then gave four practice throws before announcing confidently that he was ready for his trial. He gave a deep grunt and then made a perfect throw. It went for approximately ten feet. A fair distance, but less than any of us expected.

Finally it was my turn. I had to do better. I was their supervisor and had to prove worthy of the claim. I dug down deep in my troubled brain to the spot that contained all the paper airplane–making skills I had learned as a child, skills received by reading airplane-making books from the library. It took me less than one minute, but I was nonetheless satisfied with my modest aerodynamic vessel. I threw it gracefully, and then watched it flounder quickly to the ground three feet later.

As Jonathan left the building, I walked to the computer. I looked at the screen several seconds and told myself not to but I couldn't resist the urge. I clicked on the icon and opened up FreeCell.

Oh, how I had missed her.

Chapter 658.8	Being About Library
-READ-	Reading Campaigns
Read Five Books,	and Why Librarians
Get Mad Cow:	Have to Give Kids
	a Hard Time about Reading
	When They Can Obviously
	See That the Poor Kids
	Are Hungry

Girl Scouts have their cookies, schools have their food drives, Jerry Lewis has his telethon—and libraries? Libraries have reading incentive programs. It's their marketing plea to get exposure, to get people not only to talk about the library but also to visit the library.

It seems like a good thing, and it is. But it always turns into a chaotic rodeo to see who is the fastest hand in the West. Early in the year libraries come together and decide what they will do this year to get kids to read. Good ideas are thrown out. A plan is made. Everyone loves each other. And then the plan is taken back to the branches and all hell breaks out.

"We *will* be better than all the other branches," Faren tells us like a sergeant tells his troops before annual war games. At this point, everyone nods and somehow we all forget the point of the program. The point suddenly becomes to do better than everyone else. Faren continues. "Every minute of the day someone will be stationed at the front door. If they have a kid they *must* sign up for the program. If they don't have a kid then find out what they do have—a cousin, a nephew, a niece, a stepson, a neighbor they've never met! Everyone knows a kid, and everyone joins this program!"

"What if they already have a log?" someone would always bring up.

"Give them another. And another! This is priority one. Every kid that walks through that door gets one. Everyone!"

"So the point of this program," I asked the obvious, "is to give away thousands of reading logs, or to actually get kids to read?"

"I don't care what they do with the logs! Of course we want them to read, but kids are into TV." She paused and thought for a moment. Everyone knew she had just come up with some absurd idea. "In fact, this year encourage kids to watch their cartoons with subtitles! Tell them if they read the TV with subtitles for thirty minutes that will count as thirty minutes of reading."

"Are you serious?"

"Reading is reading."

"Well, heck," I sarcastically added, "maybe we can tell the teens to go to the liquor store with fake IDs and stock up on 'nudie' magazines. I'm sure every boy in Anaheim would be reading if they could include that on the logs! Reading is reading, after all."

Faren didn't say anything. I couldn't tell if she was offended or considering the idea.

That's what happened the first week. The second week things started getting worse. Kids were returning for a second visit and had already signed up. Then the library got desperate, and Faren decided on other plans of action. Schools were visited—some in different cities. If there was a festival anywhere near the library, then we had to have a booth, we had to sign up.

Pam rarely worked the sign-up station, but on the second week she felt we weren't being proactive enough and decided to join in. One mother refused the reading log. "My kid already has two!" she joked.

"Well, now he has three."

The mom took the log, smiled, and then threw it away. "Thank you," the woman said.

Pam smiled and marked one person had taken the log. Reading is reading.

"Who is that woman?" the woman asked me.

I smiled and dryly said, "Just a librarian trying to get ahead."

"Well, she's very pushy. You'd think she'd have a better attitude."

"She's just really eager to get kids to read."

When the stats were released, we, of course, always came out ahead. Way ahead. There were no exaggerations.[1] We were the best. We had beaten them all. Our prize? Nothing. We had beaten them all and our prize was knowing that we were the masters of the reading program, which, in all honesty, none of us could remember what the point of was to begin with because our minds had been filled with such a competitive nature.

The programs united us. Brenda and Pam, who on other months were against us, were finally for us; both set out to prove they could sign more kids up. Competition motivated all of us.

Of course, even as a team we would divide. "I signed up thirty-seven kids today!" Brenda said to Toni. "How many kids did you sign up?"

"I didn't count—a dozen maybe?"

"Ha! Yet another thing I can do better than you!"

---

1. There were, in fact, some.

"I didn't know it was a competition."

"I just wanted you to know." Brenda giggled like a little schoolgirl.

"That's very good, Brenda. Maybe you could take your salesmanship to a car lot and sell cars."

Brenda walked away with a proud smirk on her face.

"You really don't have to let her do that."

Toni nodded. "I just want to do my job and leave. I don't want to cause drama."

"Your mere presence creates drama—can't really help that."

∽

During the summer there was the summer reading program. Kids liked it; parents thought it was nice; staff got excited. But that was summer. In the spring it was a whole other can of worms, because that's when food came to town. In-N-Out to be exact.

Food changes people. Not only do they take the logs, they take them in bulk. They ask for one for their brother's wife's sister's son's cousin. They take the logs like they are sacred, and somehow the fact that food's involved does make them sacred. Everyone wanted a piece of it.[2] Even adults would come in and return them for their son who was too sick to come to the library. We knew well the person had no son, but usually we did not pursue it. I hated the In-N-Out program for several reasons. One, it encouraged beef, of which I am no fan. Two, do we really need to dangle food in front of kids' faces to get them to read? And three,[3] the library was decorated everywhere with In-N-Out. This by itself

2. It is a simple program. A student reads thirty minutes every day for a week, logs the time, and returns the log for a coupon for a free hamburger.

3. Most importantly three.

wasn't so bad. What was bad was that they decorated the places where only adults would go.

All day long adults would ask "How do I join?" "What's in the bag?" or, most annoying of all, "I can order *In-N-Out* food here?" The answer was no on all counts! Adults are dumb; you can't promote a program to them that they cannot join. They get angry. They say things like "Why do you discriminate against adults? We deserve the food, too." It was always the fat people who said this, the fat people who didn't read, who always used the library to sit on their lazy butts, and who used the computer in an effort to get fatter. If there had been a reading program for them, they would have complained that they didn't want to read, they just wanted the food.

The worst ones were the ones who tried to be cute.[4]

Normally they'd just stop at the desk and poke their fingers at the bags. "There food in there?" I wanted to say, "No, you buffoon! Why would we keep food in a bag in front of the desk?! Don't you think it would spoil? And if we did, why would we put it in a bag where no one could see it?" But I didn't. I simply answered, "No."

But *no* would never satisfy them; they would have to ask the obvious. "Well, why's it on the desk, then?"

"Just decoration."

"But there's no food inside?"

"No food."

"Just decoration?"

"Just decoration."

"You should put food in it! That would be funny."

---

4. Note to the reader: If this is you, you are not cute. Stop it.

No. It in fact wouldn't be funny. It would be stupid. But I didn't say this. I smiled. I always smiled when I thought a person was being an idiot.

FOR SHELVING

The East Coast has White Castle. The West Coast? We have In-N-Out. Unlike most fast-food chains, In-N-Out actually cooks their food made to order, and boy is it good.[5] Still not convinced of its taste? When Paris Hilton (who had formerly done commercials for Carl's Jr.) was pulled over for one of her DUI convictions, she said of the incident that she wasn't drunk, just hungry, and really wanted an In-N-Out hamburger. Does that seal the deal or what?

The hamburgers alone could put In-N-Out up there as the best, but what puts the burger chain a notch above the rest is loyalty. When McDonald's and Carl's sold out and became franchises during the fast-food boom of the 1950s and 1960s, In-N-Out refused. To this day it remains privately owned. They pay employees well above minimum wage, keep their menus simple, and sell the freshest food money can buy. They are everything a company is supposed to be.

---

5. So good, in fact, that I haven't eaten beef in several years and I can still taste it.

I don't know how I have gotten this far in the book without talking about the crazy Buddha man. I suppose there are just so many random crazy people that it's easy to forget them.

The crazy Buddha man has a long history at the library, so long that urban library legends[6] have grown up around him. I first came aware of him because he would type nonsense into the computer and put a large picture of Buddha behind the computer to protect him.[7] There was only one verifiable fact about the crazy Buddha man: he was a registered sex offender.

He liked Art for some reason.[8]

Art told me the legends. He drove a tour bus. Several years ago he had worked for the library as a page and asked out the then-manager.[9] And he had been banned for a period of time for going to see the city librarian while he was dressed in army fatigues and claiming aliens had sent him to destroy the library. All this was legend; nothing had been proven.

During the In-N-Out campaign he approached Sarah[10] and began to yell we were "Murderers, all murderers! Krishna didn't approve of the slaughter of cows."

When he was told this conduct was inappropriate, he tried a different approach. He[11] put Krishna leaflets throughout the library that said, "The library kills cows."

∼

---

6. An urban library legend is much like a regular urban legend, only it occurs in the library. It is a mysterious story and spreads in various forms to the point where it becomes fake. The main difference is that there are several parts of the story that are, in fact, true.

7. He claimed to be Hare Krishna, which made the Buddha even odder.

8. Curiously enough, the crazy Buddha man did not come to the library for several years. Then one day he reappeared with fervor; he went to a clerk and loudly said that Art had been in prison with him and now the FBI was on his case. For several days he came back to the library asking for books on the history of the FBI, the mafia, and terrorists. More than once he demanded that I find him the number of the local branch of the FBI, and on several occasions I saw him drafting lengthy letters with the FBI's address.

9. Who had quit long ago.

10. A vegetarian.

11. This was not proven.

The worse thing about the reading program was the kids who asked for more coupons. Sometimes a kid would come up[12] and ask for more. It would break my heart, because I knew how hungry they were. When no one looked I'd slip them one and an extra few for their brothers and sisters.

One boy came to the desk and asked for another and Brenda noticed me hand it to him. "He already got like twenty of those."

"Probably."

"Then why are you giving it to him?"

"Because he's hungry."

"It's going to ruin the program for everyone. In-N-Out's going to complain and stop passing them out."

But I passed them out anyway. I didn't care. I knew they weren't going to end the program on account of some kid who was just a little bit too hungry. And I didn't care if they did, because I hated the program.

An entire family of ten came in. Each had a reading log, including the baby, who couldn't read. They all looked hungry. I knew what this was. This was tonight's dinner. They were so thankful for the treat. The kids were excited. Tonight they would eat well. A hamburger and a fry was like an expensive restaurant meal for them; it was something they rarely did. I could imagine them sitting there savoring every bite, taking an hour to eat a meal that would take me two minutes to eat, just because they didn't want to finish it.

I thought about the last time I ate there. I couldn't even remember what it tasted like. I guess it was good. But them—I bet they could

---

12. It was usually a boy, a fact you don't need to know.

remember where they sat and what the person looked like who took their order. It had been that special.

"Looks like we're feeding the whole family tonight," Brenda said, trying to spoil my moment.

"Yeah, sort of looks that way."

"I remember when this program used to be honest."

"If it gets them into the library and it gets them food, does it matter?"

"It does when it doesn't teach them respect and honesty."

She would turn me in to Pam, of course, but I didn't care.

∽

When the In-N-Out program was over, the staff got a prize. A reward from In-N-Out for partnering with them to get kids fatter. The prize? A free meal, so we could get fatter as well.

I always took the coupon bitterly. Then I drove to In-N-Out. I ordered a grilled cheese sandwich and paid extra so I could get a shake. I hated the program, but I was sucked in. Free was free, and I couldn't just let it go to waste.

I ate that cheese sandwich and thought about all the cholesterol I had contributed to the world. I imagined it was some ghastly amount, the same amount to give a grown man a heart attack a thousand times over. Then I thought about how many books had been read because of the program. A lot. Would people have read anyway? Maybe. Maybe not. In the end, I don't believe the point of the program was to say "read" as much as it was to say this fast food chain supports literacy and community involvement. There aren't a lot of places left anymore that make a sincere effort to reach out to the community.

When I was a kid, Disneyland used to give out free tickets to some of the kids who read the most books, but the program had ceased long ago. I'm sure Disney cited budgeting cutbacks or something of that nature. The truth was, it didn't cost them a dime to participate in a reading program; it was even tax deductible. Companies like Disney just didn't really care about the community, except for PR's sake. If they cared at all about the community, then why would they threaten to sue a school for showing one Disney movie in a class without paying for a public performance license?[13]

When I got back from eating my free grilled cheese sandwich, I sat in the parking lot for a few moments. I looked at one of the kids. He was grossly underweight. Should I really be concerned about his cholesterol? You really couldn't do harm to a kid like that. He needed the fat. I looked around the library; almost all of the kids did. Fast food nation? Maybe, but not in this part of town. This part of town was rice and bean nation, every night the same meal because that was the cheapest thing you could get for all those kids. Was food for reading such a bad thing? I don't think so.

---

13. No joke! Disney expects schools with no funding to pay hundreds of dollars just so they can show *Tarzan* to a group of underprivileged kids on a rainy day. And if they get caught showing it without the license, the lawyers will threaten to sue. Visit http://MPLC.org to see how you can infringe on copyright laws.

Chapter 362.42088	Being the Chapter
-PRIE-	in Which I Explain Why
Is the Priest	the Mentally Challenged
in Today?	Aren't So Challenged
	After All

I'll be honest. I'm not a fan of the handicapped. It's not that I hate them or think they are a burden. I'm just uncomfortable around them. I don't know what to do when I see them. I feel like I always do the wrong thing—look at them wrong, say the wrong thing, point my finger in a way they'll interpret as crude. Is that so bad? Yes, it turns out, when the next-door neighbor to your workplace is a center for the mentally challenged.

The library I work in is literally across from a therapeutic center, which means a large percentage of library visitors are mentally challenged. At first, like most people, I didn't know how to act around them, so I ignored them. Fortunately, they didn't ignore me.

Each person, in their own way, taught me that I could come to work each day and answer questions as they came, but that was only part of my job, a small part at that. The greater part of being a librarian is about talking to people, learning who they are and why they come to the library. When someone asks a librarian for help finding something, there is no perfect place; my job is to guide that person to the right place for them, and to do that I have to know where they're coming from.

I began to see that I could sit at the reference desk bored to death, or I could try and make a little more of the job. I started to go beyond answering the questions, and began getting to know a few of the people. The more I got to know them, the more I liked my job; it made me feel like I belonged to something.

Pat was friendly; Pat always said hi; Pat thought I was the greatest guy in the world; Pat had no idea who I was from one day to the next. I liked Pat. I liked her because she could tell creative stories with certainty even though they were 100 percent false.

At first, Pat would come in like any other patron. She'd say hi to me, and I'd say hi back, and that's how it went for several weeks. You see a person every single day and you're bound to make a connection. One day Pat walked in and I said, "How was your weekend?" That's all it took.

"I was on *Wheel of Fortune!*" Pat loudly exclaimed.

"Oh, yeah?"

"Yeah! I won a car."

"No kidding. That's pretty cool!"

"It's purple. And it has four horns. And I drove my nephew to the snow."

It was summer, but I went along, "Snow can be pretty fun."

"We went snowboarding. My nephew hit a tree. He almost died. I saved him."

"Well, you sure look like a hero."

"Yeah! I got an award from the president. He said I was pretty and he asked me to marry him."

"What did you say?"

"No." She wildly laughed.

"Sure sounds like you had some weekend."

"Yeah! Some weekend."

The next day Pat came in she didn't remember me, but I remembered her. "How's that car?"

"I don't have a car!" she said like it was the craziest thing anyone had ever said.

"Well, if you did I bet it would be purple."

"No! Green!" She laughed to herself, and then said, "My dad's taking me fishing today!"

"Wow! That will be fun."

"We're going to fish from a helicopter."

"That's exciting."

"And then we're going to get raisin ice cream."

"Yum. I've never had that."

"You've never had that? That's funny!" she said loudly, and then turned to the closest person near her and said, "He's never had raisin ice cream."

Every day we had conversations like this. Some days she'd tell me about the baby she had. Other days it was about being the starting pitcher for the Los Angeles Angels of Anaheim.[1] Then she just left.

I'd see her with her coach in the park doing exercises, but she never came in. Then one day I didn't even see her in the park. The thing about the people you get attached to in the library that is so hard is they just move on. Maybe they tell their friends and neighbors that they are moving or going somewhere, but no one ever stops to tell the library. And that's what happened with Pat. She just moved on.

---

1. Los Angeles Angels of Anaheim: dumbest name ever.

A few months went by and Pat finally did come in the library again. She seemed changed. She of course didn't remember me, but she was more reserved. She didn't look up when I said hi, and she seemed uncomfortable. She was working with a new coach now, and she didn't appear to like him very much. She didn't come back after that.

I remember Pat most because she was the first mentally challenged person I had ever taken the time to get to know. She taught me to learn to like them. You should never have to learn to like someone, but sometimes people are sort of dicks like that. I make no excuse for my behavior. I'm a selfish jerk. Sometimes it takes me a while to like someone.

~

The woman looked crazy, but it's a library—who doesn't look crazy, you know? The zaniest people can turn out to be completely not insane; the most normal people can turn out to be headed for the nutty bin. You just never know.

She wandered around the library with a forced smile, her hair pulled back in this crazy-looking bun. For a while she sat looking like she was irritated. Finally she stood and walked around the library turning off every single computer that wasn't occupied.

I approached her and explained why the computers needed to be left on; she was speechless as we spoke. "Do you understand?"

"It just doesn't make any sense. Eskimos could attack."

"No—you're safe."

"I just don't know."

"Well, I'm going to turn them back on, and they need to stay on. Okay?"

She didn't answer. She spent the next hour rocking back and forth, occasionally looking around suspiciously. An hour later, a

man who looked equally crazy approached me and said, "I noticed you were talking to my wife. Is there a problem?"

"Who's your wife?"

He pointed at the woman.

"Well, she had turned off all the computers and we just asked
her not to do that."

"The computers, huh?"

I nodded.

"I'll have to talk to her about this."

He went to her and stared angrily, then the two left.

I was coming to work another day and saw them both leaving. I
watched them; I like to see what crazy people drive. She got into
the driver's side and drove the two away. The crazy woman was
the driver! It made me not want to drive. I couldn't wait to tell
everyone.

"She drives?" Toni, who was with me the day the woman
turned off the monitors, said in astonishment.

"Lots of crazy people drive," Brenda, who was standing next to
Toni, pointed out. "Toni drives."

"It's the crazy ones who are also dumb that I worry about." I
paused. "Which reminds me. Your husband's driving you to work
now, right? 'Cause if he's not, I want to leave ten minutes after
you're on the road."

"You're so mean to me. I was only kidding. You don't have to
be hurtful."

Sometimes I would go to my desk and ponder who the crazy
ones really were.

～

Sometimes you know a person is all there, sometimes you think
it, and sometimes you have no idea. The Charlie woman was
someone who looked normal, but was not. She said hello when

she entered, asked about the computers and restrooms, and said "thank you" with each answer. She said "excuse me" to someone in the way. She seemed polite and innocent, but, like I said, she was not—she was crazy.

It was at the computer that her problem really began. At first she was fine, but then she started swearing. Then she started talking to Charlie.[2] "Charlie, stop it! People are watching! No! No, Charlie! I'm going to get mad—you don't want that. You don't like when I'm mad. I'll cut you."

She was speaking quietly at first, then she got louder, then she got out of hand. I had to throw her and Charlie out. She returned on other days and it was always the same thing.

FOR SHELVING

People got it in their minds in the 1920s and 1930s that science could create a utopia; scientists convinced everyone that not only evolution was right but also the next stage in it was to manipulate genetics by creating a society free of deformities. The United States is not on the top of anyone's list for genocide, but it's sometimes difficult to wonder why not. Hitler killed Jews, Pol Pot killed intellectuals, and the United States? We killed the disabled. Why? Because that's what we do. We kill the weak.

This claim isn't as outrageous and uncalled for as it may seem. The United States[3] began experimenting with the idea of compulsory sterilization.

---

3. To be fair, so did dozens of other countries.

(Continues)

---

2. Charlie wasn't there.

(Continued)

The idea was that by forcing criminals, the mentally ill, and, in some cases, minorities[4] to become sterile a more perfect society could be formed. The philosophy was called eugenics. Not only was this a bad idea for the obvious reason that it's playing the part of God, which is always a bad idea, but also for the equally obvious reason that people tend to abuse laws such as these.

One of the earliest cases supporting the practice was *Buck v. Bell* in 1927. In this case, Dr. Albert Sidney Priddy had made petition to have Carrie Buck sterilized. Priddy believed that Buck was a genetic threat to society, that she was a slut who had already given birth to one child, and there was no telling what she would do if she unleashed her vagina on others. The courts agreed and Buck was sterilized. As it turned out, Buck had been raped.

Another fun case is *Stump v. Sparkman* in 1971. In this case, Judge Harold Stump said it was okay for a mother to have her daughter sterilized because she was "somewhat retarded" and was a little too flirty with men. The judge didn't bother to hear about evidence or even appoint a lawyer to protect the daughter's interest. A week later the daughter underwent the surgery but was told it was to remove her appendix. Two years later she married and was unable to become pregnant. When she found out why, she and her husband were rightly angry.

Science can sometimes make the world a more practical place, but this doesn't always mean a better place.

---

4. There were also cases of Native Americans being sterilized without their knowledge when they went to the hospital for other procedures.

I don't like one patron over another; I like each patron I like for distinctive reasons. I like them because they make me laugh, or think, or get frustrated, or simply smile.

I liked the crazy shoe man because he tried to take my shoe. He was a mentally challenged man who was visiting the library from the center next door as part of his training on how to function in civilized society.[5]

He came up to me while I was in the juvenile fiction area and said, "Will you be my friend?"

I nodded. "Sure. I'll be your friend."

"Can I have your shoes?"

"I kind of need my shoes to work in."

He sadly nodded. "Are we still friends?"

"Of course we are."

"Can I just feel your shoe?"

I looked at my shoes, trying to see what the fascination was in them. They were just basic leather shoes. Nothing special. It was an odd request, but I didn't see any harm in letting him touch them if it made him happy. "You can feel one, but only for a second."

He nodded, bent down, and proceeded to lift up my foot and pull off my shoe.

A little panicked, I said, "Shoes need to stay on in the library."

He knew by my tone that he had done something he should not have. He put his hands over his ears and began saying repeatedly, "I'm sorry, I'm sorry."

"It's okay."

"Can we still be friends?"

_____

5. His training included, but was not limited to, sitting next to his coach for an hour watching him write letters to his girlfriend, then spending another hour quietly sitting while the coach talked to his girlfriend on the phone.

I nodded. "But I have to go now."

The next day he came into the library looking for me while I was taking a break. He asked Pam, who was at the reference desk, if the priest was there and then went on to describe the priest as me. Apparently something about my shoes reminded him of a priest, and the reason he wanted them was so he could have the shoes of a holy man.

Every time the man came in, Andy would run and find me and tell me a patron needed my help. When the man left, Andy would always look at my shoes and say, "One day he's going to get them."

For quite some time the man was a regular—almost daily— visitor to the library. Since then he has joined the ranks of other library patrons who once were fixtures and now are simply no more. Still, not a Christmas goes by that I don't remember one last story about this shoe man of mine.

This story really begins not at Christmas but several months before Christmas, in late September. The shoe man and his gang of lovable crazies came loudly mumbling insanities into the library and did their best to act like normal library patrons (which, in my opinion, is a step down from how they normally acted). The shoe man made his way to the reference desk and asked me if I had a calendar. I hesitantly passed him the small desk calendar and wondered what he would try to do to it. I was pretty sure he would in some way deface it, but I was curious as to how. He took the calendar and carefully thumbed through it, then smiled childishly at me as he handed it back and ran off.

For over a week this went on. He would come to the desk, ask for the calendar, thumb through it, and then smile and run off to join his friends. On the second week of this, I finally asked him, "Is your birthday coming up soon?"

He let out an odd giggle and shook his head.

I waited for him to tell me what he needed the calendar for, but he of course did no such thing, and so I asked him bluntly, "Why do you want to see the calendar every day?"

He smiled, clasped his hands together, and laughed as he said, "Only eighty-seven days until Christmas!"

I have never seen someone so excited to tell me how long until Christmas—not even a child—nor did I know anyone who counted down the days until Christmas nearly 100 days in advance.

I felt sorry for him. The people who came with his group came from special needs facilities that didn't get many visitors. I imagined him opening his eyes Christmas morning and finding no presents, let alone someone to wish him a Merry Christmas. Still, I smiled and did my best to pretend that I, too, was excited that Christmas was just around the corner (even though three months away was hardly just around the corner).

This went on for the next three months. Every day he'd let whoever was at the desk know just how many days until Christmas. When December came, he started wearing a handmade Christmas tree pin, and I'm pretty sure he was humming Christmas carols, though they were always in the wrong key with a slightly different melody.

Finally, the day before Christmas, he came into the library, looked at the calendar, and could not contain himself as he laughed loudly. "Tomorrow's Christmas!"

I nodded and told him to wait. I would have felt too guilty if I had let him go away with no present from the library. I went to the staff room, got a homemade Christmas decorated cookie that another patron had brought in, and handed it to him. "Merry Christmas!"

He looked at the cookie like a sixteen-year-old who had just been given a Porsche for his birthday. Actually he looked a little more excited than that.

"Go ahead," I told him. "Eat it."

He shook his head and ran away to show the others in his group. Quickly, all five of his friends were at the reference desk saying, "Tomorrow's Christmas! Can I have a Christmas cookie?"

I couldn't say no, so I returned to the staff room and got more cookies; they weren't decorated and they were a bit smaller. I had wanted to make sure the shoe man had the best cookie of the lot. The group all went happily away with their cookies and stared excitedly at them for their entire visit. They waved at me as they left; they still had not eaten the cookies.

Several days later the group returned to the library. I was afraid to ask him about his Christmas, because I knew it very well could have been a disastrous disappointment. He came to the desk, asked for the calendar, thumbed through it, and smiled to himself. I didn't have to ask him this time what he was using the calendar for.

I got up the courage to ask him how his Christmas was. He smiled and showed me a stack of a dozen cards. "I got Christmas cards!" He pointed at his shirt, which he had worn several times before Christmas. He told me proudly, "I also got this shirt for Christmas." He then pulled the cookie from his front pocket and said excitedly, "I still have your cookie." Not much was left of the crumbling cookie, no doubt from keeping it in his pocket.

I smiled when he walked away, carrying with him the Christmas spirit of more than four dozen people. He would have been just as excited if I had given him a paper clip for Christmas.

When I think I've seen it all, there's always a crazy person who makes me rethink everything. Such was the case when the patron told me members of the international community were watching her because she had knowledge of secret documents in the government's possession and not to be surprised if federal investigators soon questioned me. I knew it was going to be an interesting night.

I have come across a number of strange things and an even larger number of strange people. Usually the strange people have a reason for their behavior, but at least once a week there is a patron who is crazy for no reason. These are the ones I get most excited about, because they really keep me on my toes.

The patron, a plump middle-aged woman with dirty hair but a surprisingly refreshing perfume, came into the library like any other patron. At first glance one would never suspect her of being who she turned out to be. She spoke coherently and seemed courteous. She had the typical grandmother looks and was very polite and friendly. She even took the time to tell me about the weather outside and told me she wanted to use the computer to e-mail her grandson.

The woman went to her assigned computer and I believed that would be it. She'd do whatever it was she needed to do on the computer and then leave. I was wrong. Five minutes later the woman came to me and said that something was wrong with the printer. I checked it out and indeed it hadn't printed her job. I apologized and asked her to print it again.

She sighed loudly enough for other patrons to turn around. "It's no use," she finally told me. "They're just hacking into the computer—like they always do. They steal everything that I want to print. I don't know why they want this stuff anyway."

I didn't know then who "they" were, but I nonetheless assured her "they" weren't. She quickly rebuked me.

"You don't know how *they* are. They're that good. And they're always doing this to me. They're all over the library. Look around. Whenever someone wipes their head, that's one of them. They're speaking in code."

It was, of course, hot and many people were wiping sweat from their brows. In fact, I believed the woman herself had wiped her head a few times. She did not speak loudly, but she spoke loudly enough that anyone nearby could easily hear the conversation with little eavesdropping effort, including the men she undoubtedly believed were talking in code by wiping their brows.

It struck me as odd at first. If she knew these men were after her, I didn't quite understand why she would let them know this. It seemed that the ball would be better played in her court if they didn't know that she knew they were watching her. But the more she rambled about her conspiracy theory the more I realized that it was, in fact, her strategy to let them know that she knew that they knew and she didn't care that they knew it.

The strategy wasn't too bad. I imagined her goal was to make them uneasy. She knew, so now they'd have to be more careful. And they'd have to nervously question what they had done wrong; they had slipped up somewhere and in doing so they had given away their position. Perhaps they were even considering aborting the mission or sending in new agents. In either case, they'd have to be very thoroughly debriefed as to what went wrong with their operation. But the more I toyed with this idea the more I became aware that I had seen way too many conspiracy movies and I was falling hard into the incoherencies of this woman's mind. Still, I was nonetheless intrigued and amused by the woman and gave her way too much of my time.

I convinced her to print again and stood with her at the print station to make sure she did everything right. As we waited for her document to come on the screen, a pregnant woman soon stood behind us waiting to print her own document. The first woman turned and became hostile, saying to the pregnant woman, "I know what you're doing—you're a suspect." She looked at others nearby and then at me. "Everyone is a suspect. You can't be too careful." She pointed at the pregnant woman. "This woman here has been watching what I've been doing since she got here. And the stomach's not fooling me. They probably hired her just because she's pregnant. But she's still a suspect."

"Sure, go away," the first woman said, watching the second carefully, "but you're still a suspect. You watch me and I'll watch you."

The pregnant woman backed away slowly and I did my best to apologize to her with my eyes. The scenario was amusing when it involved only me, but I knew it could escalate into far worse problems when she began accusing everyone in the library of being a suspect.

She looked at a small boy who was wandering around the library with his mother and said, "They've been training kids for years now. They used to only use them in other countries, but now they're using them in the U.S.—have been for at least two years."

It took us two tries to get her documents to print. I saw the documents disappear from my print screen with my own eyes. When they at last printed, she switched her focus from hacked computers to the copy machine. She needed to make multiple copies of her document to, in her words, "be safe." She was able to recognize a national conspiracy against her, but she was not able to work the library's very basic copying machine and thus required assistance. Normally I would have asked a page to assist the woman but I felt too involved now.

The woman said the copying machine was slow and wanted to know who the library's vendor was. I was impressed that she knew the library used a vending company for its copying services and told her immediately the vendor's name was ASP.

"I'm not surprised," she replied in a tone that said, while she wasn't surprised, she was disappointed. After a long pause, as she looked carefully around the library to, what I figured, make sure no informants were listening (or perhaps to make sure they were), she told me quietly, "ASP is funded by our government. They make copies of everything xeroxed on their copiers and forward it to analysis at the NSA. Every time copies are made, it's stored on a tiny chip inside the copier." She looked quickly around the library and said in an almost incoherent whisper, "I'll show you where the chip is if you want to see it."

I was curious, but didn't want the woman to think that I was taking her too seriously, so I declined the offer.

She nodded and said, "It's better you don't know where it is, anyway."

She had more theories. The whole idea of the religion of Islam was founded by a secret society of world leaders. George Washington and almost every other president had been in the group. So were Napoleon and Hitler. World War II was thought up during a game of poker between Churchill and Hitler. I imagined if any of this was even remotely true then Dan Brown was hard at work on the novel.

She went on to tell me why she came to the library. "I'd do it at home," she explained, "but it's too dangerous, so I had to come here." Her face became sad. "And I had to leave my dog—my poor dog—in the car. It's their fault that my poor dog is suffering in my hot car. And I can't roll my windows down because they'll take him—they have before."

I thought about that poor dog suffering as I watched her leave the library—then wait at the bus stop—then get on the bus. That settled it. I could be satisfied that the woman was simply paranoid and crazy.

Then two young men with army buzzed heads and crisply ironed white T-shirts walked by and quietly said, pointing at the bus, "There she goes. Let's roll."

Everyone was "suspect" to the woman, and I imagined she had left believing I was innocent. Nonetheless, I would have to give an interview of what she had said to me to the secret agents upon her departure.

Toni was working with me that night and had witnessed most of the scene. "Was that for real?"

I shrugged. "Does it matter?"

Sometimes it sadly happened that staff could officially join the ranks of the crazy library patrons. This became the case with Michael, the computer clerk.

Michael continued a downward spiral for several weeks. He couldn't start the day without spending at least one hour doing some form of cleaning. This would have been fine because it helped keep the library clean, but it wasn't fine, because his cleaning involved more studying of dirt particles than actual cleaning. He would spend ten minutes organizing a stack of free local magazines, then spend another five minutes studying the magazines' straightness from different angles only to spend another ten minutes straightening them a little more.

I didn't think much of Michael's behavior because I was too busy to care; but it became the water cooler talk among staff.[6]

---

6. There is no water cooler in the library.

"What's the deal with Michael?" the gossip would usually begin, which would be followed by long detailed accounts of what exactly the deal was. Most were convincing theories on why he was having a mental breakdown of some kind based on the mental breakdown that someone else had that they knew.

Brenda was the first person to come right out and ask Michael what his deal was. She could have done it tastefully, but that wasn't exactly her style. "What's going on, Michael?"

"What do you mean?"

"All of this cleaning? You're acting like a nutcase. You're kind of starting to look like one, too."

Michael tilted his head and stared at Brenda like a confused puppy. His eyes matched his confusion. "I don't know what you mean." Then he started cleaning again.

One day Michael stopped coming to work. He didn't call in; he just didn't show up. It happened while I was the librarian in charge of the building, which meant I had to call to see why he was a no-show. When I called, his mother informed me that he had gone to Mexico to deal with a family crisis.

Two weeks later Michael came back to the library. He looked like he was sleepwalking. Everyone said hi to him, but he just continued walking, straight to Faren's office. He put in his two weeks' notice and apologized that he was two weeks late turning it in. Then he left. He said nothing to anyone else.

Two months later Michael returned again to the library to get books with one of his nephews. He looked refreshed for the first time in months. I was working with Cindy and Brenda that night.

"How you doing?" I asked when he came to the desk.

"It was a rough time for a while, but I'm doing better. A lot better."

"So, what happened?" Brenda asked and then added with a laugh, "Have a nervous breakdown?"

Michael looked embarrassed and nodded. "Kind of. I was seeing things."

"What?" Brenda asked, suddenly more curious.

"Just people—family—friends—people from work. I would be sleeping, only I was awake. It just felt that way and these visions of familiar people and places would come to me and I'd get lost in it. I was possessed by Satan. But I'm better now. I spent the past month in Mexico; my parents sent me there to see an exorcist."

"Exorcist?" I said, surprised that people still did that.

He nodded. "They did magic on me and I got better."

"Were you taking anything?" Cindy asked. She was usually a reserved person; when she wasn't washing her hands she was minding her own business. I was surprised to see her become so chatty.

"What do you mean?"

"Like drugs."

Michael shrugged. "Nothing serious. Speed mostly. And sometimes I do a little bit of coke. That's it."

"Nothing serious?" I said.

He nodded.

"Michael, you weren't possessed by demons, you were addicted to drugs."

"No! Drugs don't do that."

"They sort of do, Michael," I said.

"Are you taking anything now?" Cindy asked.

He shook his head.

"Have you seen the visions since you got off it?"

He shook his head again.

"Well!" I said.

"The priests are certain of the demons. They're good about that."

"The demons you had are best removed at drug treatment centers," I said.

"It wasn't the drugs—the priest said."

"You told the priest you were on drugs?"

"No. They didn't ask. After talking to them, they knew right away what it was."

Michael came in now and then. He claimed he was staying clean and was planning on entering college again. One day he stopped coming in and I only hope that he did stay clean.

That was that. It summed up what my job would always be. I would maintain friendly relations with patrons and staff but there would always be another part that I would never know. I wanted to hope that I knew Michael well enough that he would have sought me, or at the very least someone on staff, for help. But that's not how it worked. People came to me in confidence—not for help but for directions.

What I began to see when Michael left was that I wasn't supposed to know people. I was merely supposed to be their guide. The person who pointed them to the person they wanted to know.

Chapter 973.917	How I Said Good-bye
-FRON-	to the Library
The New	That Had Raised Me
Frontier:	

How do you say 'bye to something you've known for so long? Nearly every day for the past several years I had walked in and out of that little building. I knew everything about it—where it leaked, where paint was chipped, and even what made the paint chip. I could close my eyes and find anything in the building by simple intuition. How do you say 'bye? You really don't. You just let it fade away. One day it's there, another day it's gone, but the memory still stays. The library had received a grant, and the old library would be torn down to make way for a bigger one.

The last month we had all kinds of festivities planned for the closing.[1] There were dozens of opportunities for people to come

---

1. A committee was of course organized; committees are formed for everything at libraries.

and share their memories of this small building where the community had come for nearly fifty years to learn, to read, to love.

Older patrons would talk about how they had personally known the librarian the building was named after; teens would share memories of how they had come to hear stories when they were barely old enough to walk. Everyone had a story, a memory. That entire month it was all memories. No one talked about the library closing. No one wanted to think about that. Everyone had accepted the fact; everyone knew it was for the better. Still, this was their little library, their little place to go and learn and grow. That was being taken away.

Some people would come in and say, "I didn't know they were closing this place. I saw the sign. I haven't been in for years." These were the ones that made me smile. Even as the library closed, people were coming and discovering it all over again, one last time. They would have memories, too.

You work at a public place so long and you know you're going to miss it, but you'll miss the people more than the place. People who were fixtures in your daily life would suddenly, and somewhat abruptly, be gone. They would say they'd visit, and some in fact would, but it would never be the same. It was never the same. But there was still that one month to spend with them.

~

Lynnette liked to talk. She lived in the house her parents had left her when they died. She was a bit slow. She had never worked an honest job. She never went to college. She didn't really do anything. In short, she really didn't have much to talk about. But she sure liked to talk.

She also knew my grandma.[2] Usually our conversations would go something like this:

---

2. By knew, I mean that thirty years ago, when she was in her twenties, my grandma had attended the same sewing class, and she would occasionally say hi to her.

"I'm reading a book on President Washington. That's impressive, huh?"[3]

"Sure."

"He was the first president. You know that, right?"[4]

"Yep."

She looked around the library awkwardly, as if she was trying to think of something else to say so she wouldn't have to go home. A library clerk walked behind me and she said suddenly and loudly, "I'm going to check this book out because I haven't done that yet. He knows I'm going to check it out, though. Huh. You know, right?"

"Right."

The clerk seemed confused and just said, "Okay."

"He and I go way back. I know his grandma. Right? I know your grandma, right?"

I shrugged. "That's what you say."

"She used to go to my sewing class. I know his whole family. Right? I know your entire family, huh?"

"I guess."[5]

At some point she'd run out of things to say and she'd leave. I'd then spend the rest of the afternoon assuring everyone that I was in no way associated with the woman and she did not, in fact, know my grandma.[6]

During most of the month of closing, Lynette would stand close[7] to people and listen to their stories. Then she'd tell hers

---

3. In fact, the book was written for little kids, and she probably only wanted it for the pictures.

4. All of her sentences ended with either "huh" or "right."

5. No one in my family had a recollection of her.

6. In fact, I had asked my grandma about the woman and she only vaguely remembered her.

7. Like invading-my-space close.

loudly, with food in her mouth. It would go a little like this: "I am a friend of this library. Everyone knows me. I've been going here since I was a little girl." She told me this exact phrase at least twenty times. She told everyone. She just wanted to be involved in something. Be a part of something.

I think that's what most people wanted. They wanted to be a part of something. They wanted to share their stories and feel a connection to this little branch one last time before it closed.

Ernest told stories mostly about the employees. He loved the books, but I think he loved coming in and talking to the workers more.

"I'll tell you what I'm going to really miss about this place," Ernest said. "The way everyone jumped whenever you made the announcement that you were closing. You got a creepy voice."[8]

"It's like a family here," Ernest said another day. "You get to know people and it's not like the library is going. It's like you guys are going."

"We'll still be around," I insisted. "Just at different places."

"It won't be the same."

I didn't know then how prophetic Ernest's words would turn out to be.

Another day Ernest said, "The staff here is like a family. I love coming in and seeing all of you fight and laugh and get sad together. It's like watching a soap." He looked at Brenda. "She's like the bossy older sister—always tell you what to do even though you're her supervisor. And Michael's like the pothead younger brother whose always getting into trouble. And

---

8. No one had ever told me this before.

Tim[9] is the outcast because he's gay. Then Faren's the mother that nobody likes to listen to and everyone complains about but nobody can quite live without."

Ernest had observed us well and he knew us well. Indeed, we were a family, but soon the family would fall apart.

~

Some people didn't quite make it to the end.

Pam turned out to be right; two months before the library closed, she announced that she would be a manager. She wouldn't be manager of any library near me, or in the state of California, but she would be a manager—in Louisiana to be exact. She would move thousands of miles, for less pay, in an environment that was less than ideal, just so someone somewhere would call her a manager. It was that important to her.

No one seemed to care. We all said we'd miss her, of course, but in all actuality it was only Brenda who would miss her. They were a team, a tag team. They found problems together; they pretended they were the boss together; they complained together. In terms of coworkers they were soul mates. Brenda knew, no matter what, she'd always have one person backing her.

What I learned from the two was that business wasn't like *Survivor*. You didn't form alliances with coworkers and engage in tribal wars. You could do that if you wanted to, but it would get you nowhere. Business was simply that: business. There wasn't room for alliances and friends. There wasn't room to spread gossip. You simply had to come each day and make it new. If there was a problem with someone, you couldn't answer like they were your friend. You had to answer like it was business.

---

9. A page in high school.

Anaheim is one of those Cinderella stories that every city dreams up. Its rich history can easily be summed up by looking at three different periods: the pre-Disneyland era, the Disneyland era, and the post-Disneyland era.

German settlers originally came to Anaheim in the 1850s to start vineyards. They made up the word Anaheim by combining two words: *Ana* because it was along the Santa Ana river, and *heim*, which is German for home. Thus it was those first settlers' home by the Santa Ana River.[10] A plague wiped out most of the vineyards in the 1870s, and the settlers planted fruit trees and chili peppers in their place. Anaheim became an official city in 1876, about twenty years after the first settlers arrived. It had grown from a handful of families to almost 1,000 people.

As a side note to this side note, the city had a bit of controversy in the 1920s when the Ku Klux Klan managed to get four of its members elected to the five-member trustees board. The Klan wanted to make Anaheim a model KKK city. They lasted almost a year. When they were discovered, a recall election was held and the members were ousted.

In the 1950s, a person could travel from Kansas to Los Angeles for as little as a dollar. This led to a boom of families flocking to Southern California. Anaheim was still a small city, which made it appealing to young families hoping to buy land and start a new life after the war. By the start of the 1950s, the city's population had soared to 15,000, but the real boom was just beginning.

---

10. The Santa Ana River isn't much of a river today; half the year it's pretty well dried up and the other half it's flat-out ugly. Unlike many rivers that are lush with vegetation, the Santa Ana River is full of dirt and a bike trail that goes to the beach.

One afternoon a few weeks before we closed the library, a junior high kid came up to me and smiled. "You don't remember me, do you?"

I looked at him carefully, but I honestly didn't remember him.

"You used to read to our class."

It made me feel old. He wasn't an old kid, but it had probably been several years since he was in third grade.[11]

"No kidding. Who was your teacher?"

"Ms. Griffin."

"She taught first grade."

He nodded.

"That was a long time ago."[12] I added, "I hope I didn't scare you too much."

"No. You were funny. That's what I remember about this library. Coming in and hearing stories."

That single memory made my day, to know that a kid's biggest memory was something I did. A car can go a long way on that kind of fuel.

~

I liked the memories of the elderly the most. These people were old school, dating back longer than me. They would tell me stories about what the library used to look like. About the old staff members. About when there was no computerized card catalog.

"I used to come when Elva[13] would read us stories." Or "I remember when it first opened; I was one of the first people through the door." I liked them most because they brought us food and cards. Old people know how to send someone off.

---

11. The cutoff grade for getting stories.

12. Now I felt even older.

13. The library was named after the city's first children's librarian.

I get worried when I see them, because younger people don't know how to behave like that. They don't know etiquette. They don't know the civilized behavior of older people. They don't know Emily Post. It's generation Stewart, and while Martha Stewart is okay,[14] she doesn't know how to behave like a lady.[15] I want the elderly to sit down and teach this generation a thing or two about manners. Then again, old people drive me crazy and sometimes I wish they'd just shut up.

Mrs. Hubbert would come in with her husband and say, "It's really great that you're building the community something a little nicer."

I nodded yes.

"I don't believe I'll ever get to see it, though."

"Why's that?"

"Well I'm not getting any younger. I'm seventy-nine. It'll be two some-odd years before it opens back up. I've been smoking for over fifty years. You do the math."

How do you reply to something like that? I replied like this: "Well, you never know."

"Of course you don't, but I'm not going to kid myself. You get to be a certain age and you wonder every night before you sleep if you'll wake up in the morning."

This was turning into one of the saddest conversations I had ever had. "Well, you look healthy enough."

"I'd be in a hospital if I didn't. But that's how I expect I'll go. I'll look healthy enough, and then one day I'll just die. I don't want any of that stroke stuff. No waking up one morning and not being able to feel the right side of my body. That's bull. I told myself a

---

14. In fact, she is not.

15. Ladies don't get caught doing insider trading.

long time ago I wouldn't go like that. One day I'm just going to shut down and not turn back on. It'll be that simple. None of these years of pain and suffering crap. I won't see to any of that."

And that was indeed that.

～

I hated teens, but there was one group of teens that I kind of liked. They were a group of sisters and cousins. There were five of them. They'd come every day after school to do homework and read. They were the kind of students I hoped my kids would be, because they never caused problems or got into trouble. They even apologized if they giggled too loudly.

They told me how much they would miss the place. It was odd hearing that from teens. It almost seemed odd hearing that libraries really did make a difference to them. You want to believe they do, but you rarely get to see it. The last week we were open we gave the teens a permanent marker and let them write on the wall.

～

The staff remembered the past but they also thought a lot about the future. We talked about what it would look like in two years and how we would all return. The sad part was how few of us would. You make lots of broken promises when your emotions are full.

"We'll all be back together in two years," we would each at one point say. "And we'll get together at least once a month for drinks." It seemed reasonable then, but they were all broken promises that never saw the light of day.

～

The last day the library was open to the public came and went like any other day. People came in and used the computers and checked out books.[16]

_____

16. Which they would have to return to other libraries.

As I greeted patrons one last time, I wondered all day how it would be when we closed the doors for the very last time. Who would be the last patron? Would I have any final words? It seems silly how many emotions went through my head, but this had been my life for so many of my young adulthood years. This was the place where I started to discover what it meant to have things like a career and what it meant to be professional. It had taught me not only about people but also about life.

As it happened, Ernest was the last patron. It was fitting. He was a friend, and probably the patron who had spent the most hours in the library in the final years of its old life. He was just the person I hoped would give the library its final respects.

At closing, I walked Ernest to the door. I said maybe he could be the first person who walked into the new library in two years; he smiled and said "of course." He swore he would come often to the library most of us would be reassigned to. (These two promises ultimately would not be entirely kept.) Then we shook hands and he left.

Only three employees were in the building when the door was locked for the last time. In the end, no one really cared about being there when the doors closed. No one but the three of us. We all looked at each other. We didn't speak. We all knew what we were thinking, though. *Thanks for the memories, little library.*

∾

The next day I traded in my slacks and dress shirt for T-shirt and jeans. For the next month the library would be boarded up and employees would begin the process of moving out fifty years of books, furniture, and memories.

There was a lot of messing around, a lot of throwing airplanes, throwing Frisbees, and listening to loud music. It didn't seem like a library. It wasn't a library without the people. It was simply a building that we were packing up. It was as if all life had left the building the day before, left when we closed the door.

What was it about a church that made it sacred? It was just walls when it was built, just a building when the pews were put in. But sometime between then and when it had its very first service it became a church, a sacred institution for those who believed. That was the library. That's what I thought of during that final month of packing. What made it sacred? What made it a library?

A library was nothing without its people. You say *library* and there's this iconoclastic image of an old-lady librarian telling people to be quiet and not to run. But the thing was, that lady— that iconoclastic lady—was with us when we cleaned. She wore blue jeans, too. Maybe she was what people thought about when you said library, but she didn't make the library. People made the library. That's what made a library. Without them, all the sacred-ness was gone. It was just a building with books.

We'd share occasional memories about stupid things we had done. We wrote on the walls because we could. We spilled things on the carpet because what difference did it make? We were care-less because we could be. We harmed that little library and gave it no respect. It had cared for each of us, but to us it no longer seemed important. How did that happen?

We snuck little mementos out of the library. I took one of the ugly egged-shaped meeting chairs that had gone in the community room. I put it in my bedroom. Sometimes I sit on it and remember the old building. I also took the huge black sign that hung from the ceiling that said "Restroom" in bold white letters; I gave it to my brother.[17]

---

17. A collector of all things tacky.

When the movers came, they were careless. They were slobs who probably had never been in a library before. They didn't know how to handle books. They tossed them quickly in boxes and then tagged them up. And we let them do it. We didn't care. The books had no meaning without the people there who read them, who told us stories about how well they liked a particular author.

Every now and then I would catch the movers tossing in a book from an author I remembered a patron telling me they liked and I cringed. I wanted them to be careful—protect that little book for the sake of the person who read it.

~

Toni stayed to the end, but that was it. Ultimately, she didn't want the hours. She wanted fewer of them. She took a job in yet another division for fewer hours and less pay. Which meant once more Brenda wanted the job, at least until someone else got it, in which case she would have turned it down had she been offered it.

~

Some of us would see each other again at another library, but many would be transferred away to other locations. In the end, my relationship with these people finished with a simple handshake.

"It's been nice," Andy said and extended his hand.

I nodded. "We'll still see each other."

"Of course. It's only another library."

And that was it. He went to one library and I went to another. The next time I saw him was over a year later. He had changed; so had I. I've never quite understood how your good friends one moment can be someone totally different the next. Does friendship just blind us? So much that the person doesn't appear changed unless we're away from them for a long time?

Cindy shook my hand and then washed her hands. When she finished she washed them again. She washed them several times before she actually left the building.[18] She was crazy, but it's those things that you miss the most, those crazy little details that make people human. We say they annoy us, but in the end they don't—we love them. We love them because it's what makes our day beat.

~

It took several months for the library to be torn down. It was behind schedule. We had heard rumors of when the old ship would go down, but those rumors all came and went. Ernest would visit me at my new library often and tell me how he couldn't believe that building was still standing and would ask what was taking so long. He would go to the library parking lot every day and stare at the building all boarded up and waiting for its day of judgment. But every day it got a stay of execution.

Then one day, as I drank my morning coffee, my cell phone rang. It was Ernest.[19] "Today's the day!" he said excitedly.

I got my camera, put on my shoes, and left. I was there in time to see the first wall go down. It was bittersweet. Alone except for Ernest and another coworker, I watched these men—these laborers who had never been in *our* library—tear down the walls. Occasionally, another coworker would show up and snap a picture or two.

When no one was looking, I tore the name of the library letters from the building. Each letter was large and metal. I called my mom

---

18. A month after the library closed, Cindy received a full-time position in another city. (I was told by an acquaintance who happened to work at the library that she no longer sits on newspapers.)

19. He was the only patron who had my number.

and told her to bring her van, which was the only thing I knew that was big enough to hold them all. I don't know why I took them. Why not? They ended up going in my mom's garden. I didn't want them. I just took them because why not? So now, in my mom's garden, to this day the name of the library is spelled out in the ground.

It took several days for everything to be completely knocked down. When it was gone and the ground was leveled it sat there for several more months, and nothing more was done to it. That's the way you treated something that had been so sacred.

One day I went to the park and ate my lunch staring at that empty lot. It just looked like dirt. I had suspected staring at it would bring back memories. There were no such memories. It was just dirt, nothing more, nothing less—just dirt. It made me remember nothing.

Several months later, the city officially decided to give its blessing with a groundbreaking ceremony. Tents were put up; important city people were called; the mayor and his council members were all invited to give speeches.

I looked around at all the people who came. I knew only a few; the rest came and pretended they cared. There were no kids or their Spanish-speaking parents, even though that's what our library largely consisted of. There were lots and lots of white people in suits who came out to make it seem like they cared.

I looked at the mayor. His mouth moved, but what came out was mere propaganda. I doubted he had ever been in a library. Who needed libraries for this man? If he read at all, he read books he purchased from other cities.[20] He lived in a huge house miles away from this library in a much nicer, cleaner part of the city.

---

20. Anaheim had a baseball team, a hockey team, a convention center, and a theme park, but no major retail bookstore.

His speech was about how wonderful it was that the city was building a new library. He talked about this fact for less than a minute. He used the remaining time to talk about all he had done for the city and all that he would do. He talked about community centers, the wi-fi campaign, and a lot of other stuff that didn't really pertain to the library.

When he finished, one of the council members talked about the importance of literacy in the city. He said he was going to see to it that the council cared a little more for the city's libraries (and for a while they actually did). I liked this guy; I couldn't believe my ears. I noted his name and voted for him the next time he ran. I did not vote for the mayor, even though he ran largely unopposed and won favorably over the other candidate.

When the mayor and his council finished, they rushed to talk to the cameras and other important people. They smiled at me and the rest of the library staff; they didn't dare speak with us and tell us thanks for being public servants. We were public servants, and that's how they treated us, like servants that you appreciated because they brought you your things but that you didn't actually talk to. But we weren't bitter, because we didn't want to talk to the man and his puppets anyway.

We simply ignored them, took pictures together where the new library would soon be, and left.

Intermission:	Starring Roland,
	Who Is a Library Tech and
	Whom You Shall Meet Formally
	in a Coming Chapter

(Picture yourself sitting in a theater several years ago. The movie is *Ben Hur*; the time is intermission. The music begins to play. It's annoying and repetitive and actually makes you want to leave the theater to stretch. Don't you miss that annoying music? Then read a little further and you will find an homage to those days. When you're sick of reading its pointlessness, skip ahead to the next chapter, which will surely be better than this.)

FADE IN:

EXT. ANAHEIM, CALIFORNIA, LIBRARY BREAK ROOM—
SUNNY DAY

CUT TO:

INT. INSIDE LIBRARY STAFF ROOM—DAY

The room is empty except for two young homely looking library employees. They are sitting in a gay fashion (but not that gay—the happy-go-lucky Great Gatsby gay). Roland, the younger of the two, is eating a bag of chips, which will surely make him fat and uglier. (Also, he has not washed his hands. They are greasy.) Scott, the older, is typing on a Toshiba laptop.

SCOTT

Tell me about your shoes. What kind are they and how are they on your feet? Are they appropriate for your job?

ROLAND

(looking down at shoes)

They're black ones. A little scuffed up. I think it's Alfonie—generic brand, perhaps? They have no cuss words, so of course they're appropriate for work.

SCOTT

So, as long as it has no cuss words you can work in it?

ROLAND

Yeah. And they can't be comfortable.

SCOTT

Mine are comfortable.

ROLAND

(bitterly)

You get paid more than me. Plus I don't know how to shop for shoes.

SCOTT

Do you think people look differently at you because of your shoe choice?

ROLAND

I don't think they care as long as they get their books. And shoes can't stink. Well, mine kind of stink, but no one has complained.

SCOTT

If they complained, would you buy new ones?

ROLAND

(suspiciously)

Are you basically trying to make this the worse interview in the history of man?

SCOTT

(shrugging)

It's intermission. Do you really think anyone will notice? Everyone is in line at the snack bar or peeing.

(beat)

Answer the question.

ROLAND

I would take it up with my boss.

SCOTT

Have you ever had a bad experience with your socks? Like a hole in the front that you just had to work with for the whole day?

ROLAND

(embarrassed)

I had to come to work with dirty socks.

SCOTT

Did it change your attitude that night?

ROLAND

I think so, yeah.

SCOTT

What about people who wear white socks with dress shoes? Would you ever engage in that kind of activity?

ROLAND

Yes. I've done that a few times.

SCOTT

Did you feel tacky?

ROLAND

Yes. I knew I should have worn the black socks.

SCOTT

You're at a movie. It hasn't started and those stupid commercials start that come on before the preview comes on. What do you think about during those commercials?

ROLAND

I normally lean over and discuss my disgust with the person I came with.

SCOTT

What if you're alone?

ROLAND

Then I make loud grunts of disgust.

SCOTT

What do you think about the library's carpet?

ROLAND

I don't think I've ever paid attention to it. It's okay, I guess.

SCOTT

How often do you get bored at work on average?

ROLAND

3.14.

SCOTT

That's pi?

ROLAND

No, wouldn't that be a bunch more numbers?

SCOTT

Okay. You're right.

ROLAND

This is probably the worst interview ever.

SCOTT

Do you remember that time the doorbell rang in New York at three in the morning, and you pretended to be sleeping, so I had to open it?

ROLAND

Yeah.

SCOTT

So what question would you ask if you were conducting this interview?

ROLAND

Who cares about library staff?

SCOTT

Is that a question?

ROLAND

No.

SCOTT

(annoyed)
So?

ROLAND

Why do you work here? Because you have a passion for libraries? Or do you work here because your dreams got crushed? My answer would be the latter.

SCOTT

Have you ever thought one of the old-lady patrons that come to the library is hot?

ROLAND

How old is old?

SCOTT

The grannies that demand mysteries.

ROLAND

Well, some might have been fetching in their younger years, but I'm not changing their diapers. You don't have to put that.

SCOTT

You didn't tell me it was off the record.

ROLAND

Oh. Okay.

SCOTT

Tell me about this French pop crap you're into.

ROLAND

It's pop music in French. It's pretty self-explanatory. You'd have to be a
complete moron if you did not understand what it means.

SCOTT

So, is it like pop music that people sing in French?

ROLAND

Yeah.

SCOTT

Do they do dances and stuff?

ROLAND

They twist. The twist was like Beatlemania over there.

SCOTT

So is there French pop now? Or is it a thing of yesteryear?

ROLAND

Did you seriously just use yesteryear in a sentence?

SCOTT

I like to bring olden words back.

ROLAND

When did people ever use yesteryear?

SCOTT

I'm asking the questions.

ROLAND

It's more electro now.

SCOTT

When are you going to get me that French guy singing Bob
Dylan?

                    ROLAND
I keep forgetting.
                    SCOTT
Well, remember.
                    ROLAND
Tell me when I'm at home. Not while I'm working and am obviously not going to remember to make the tape.
                    SCOTT
Fine. I think our lunch is over.

    FADE OUT.

(Now imagine here that everyone is returning to their theater seats. The lights dim again. The feature presentation will return shortly. Thank you. That is all.)

    END

Chapter 428.2461	Being the Incomplete, Irregular,
-SPAN-	and Inappropriate Guide
Spanglish:	to Being a White Guy
	Who Can't Speak Spanish
	Working in a Library in Which
	English Is Only Kind of
	and Sometimes Spoken

I didn't think too much about it when four cops in a police car came from behind my car and raced up the street with their lights flashing and sirens blaring. I did, however, think much about it when I drove a little further and saw that the cars had stopped less than a block from the front of the library I was going to. They had joined a handful of other police cars to barricade the street. A helicopter circled above. An officer in the street laid out flares and directed cars down another street.

This was my first day at the branch library that I had been reassigned to. I called the library on my cell phone to let them know I'd be a bit late. I had worked at the library before on the occasional weekend. I knew the back streets and how to get into the library the long way. I wasn't worried about any of that. I was worried because what kind of way was this to start at a new library?

By the time I got to the library the police had opened up the street again. I found out later in the day what had happened. Shooting. Someone had been shot at the liquor store one block away. I silently hoped to myself it had not been one of our patrons doing the shooting. This neighborhood was everything the old library was not. It was on a busy street next to apartments that weren't exactly luxurious. Its nearest neighbor was a high school.[1] The old library was like a small neighborhood library; the new library was like a city library. It was in front of a bus stop, which meant a whole different sort of person came into the building. I don't think it's fair to say if you take the bus to the library you're definitely crazy and there's a good reason why you don't drive; but I think it's fair to say if you take the bus to the library there's an 85 percent chance you're clinically crazy and a danger to society.

When I went in the building it was loud, dimly lit, moldy, and unfriendly in every way, from the way the doors squealed to the color of the paint. At the front desk were a few familiar faces. They looked the same, but their eyes told another story; they appeared sadder and chaotic. The old library had been warm and friendly; the new library was simply intense.

"Hi, Rosie!" I said when I walked by the desk and saw the familiar face.

She did not say hi back. She simply nodded and forced a smile.

"So what do you think of the new place?"

"It's very busy."

---

1. The very high school, in fact, that much of the gang from No Doubt, including Gwen Stefani, had attended. As a footnote to this footnote, just down the street from the old library was the golf course Tiger Woods had golfed in high school, so both libraries, technically, had a small claim to fame.

Indeed, it was busy. And not very grateful. People came and got books and acted like they weren't getting a treat; they acted like they were owed the books—like it was no privilege for them. All day long I watched people get their books. "Thank you, come again!" the clerks would say. And all day long people would simply take their books and walk away without even a smile or thank you. This library, for better or worse, had attitude and a personality all to itself.

∽

There was no full-time clerk when we transferred. Brenda took it upon herself to fill this role. "I've been here the longest and know the most," she told all the incoming clerks. "And besides that, everyone knows I'll be the full-time clerk just as soon as they hire me."[2]

∽

There were many new faces at the library. I had imagined that somehow things would be the same, that people like Andy and Cindy would be gone but in their place would be people just like them. This was not the case. The person who did the job of Andy was Hon, an aging Asian woman. She knew little English, despite

---

2. Not true. A week before Brenda went to interview for the job she had already interviewed for a half dozen times, we had the following conversation: "Maybe you should just try not being yourself," to which she replied, "What's that supposed to mean?" I shrugged. "They know who you are. You're not there to tell them what they already know. You're there to sell yourself. You can't just go in there and say 'hire me because I've been here the longest.'" (I don't know why I was coaching her on what to say when I wasn't exactly in favor of her getting the job.) "So how do I impress them?" "Lie. Rave about how good you are with customer service—how the patron is always right." "But they're not always right." "Now see! That's what you don't want to say." "It's true. And honesty is the best policy—that's what everyone says." "Maybe to a clerk who only wants to work part-time for the rest of her life, but if you actually do want this job, then tell them what they want to hear." "I'm not kissing butt." "Then you're going to lose the job to someone who will. Attitude is everything. You want a job, sell yourself." "I'll just be myself."

having lived in the United States for over thirty years and working in a job where English is the only language spoken.

Despite the language barrier, I liked talking to Hon—mainly because of our language barrier; not even a week had passed and we already had a morning greeting. Each morning Hon would come in and ask, "How you do day?" I would reply, "Fine. How are you today?" And Hon would say, "Yes."

About a month into my stay at the new library, Hon got mad at me. I'm not sure why exactly, but she came to me and said, "I mix peanuts in your shoe."

I didn't know what she meant, but I could tell by her tone that she was angry. "What's wrong?"

"Cements in the paper, plus I need a bag."

I looked at her, confused. She got angrier. "Cements in the paper!" she said.

"Okay."

She walked away from me, and we didn't speak for two days.

⌇

If Hon technically replaced Andy, then Roland technically replaced Cindy. He came to the library as a library technician about a week after I arrived. He liked to impress people who could give and take away my hours, which meant he didn't impress *me*. He also carried a notebook to write down what tasks he should do that day. Each day he would bring a notepad to Faren's office and ask diplomatically what she expected him to do that night. Some days she would actually give him a task; other days she was too busy and would send him to me just to get him out of her office.

I gave Roland nothing but bad advice. I told him not to help teens because they could help themselves. I told him to point out where books were instead of walking the person over to them. When a person called on the phone to ask if we had books, I told

him to simply say, "We're not allowed to divulge that kind of information over the phone," and then hang up. And finally I told
him it was okay to say, "I'm not too sure about that—sorry I can't
help you," and then walk away. In general, I gave Roland advice
on how to give the worst library customer service humanly possible. I did this for two reasons. One, just to be a bit of a dick; two,
because he would write down my advice in his cheesy little notebook, as if he planned to actually use it.

I didn't like Roland. He was a go-getter and a yes man—and
he made everyone look bad. Supervisors, on several different
occasions, told staff about how they weren't meeting expectations, and used Roland's performance as an example of what a
model employee should look like.

"Why don't you just tone it down a notch, Roland?" I told him
his second week. "It's one thing to look good, but it's another to
make others look bad in the process."

"It's not my fault if people aren't trying hard enough."

Now he was just making me mad. But as much as I hated what
he was doing I couldn't help but have some admiration. He was a
lot like me in my younger years. I had spent a lot of time impressing
people; now I could reap the rewards of my effort. If I was late for
work, no one noticed; if I took thirty minutes on my fifteen-minute
break, no one noticed; if I left early, no one noticed; and if I spent
the entire day in a chat room, no one noticed. People trusted that I
was doing my job because I spent so long doing my job right that
when I slacked off they still figured I was doing the right thing.

One night Roland commented on how I tended to point in random directions when people asked for books. "Don't you feel
guilty not helping people? It's kind of your job."

"I help them when they need help," I explained, "and I'm really
busy right now."

Roland looked over at my computer and sarcastically said, "You're reading about Hollywood gossip."

"Part of my job is to stay informed. When people come in here asking for books on something that's in the news, I have to know what current event they're talking about."

"Yeah, but doesn't current events usually mean Iran getting nukes? Not some celebrity breaking up with his girlfriend."

"The only definition of current events I know about is news that is current. That's why checking my e-mail also counts as current events. You never know when I'm going to get pressing news from someone that is current."

"Like the movie of the monkey drinking his urine as he peed that you showed me the other night?"

"Exactly! What if a kid was doing research on monkeys that drink their own urine? Now I know what direction to point them!"

"That's so unprofessional."

"Yeah, well, a monkey says what?"

"What does that even mean?"

"You said what!"

"So unprofessional."

FOR SHELVING

The next era in Anaheim's history began when Walt Disney came to town.

Disney was a young father disappointed that all the local amusement parks he visited with his kids really had no imagination; they were just rides. He started thinking up a dream for a theme park where kids could live out their childhood fantasies. His original plan was to build the park on an eleven-acre piece of land next to his animation studio in Burbank. City officials, however, rejected his plan. While trying to come up with a plan that the city would approve, Disney took a drive down the Santa Ana Freeway. He ended up in Orange County, where he felt he had been transplanted back to the Midwest, where cities were small and everyone knew your name.

Disney suddenly began to dream a lot bigger. He went from planning a small park that would cost $10,000 to planning a large, multisectioned park that would cost $4,000,000 and encompass over 100 acres of land. There were two problems he first had to solve. One, where to put the park, and two, how to fund it. Canoga Park, Long Beach, and Palos Verdes were all considered as possible locations, but in the end Anaheim was decided to be the best choice.

To fund the extravagant venture, Disney was able to convince ABC Network to invest $500,000 and make available another $4.5 million in loans in return for a partnership. In return, Disney agreed to produce a weekly hour-long series. The series Disney created allowed him to freely advertise his theme park for an hour each week.[3]

Disneyland opened its doors in 1955 and was famously a complete and utter disaster. The first day, a gas leak closed Fantasyland; it was a hot summer day and water fountains had not been installed; and the heels of women's shoes left marks in the newly paved asphalt. Critics complained that the park was simply not ready. Despite poor reviews, 1 million people came to Disneyland in a mere seven weeks.

One could say the real birth of Anaheim was 1955—the day that Disneyland came to town.

---

3. In a twist of fate, in 1996 the Disney Corporation bought out the company that paved the way for its success.

The first thing any librarian should do at a new library is get to know their community. I'm no expert on libraries, but the reason so many libraries fail in lower-income communities isn't so much a failure on the part of the community as a failure on the part of the librarian. A servant must know its master. I believe in taking it one step higher, going so far as to live in the city where I work. This wasn't a stretch, since both libraries are in the same city, but I did spend more time just hanging out there, shopping at the stores nearby and eating at the hole-in-the-wall restaurants.

If I just went to work every day and did my job I didn't believe I was doing my job. You have to go the extra step—you have to know who you are doing the job for. Not long before I started working at the new library, my manager had warned me about streets that I didn't want to drive down; she was right. There were streets I shouldn't be driving down. Instead, I needed to be walking down them.[4]

What was this new community? Mexico. I was lucky, because, as it happens, this is one of the easiest nationalities to get to know and love.

Nearly every day someone would come in and say something to this effect:

"You speaka Spanish?"

I would shake my head and point at a clerk up front. "She can help you."

"No. I looka for eh book English."

"Book English?"

"Sí!"

"A book in English?"

"No. No! I learn."

---

4. To be fair, this is Anaheim. Not exactly Thug City, USA.

"You want to learn English?"

"Sí. Sí! I want to learn!"

How could you not love a nationality like that? How could you not be impressed when someone came and said I want to learn? It was usually someone who didn't speak English who wanted to learn something. Sometimes it was learning English. Sometimes it was learning to write. Sometimes it was something entirely different.

~

I don't like white people.[5] They say they are not racist to be polite, but that's a lie. We are all racist: blacks, Mexicans, whites, and Asians. We can deny it all we want, but there's not a single race that does not have some racist thoughts toward another. One race will always help their own race simply because that's what we do. We're shallow, in the end. We help because we identify with people, not so much people of our color as people of our background. It's not that we intend to do this. It's just that we're too lazy and self-absorbed to make a conscious effort to help the people we don't understand. Sometimes a person comes along to prove my point so strongly that I want to smack them upside the head. One such day brought the old man who was the fartiest old dick I've ever come across.

"I want to check these out!" he said, throwing his books at me.

"The circulation counter is right there." I pointed. "Rosie will happily check you out, but you have to wait in line."

"I can't understand a word that damn Mexican says."

"I'm sorry, you'll have to wait in line."

He looked at the desk and saw Rosie speaking Spanish to a woman. "Look at that! Talking Mexican to her!"

I didn't speak. I didn't really know what to say to that.

---

5. I am white.

"I'm not trying to sound racist. I got nothing against them. My parents came here and they learned the language. They didn't get jobs talking German. They had to learn American before they could get a green card."

"I'm sure they're trying."

"Oh, they're trying alright! Trying to take over this country and making Mexican the national language."

"Actually Mexican isn't a language. Neither is American."

"You get what I'm saying."

"No. Actually I don't. And if you want those books you're going to have to get in line like everyone else."

"Don't be like that—we got to look out for each other."

"Sorry. I can't help you."

"Oh! I get it! You're one of those young kids who thinks the world is perfect. I'll tell you what—ten years from now you're going to get what I'm talking about. You're going to know why we people have to look out for each other."

"I hope by *we* you mean Americans."

"You won't help me?"

"No puedo ayudar."

He walked away and shouted, "Damn Mexicans! Damn you all!" as he walked out the door.

~

The longer I worked with Roland, the longer I saw that he sort of valued my opinion. Sometimes I acted like I didn't give a damn about my job, but he knew, as much as I played it like I didn't take my job seriously, he knew that I in fact did and that I knew quite a bit about the profession. This depressed me. It depressed me because that meant someone thought I had worked at something long enough to be an expert at the job. Maybe one day I did intend to be an expert at a job, but certainly not now, because that would mean I had, in fact, entered into a career, which I wasn't exactly prepared to do yet.

"So what is it that you actually do?" Roland asked me one day, as I checked my e-mail.

I hated this question, but I hated it even worse because he actually worked at a library. With most people I could reply by saying, "Oh, you know, just library stuff," which somehow appeased them. With someone who actually worked in the field, this was a bit more complicated, because they knew that was a lie. I gave him the most generic answer I could think of: "What do you mean what do I do? You've seen what I do."

Roland nodded. "That's the thing—I really haven't. I've seen you check e-mail and visit mindless Web sites, but I haven't actually seen you do something librarian-like. Yeah, you help people, and you actually do know what you're talking about. But I want to know what you do when you're not doing those things."

I laughed at the suggestion. "I do plenty."

"I'm sure you do. I'm just thinking of one day becoming a librarian and I want to know what you do."

My mind raced. I couldn't just make something up because he would know. "I process books. Research book trends. Stuff like that."

He nodded. "But I do that, too. More than you sometimes. Isn't there anything you do that I don't? Something that makes our two jobs different?"

I nodded enthusiastically and said sarcastically, "Of course! I get paid more than you."

$\sim$

The lights and atmosphere were a little dim at this new library, but it certainly wasn't short on people who wanted knowledge.

I became a librarian because I liked books. The longer I stayed the more I saw that I wasn't staying for the books, I was staying for the people. I was staying because I liked helping people, staying because there was always someone out there who needed help knowing something.

The building was different. It wasn't the old library. But it was still a library. You could go to any library in the world and it would still be the same. Maybe cosmetically it would be different, but you close your eyes, and there's nothing different about it. The noises you heard, the scent you smelt, the people who came in, the questions they asked, the way teens behaved, and the way kids behaved—it was all the same. How many other professions did this happen in?

Chapter 808.87	Being Things Librarians
-KEEP-	Must Do to Keep Themselves
Keeping a	from Cracking Up
Straight Face:	

The first few weeks, people came off and on from the old library. They'd say hi and that they missed us and that they couldn't wait for the new library to open. It was always good to see a friendly face.

Ernest stopped in on my first day of work, and continued to stop in every other day for two weeks. About a month after starting work at the new library, Ernest stopped in and didn't look too thrilled.

"How's it going, Ernest?" I asked cheerfully.

"Not too good. Not too good at all."

"I'm sorry to hear that."

Ernest was quiet. I thought he was going to say something, but he didn't. I slowly began to back away. A tearful sentence from Ernest's lips stopped me. "I'm moving to Texas."

"Texas?"

He nodded and wiped away his tears. "My son's out there. He's going to take me in. I'm going to watch his kids."

I could hardly see Ernest as a nanny. Maybe a crazy grandpa who gave bizarre gifts and occasionally took the kids fishing, but not someone you would leave your kids with for extended periods of time. And the way he was acting I suspected there was something else to the story.

"When?"

"Friday."

"This Friday?"

"Yeah."

"That's in two days."

He nodded. "I really wanted to stick around until that new library was built."

"Well, you better come visit when it's done."

He nodded yes, he would.[1]

"I really don't know what to say. There's not a single person here who's not going to miss you. You became a fixture in our library lives."

"You're a hard group to replace."

And that was that. That was the last thing he said before he left the library, and he didn't come back. Staff speculated as to why he went. A family member was ill or he was in trouble with the law were the top favorites. Maybe he really was going there to care for his grandkids. It didn't matter. What mattered was he was gone.

Ernest's slot as favorite library friend was vacant for several months. Everyone looked for patrons who could replace him. In the end, no one could. The one we ultimately chose was named

---

1. He didn't.

Woody. Woody was a retired policeman and recovering alcoholic. But Woody, as Jonathan pointed out, did not have the wit and wisdom of Ernest. And he sort of smelled.

Ernest's departure, in some ways, was the end of an era for me. Eventually, all the old patrons either stopped coming or morphed into something entirely new. They became patrons of the new library. They were not remembered as patrons from the old library. I had a new family now.

～

No one likes it when his car battery dies; it just makes a bad start to what could otherwise be a nice day. But when you have an uncle who lives, literally, across the street, a dead battery doesn't have to be a bad thing. Unless it turns out that his battery is dead, too, and you have to ride on the backside of his motorcycle.

At first it sounded like a good way to boost my image. Motorcycles have a way of making people look cool. I imagined myself arriving at work with helmet in hand and pretending that I had indeed just ridden my new bike to work. Maybe I would even shake my hair[2] the way I always saw it done in the movies. I had been looking for a way to sex up my image at the new library so that I wasn't the same old person from the old library. I thought this short trip might be my ticket.

My fantasies never really panned out quite like I expected. In fact, they always failed quite miserably.[3] As soon as I started having fantasies about this current scheme, I should have

---

2. It was long at the time.

3. All of them, from meeting and marrying a famous actress all because I used the expensive shampoo they had on sale at Target, to becoming a professional gaming player because I almost beat my brother's high score on *Super Mario Brothers*; or my personal favorite, becoming the head coach of the Los Angeles Lakers simply because I had taken the team all the way to the finals on my Xbox (granted, on easy mode).

known it was going to fail, but, as I always did, I had hoped, for some ridiculous reason. How could it go wrong?

Of course, it did go wrong. From the moment I got on the back of my uncle's bike and my uncle told me "Just put your arms around me—I won't bite," it went wrong. I never imagined that riding a motorcycle could be so gay, but having your arms tightly wrapped around the stomach of a sweaty overweight man just gives people the wrong idea about things.

I wasn't worried as much about people staring as I was about falling off the back of the bike, so I held on tight and imagined how I would still look cool walking into the library with my motorcycle helmet under my arm and that no one had to know I had really just spent the last ten minutes strapped to the backside of my uncle. But, like I said, my fantasies never quite panned out as I expected them to.

I knew my fantasy in all its capacities had been defeated when my uncle pulled into the parking lot and Faren and every other manager in Anaheim were standing in front of the library. They looked at me oddly and then pretended not to notice. It's bad when even librarians feel bad for you.

My uncle took off his helmet as I got off the bike and said as loudly and as gayly as he could, "Have a good day at work, honey!" Then he rode off. I watched him speed down the street and wondered how he could make it look cool, while I simply gayed it up like always. Then I turned to the managers. I nodded, but they did not nod back. I wasn't cool. I was a librarian, and not being cool was as cool as I'd ever get. My image could not be changed from one library to the next.

❧

Among the library's new extended family was a fire station that had just opened next door the year before, after the old, smaller firehouse had been torn down. Some think that is every woman's fantasy—working next to a fire station—and maybe it is. I thought the firemen were a bunch of arrogant jerks and not very neighborly in any way. I hated them, even though everyone loved them.

This was during the post-9/11 phase where firefighters were everyone's heroes and everyone went around wearing "I [heart] Firemen" T-shirts. I hated those T-shirts because I hate firemen. Sure, they're nice when you're having a heart attack or when your house is burning down, but they certainly don't make good neighbors.

It seemed nice at first. If anyone tried to kill me they were a quick walk away. I'd imagined them helping us at the smallest of things just to be a friendly neighbor. But they never came over to say hi. They were like the football players of the city departments. They know they are heroes; they know everyone likes them and wants to be them when they grow up. They are simply not very humble or even sort of friendly. Like I said— they are sort of jerks.

At first I just thought they were shy. They didn't want to come in and see us because they just weren't *people* people. This I could understand. Then one day someone came in the library and said there was a car parked in the middle of the parking lot and no one could get in or out. I went outside and saw that indeed a car was in the middle of the parking lot. It was actually positioned in front of a space and appeared to have somehow rolled forward to its current location.

I returned to the library and made a quick announcement. I described the car and asked if it belonged to anyone. No one claimed it. The next plan was to push it into the spot. But there was a problem; the library staff that day was me—a skinny white guy with bony arms—and a bunch of women. Not exactly the types to be pushing around cars.

Kate, a library technician, suggested talking to the firefighters about it. It seemed like a good idea. That's what friendly neighbors do for each other. We rang the doorbell. I let Kate do the talking. It seemed best to let her play the role of damsel in distress.

"Hi! We seem to have a car parked in the parking lot, and none of our library patrons can get out of the lot. We were wondering if you could help us push it back into a space."

He walked outside, stared at the car, and admitted, "Oh, yeah, that's the car that caught on fire. Lady was in the parking lot and the engine got on fire. She had to go get a tow truck."

Thanks for telling us! I wanted to say.

"So, do you think you could help us move it?" Kate asked

At this point another fireman came out; he looked like a captain. "They want us to help push that car in a stop. Seems it's blocking traffic," the first fireman explained.

The one who looked like a captain shook his head. "Be our rears if something happened to one of us while we were pushing it— since it's not an emergency. Wish we could help, but it's a liability."

What a dick! I thought to myself.

"But you really do need to get it moved. If we go out on a call we wouldn't be able to get our truck back in—it *is* blocking things. So if you could go ahead and move it, that would be great."

That was my first encounter with the firemen next door.

A few months later a guy came into the library out of breath and said in a panic, "There's a lady in front of the church next door with her panties down and a longneck bottle in her hand. I think she might be dead."

"Did you go to the fire station next door?"

He looked across the way. "That's a fire station?"[4]

I nodded. "Come on. Let's go next door and see if they can help."

Two things crossed my mind as we walked across the street. One, this guy kind of looks like the type of man who would rape a woman and then kill her and come to the library for help; two, and more importantly, I had just heard the fire trucks leave on a call. I was really worried that no one was there, and I was about to go take the vitals of a woman lying half naked in front of a church, with a bottle of whiskey in her hand. That wasn't in my job description.[5]

We rang the doorbell. No one came. I pounded on the glass. No one came. I rang the doorbell again. Finally a guy came from the office. He looked like he was the guy that stayed behind because he was a bit of screwball.

"Hi. I work at the library next door. This gentleman just came in and said there was a woman down the street that might be dead."

"Well, everyone is out on a call."

"There's no one who can help?"

He sighed and finally said, "I guess I can go take a look."

The firemen came into the library only a few times, once on an emergency call. An elderly lady had slipped while taking a crap and couldn't get up. I wasn't there that day and I was glad. Apparently it had been a pretty messy job for them and not a pretty sight when they brought her out.

---

4. It's a large fire station with several fire engines; two stories; and the words fire station clearly marked. It's pretty hard to miss.

5. Actually, most of the things in my job description were things I never did.

The only other time they entered the building was when they needed to check e-mail; this lasted only a few weeks because one of the guys got a laptop and saw we had wireless access and came over immediately. "Hey, I noticed you have wi-fi, and I was wondering if I could get the encryption key."

I thought back to how they hadn't helped us. I wanted to say no or something clever like that but didn't, because it would be my rear. In the end, I gave it to him. I realized that if they were the cocky jocks, then librarians were the nerdy guys they picked on. We gave them our lunch money and they let us go on our merry little way.

It's just the way things went. We weren't heroes—we only inspired them. And apparently gave them free wireless Internet access.

FOR SHELVING

Maybe I wasn't ready to grow up, but it could have been worse. The rite of passage in some cases borders on scary to flat-out bizarre. As the BBC reported in 2003, a nine-year-old tribal girl from India married a dog. Whenever you feel you are facing a life-changing decision, consider this: at least you don't have to marry a dog. The girl had a tooth rooted to her upper gum, and members of the village believed that if the girl did not marry the dog she would face a bad omen. By marrying the dog, the omen would be passed on to the dog. The marriage was attended by over 100 guests.

The practice of marrying pets is not common in India, but is not unheard of; the incident was not the first of its kind, and will likely not be the last. While the girl would not consummate the marriage, she would be required to care for the dog. If she chose to marry in the future she would not have to divorce the dog.

A full-time clerk position opened a month after I moved to my new location. Brenda applied and did not get the job. I was relieved. Who wouldn't be? But on the same note, I pitied her. It had to be taken as an insult to be working for the same job for fifteen years without a single promotion. Ultimately, the promotion went to Rosie.

Brenda told me she was herself in the interview, and this is where she failed. She answered questions about how she would handle a difficult patron in this matter: "Well you know me! I've been here for fifteen years!" Despite what I told her she still went ahead and answered questions as if the interviewers were not professionals but her friends.

"I wouldn't have taken it anyway," she told me.

I nodded. It was all I could do to say I was sorry even though I was not. The truth was I was scared. I was scared because the person who got the job had been at the library for only five years. She was nicer, sharper, and more qualified, but I feared for the poor woman's safety. Brenda would be bitter, and she would do all she could to screw the woman's job up.

"I'm tired of this place," she told me. "I'm not doing any more favors for it. I'm just going to do my job and nothing else. They treat me like this and they'll get the kind of employee they deserve."

"Just be professional."

"I'm always professional!" She then looked to the back of the library where Rosie, the clerk who had been promoted, was processing books, and she said, "I'm going to go over there right now and give her a piece of my mind. Just lay down the law and tell her she may be my supervisor, but she's not my boss and I don't have to answer to her."

There was enough bitterness and drama at the new library that a break should have sounded good—even if it was a small one. A company picnic should have sounded ideal to me, but in truth it did not. The annual city summer picnic was nothing more than listening to a speech on how great everyone is, hearing someone give kudos to people who had suffered with the company the longest, and cheering on someone who was brave enough to retire. When lunch finally was served, you ate quickly, so as to get away from the guy next to you who wouldn't shut up about how great his IRA was doing.

I would take real work over the picnic any day. But sometimes luck isn't in my deck of cards and I have to suffer through the thing. Such was the case the year I started working with Matt.

Matt was a young kid, out to conquer the world, who started working at library the same week that I was reassigned. He looked eagerly at any get-rich-quick scheme that passed by him and would do anything not to go to school. Matt was in love with two things: himself and his iPod. Matt was also a pothead. A fact I knew but tried not to dwell on. I was his supervisor and I really just wanted not to know such details. Don't ask, don't tell—it's the American way.

Faren decided to send the two of us to the picnic to give us some time to break away from the female-dominated workplace and experience male bonding.[6]

"Should I drive?" I asked Matt in the parking lot.

"No way! You have to check out my new sound! It's brilliant!" He told me proudly, "I have it hooked into my iPod! It's insane!"

Great. I didn't like driving with other people because I'm not one to trust anyone. It takes a lot to earn my trust, and he hadn't

---

6. Actually, it was because she didn't want to go herself, and someone had to represent the library.

earned it. Nonetheless, I nodded. If anything else I'd save a couple bucks in gas.[7]

Matt opened the door and the stench of pot immediately exited. I gasped.

"Relax! I'm not gonna smoke it."

"Maybe I should drive?"

"Stop being such a pussy. Get in."

I don't know why I obeyed. I just did.

"We can roll if you want to."

"No thanks."

"You ever seen it?"

"Yeah," I said, trying to sound hip.[8]

Matt peeled out of the driveway and I said a quick prayer. He drove like he acted: sporadic, wiry, and utterly insane. We wove in and out of lanes, cut people off, and stopped for no reason at all. He cussed at cars going too fast, cussed at cars going too slow, and cussed at me just because.

I tried not to be nervous. I tried to sound cool. I did the first thing that came to my mind; I quizzed him on pot. I asked him where he bought it, how he smoked it, and why he didn't stop. He told me all kinds of details I preferred not to know, about bad weed, going to East L.A. for a cheap bag, getting into a fistfight during a deal, and how he didn't use protection when he had sex because he shot blanks. He went on to tell me how he smoked it nearly every break and during his lunch.[9]

We got to the picnic and I worried that I reeked of the stuff. Two librarians from other branches did look our way as I got out

7. Yes, I am that cheap.

8. I had seen it on some narcotics show on the Discovery Channel.

9. He also came back regularly from lunch a little drunk.

of Matt's car. "Do you smell that?" one of them said. I thought we were busted until I turned around and saw they were referring to the barbecue starting behind us.

The barbecue was a joke, as always. Matt made his way to the food line and I lagged behind. He found a table in the shade, but I did not join him. I wanted to look professional, not like some young kid slacking off and at the event only for the free food.

I sat next to a man from HR who had been with the city for thirty-seven years.

"Lot of good times," he told me, like he was trying to pass down wisdom. "Lot of bad times, too. But it's a job. It's a good job. It fed my family, put my kids through school, and got my wife the trip she always wanted to Europe. How can you complain about that?"

"I guess you can't," I said politely.

"No, you really can't. I'm retiring next month."

"Congratulations," I said, trying to sound like I sincerely was happy for him.[10]

He nodded proudly.

"What will you do?"

"Oh, I'll be coming back—just in part-time capacities. They really can't fill a position like mine. I'm too hard to replace."[11]

I sat with the man as long as I could, then excused myself and joined Matt in the shade.

---

10. I couldn't have cared less.

11. I had discovered that this was the new trend. Retire and then come back to work part-time. That way you get the benefits of a retirement check and you get another check on top of it. It was wonderful for businesses because they didn't have to hire a full-time replacement; it was really quite crappy for my generation because they were having a harder time getting ahead. When I retire, I plan on doing just that.

"This is my sixth hot dog!" he proudly exclaimed with food in his mouth.

I nodded and meditated on the cars passing by.

"I wish I could light up right here. Just lean back against that tree over there, close my eyes, and just get baked in the sun."

I turned my head and looked at the division head, who had just started speaking.

"This really blows, huh?"

"Yeah."

On the way back I was honest with Matt. "Look, I think it would be better if you didn't tell me about what you do after work. What if the manager asked me if you do it? I'm not going to lie for you."

Matt laughed and said, "Relax! I know you're cool like that."

It really made me think: *Was I cool like that?*

Not too long after that another employee had said jokingly to Faren about Matt, "Everyone knows that if he's not stoned, he's drunk."

Faren laughed. "You don't really think he's done that, do you?"

"Um, yeah!"

"I don't want to hear that!" She laughed and then ignored it altogether. The truth[12] was she liked Matt because he could put things together and paint; he was cheap labor for the library.

As it turned out, I didn't really have to be cool like that. It wasn't going to be an issue, apparently.[13] But that still didn't solve my dilemma. It wasn't about whether or not I was cool like that. What mattered was that I was twenty-five in a position I wasn't

---

12. Actually, the employee had been known to exaggerate, and she didn't ignore it because it wasn't important but because his claims didn't always carry much truth.

13. He was good at hiding it.

sure I was ready for. I was facing ethical questions; I was being asked to supervise; I was in charge of a building. Did I really want any of those things?

Not long after that I went to Del Taco for lunch. I saw a kid who still had to be in high school yelling at a Spanish man twice his age. As it turned out, the little kid was the supervisor. I thought about how maybe I was making too big a deal out of it. Even the punk little kid at Del Taco had important responsibilities. But that was Del Taco! The truth was, I had always wanted a nice desk job where I didn't have to be in charge of anyone or anything. I didn't want stress. I just wanted a nice job to get me a paycheck so I could go home. I had that.

Maybe I just wasn't quite ready for a career.

Chapter 650.13 -MYSP- MySpace:	Being the Part Where Our Hero Discovers He Has a Place on the Internet, and People Like Him, They Really Like Him

MySpace.com. That's all you need to say in any library. MySpace.com. That one word (or Web site, if you will) will surely spark a debate. There are haters, lovers, and in-betweeners.

I myself think it's a great tool. A library tool? Not so much. Before it was banned at my library, teens would flock in groves to the library to use it. Noise level increased. Rowdy behavior increased. Swearing increased. Attitude problems increased. And that was just the kids.

ABOUT ME

I'm a librarian, freelance writer (meaning I get paid enough writing to pay taxes on my income, but not nearly enough to make an honest living), and

(Continues)

(Continued)

all-around disturbed person. I don't enjoy meeting new people, and quite frankly don't like people in general (though I have found some to be quite nice). I like dogs. I have a home page that is sometimes updated (www.scottdouglas.org), and an e-mail address that I sometimes check. I also have an e-mail address that I often check. I like books, plays, and foreign films, and I'm not gay, which is becoming a difficult feat. I also like the color green and the numbers 7, 13, and 21, but I'm not sure why. I'm a conservative Christian, but, by and large, I don't really like other conservative Christians, which doesn't really make sense. Sometimes I wonder if the world really is flat; other times I wonder if the personification of time in Shakespeare's sonnets meant something deeper or if he was just trying to get laid (I never really liked Shakespeare, btw, but I like Jane Austen). Still other times I wonder what their baby would have been like if Flannery O'Connor and Mark Twain (had he been alive when Flannery was) had had one.

One day. That's how long it took for Brenda to have her first official run-in with Rosie, the new clerk. Rosie was entering new videos in the computer and then putting rental stickers on the covers.

"That's not the way we do it," Brenda pointed out, as the clerk put a dollar rental sticker in the right bottom corner instead of the left bottom corner.

"We're changing it," Rosie explained. "It's better this way because it doesn't cover up the movie's title."

"Well we never did it like that before."

"We're changing that way."

"It's too confusing that way," Brenda pouted.

"I'll train you."

"I'm not stupid," Brenda said, offended. "I know how to apply a sticker." She walked away and told Faren that Rosie had verbally

harassed her and treated her like she was a child. And she wasn't
doing the stickers right.

You can only take so much of this kind of petty behavior;
sooner or later you either go crazy or you find the therapy you
need to get through it. What did I find? I found MySpace.

SCOTT'S INTERESTS

GENERAL: Writing, reading. I'd like to dispel the cliché that librarians
are boring, but that simply just doesn't seem true to me. Watching paint dry
seems like a pretty swell day to me, although watching a movie might also
be fun.

MUSIC: Collective Soul; Led Zeppelin; The Doors; Nirvana; The Beatles;
The White Stripes; The Who; Johnny Cash; Elton John; The Eagles; Bob
Dylan; Bo Bice. Don't laugh, we all need one guilty pleasure!

MOVIES: *Wild Strawberries; Il Postino (The Postman); Dr. Strangelove; The
Last Time I Saw Paris; The Gods Must Be Crazy; Roman Holiday* and pretty
much everything else with Audrey Hepburn; *Some Like It Hot; Adventures
of Buckaroo Banzai; The Agony and the Ecstasy; Tae Guk Gi (The Brotherhood
of War); Donnie Darko.*

TELEVISION: *The Simpsons; The Office; The Daily Show; 24.*

BOOKS: *The Crying of Lot 49; East of Eden; Wise Blood; The Adventures of
Kavalier and Clay; Rabbit Run; 1984; The Great Gatsby; Brief Interviews
with Hideous Man; Pride and Prejudice; The Sun Also Rises; Mere Chris-
tianity; The Handmaid's Tale; Just As I Am: The Autobiography of Billy
Graham.*

It didn't take long for things to get out of hand with MySpace. Teens started stealing library cards so they could get extra time; adults would constantly argue about why they deserved more hours; and even little fourth graders were asking older kids for advice on how to "pimp out" their MySpace page.

When teens found out I had a MySpace page, the conversation would go a little like this:

"You have a MySpace page?"

"Yeah."

"Will you be my friend?"

"No."

I did become friends to a few of them just to get them to stop asking me to add them. When I did add them and saw their pages, I was a bit frightened at what I saw. I expected obscene comments and behavior; what I didn't expect were suggestive pictures that, I was pretty sure, were taken right at the library.

Ultimately, MySpace was blocked because it was slowing down the network. This wasn't the real reason. The real reason was because it was making all the librarians mad. Actually, the straw that broke the camel's back was when a manager saw a teen posting a photo of girl's nipple piercing to his page.

The day it was blocked, it was like the library rolled back in time. The kids were polite. They didn't scream or run. They of course found ways around it, but that didn't matter. For a few days there was peace. I loved that day. I requested to work it. I wanted to see the looks on their faces when they ran to their computers and saw for the first time their beloved friend was no longer there. I wanted to hear them say "What the heck?" I wanted to be the one they ran to and cried, "Why can't I get on MySpace?" And I certainly wanted to be the one to tell them "Because it's been blocked." Seeing their sad faces and crushed hearts was my reward for spending so many hours with that site. So many hours telling them to settle down and not fight because someone posted a comment another kid didn't like.

"It's *so* not fair!" Casey, a teen girl who regularly came to the library to check MySpace, said.

"Maybe it's for your own good," I would reason.

"Whatever."

"Do you know about all the old guys who use MySpace to meet young girls like you?"

"I'm safe." Casey assured me. "I don't put any information about where I live or even my school."

"Do you put photos of yourself?"

"Of course! Everyone does that."

"And do your top friends all go to your school?"

"Yeah."

"And do they put where they go?"

"Yeah."

"Wouldn't be too hard for some creepy old man to track you down just by looking at all your friends' pages, then, would it?"

"What do you mean?"

"Well, if all your friends go to that school, wouldn't you assume you went there too?"

"Stop scaring me."

"I'm not the one using MySpace."

"Well, I don't talk to old men anyway."

"Do you talk to any guys you've never met?"

"A few."

COMMENTS

MARK TWAIN–Thanks for that one night in Tokyo. It was fun. Let us never speak of it again.   (Continues)

(Continued)

BO BICE—So you're the one!

FLANNERY O'CONNOR—Enough with the love letters, I get it. You like me. I just don't feel the same way. And I'm dead.

SCOTT DOUGLAS—I wish people would stop mistaking me for you. For the record, people, I'm the Scott Douglas who used to be in the Christian rock group White Heart and was later arrested on sex-related crimes. I'm not the Scott Douglas who wrote this book.

DICK CHENEY—Let's go hunting sometime, yeah?

SPOT—See Spot comment. Comment, Spot, comment!

"So what makes you think they're not just posing as young guys?"
"I don't know. They're sweet to me. I just know they aren't, I guess."
"I'm sure that little teen murdered last week by some guy she met on MySpace thought that, too."
"Shut up! There wasn't a kid murdered."
"It was in all the papers."[1]
"Serious?"
"Yup."

SCOTT'S TOP FRIENDS

Kevin (Brother)

Beth (Cousin)

d (muse)

---

1. It wasn't. I was making all this up.

The Wittenburg Door (satire magazine)

Bob Dylan

The White Stripes

NOOMA (great organization, check them out)

The Long Blondes (librarians turned rock stars—sort of)

MySpace is a great tool. Just not in the library. What I learned from it was there was an entire world of librarians my age and even younger. I joined groups, made friends, and ultimately saw that maybe I had no idea who I was but there were people out there like me, and that made me feel better.

I had lived in a sheltered world for several years. I was the young man in the pool of old ladies. The closest person to my age who was a librarian was in her mid-thirties. MySpace showed me an entire world of younger librarians who in fact had their own online community. We talked about random things, from best film to feature a librarian to should food be allowed in the library? We encouraged each other because we knew we were the future. We were the ones who had to come up with the ideas to take the library to the next level.

"Do you ever wonder if you need a career change?" one of my online friends asked in a chat one day.

It was like he knew exactly where I was coming from. I wasn't alone. As much as I was unsure of everything, I felt fine about it, because as unsure as I was there were other people out there who were just as unsure. There's always comfort knowing you're not alone; it's so much easier to give up when there's no one else out there who can relate.

Do I ever wonder about a career change? Who doesn't? That's what I learned from MySpace.

Information professionals have been throwing out the phrase Web 2.0 for the past several years; many believe that the next phase of the Internet is the idea of collaborating and sharing with other users.

Social networking and Wikis are both examples of this. While some[2] have taken this coined term and presented it as the next revolution in the development of the Internet, others, such as the godfather of the Internet, Tim Berners-Lee,[3] wisely called this new revolution no revolution at all, since the technology has always been there.

What is Web 2.0, really? A joke. The same general ploy that greeting card companies use to make up holidays also applies to people who try to present Web 2.0 as something new. Web 2.0 is a coined term used to get people excited at lectures, but is something that really means nothing because the term has no set of standards and is defined differently depending on who you ask. In all actuality, the term is most commonly used to refer to technologies that have been around since the early 1990s. Social networking sites like classmates.com began in 1995; that same year c2.com became the first site to employ the use of Wikis; and sites like Amazon.com have allowed users to post reviews of products almost from the beginning.

There's nothing new about the technologies. What's new is that people are finally using the Internet and learning how to use the technologies that have been around since the beginning.

---

2. Such as many information/librarian professionals.

3. The person most often referred to as the creator of the Internet as we know it today.

SCOTT'S SCHOOLS

2001 to 2003:

San Jose State University

San Jose, CALIFORNIA

Graduated: 2003

Student status: Alumni

Degree: Master's

Major: Library Science

1999 to 2001:

California State University–Fullerton

Fullerton, CALIFORNIA

Graduated: 2001

Student status: Alumni

Degree: Bachelor's

Major: Comparative Religion; English Literature

1996 to 1999:

Fullerton College

Fullerton, CALIFORNIA

Graduated: 1998

Degree: Associate

Major: English

1992 to 1996:

Valencia High

Placentia, CALIFORNIA

Graduated: 1996

Student status: Alumni

Degree: High School Diploma

MySpace is also good because you can find out so much about the people you work with, especially when they blog. I found someone who had a fear of glitter, someone who didn't like clowns, and someone who honestly believed they could kill Ronald McDonald in a celebrity death match. A few months before the library banned MySpace, I also found out that Brian, the new librarian for teens, had created an account and appeared to be using it to find out more information about employees. I could have complained that this seemed to be slightly invasive, but there was really nothing I could do to stop him. So I decided the best thing to do with it was just have a little bit of fun.

"Do you think everything on there is true?" he asked me a few days after he told me about his account. There seemed to be concern in his tone.

"Definitely," I lied.

"I read that most people lie on MySpace."

"That's a misconception. They lie about their favorite band and stuff like that. But not everything."

"What about when it says someone is bisexual?"

"It means they're bi. Why would someone lie about that?"

"I guess they wouldn't." He leaned back in his chair and seemed to be dwelling on the notion. "Is that where guys like girls, but they dress up like girls?"

"It's where they like to mess around with guys and girls." I couldn't believe I was having this conversation with him. "Also, any person that wears a pink ribbon is supporting the bi community."

"Really? I thought that was breast cancer?"

I shook my head. "Most people think that, but it actually started in support of the bisexual community; in the 1980s, scientists discovered that people engaging in that kind of sexual activity were four times as likely to develop breast cancer."

"That's not true!"

"No. It is. It's on Wikipedia. I read it the other day. I was just as surprised as you."

He looked at his computer screen. I knew he was tempted to look, but not in front of me.

I started to leave his desk, but he stopped me with one final question. "So when Roland's page says he's bisexual it's the truth."

"Yep."

Roland actually had a girlfriend, and the thought of him liking the opposite sex had definitely never crossed his mind, but he was the one who had set up the page like that, so he was the one who had to answer the questions.

"Oh." He seemed thoroughly confused, but simply added, "Well, you just never know do you? He seemed like a nice young man."

I nodded and left. Brian acted different around Roland for several days, until he got the courage to start asking him questions. Roland came to me a week later and said, "Brian's been acting really strange lately. He keeps asking about my girlfriend—like he's trying to probe me to figure something out."

"That's because he thinks you're bisexual."

"Bisexual?"

"He saw your MySpace page."

"Did he ask you about it?"

"He asked me if it was true."

"What'd you tell him?"

"I said it's MySpace—everything is true."

"Oh. Well, thanks a lot."

"Just go with it. I think he's excited because he doesn't know any bisexuals. I bet he can't wait to tell all his friends."

"But I'm not bisexual."

"Trust me, Roland, I think it's best not to ruin it now. He'll only wind up disappointed. You're new—just tell him what he wants to know. Tell him your girlfriend is into it, too. That you have bi parties and have sex with multiple partners at the same time."

"I'm not going to tell him that."

"Do you want to impress him?"

"I'm not going to tell him that."

"Fine. If you want to go any place in this job, though, you need to learn to stand out from the rest and set yourself apart. It's a competitive business."

I laughed at the ridiculous notion, then looked up at Roland—he was writing down what I said in his notebook.

SCOTT'S DETAILS

Status: In a relationship

Orientation: Straight

Hometown: Anaheim

Body type: 6'0"

Ethnicity: White/Caucasian

Religion: Christian—other

Zodiac Sign: Aries

Smoke/Drink: No/No

Children: Some day

Education: Grad/professional school

Occupation: Librarian

Chapter 305.26	Being the Old People
-NICE-	Who Make Our Librarian Feel
A Nice Young	All Warm and Fuzzy,
Man:	and Whom the Librarian
	Wishes Would Just
	Die Already

Old-lady patrons add a unique flavor[1] to the library. For the most part, they're either warm and fuzzy or bitter and rude. Either way, it's fun to listen to their rambling theories about life, happiness, and why everyone should read Dick Francis. Libraries, however, wouldn't be quite right if there weren't at least one woman who was loud, crude, and sometimes a little drunk. For me there is Ms. Haskell.

I knew Ms. Haskell was special the first day I met her; she asked for the dictionary—on audiotape. Not an abridged version, or a *500 Power Words Everyone Should Know*—not even a collegiate dictionary would do. She had it all scribbled out on a stained napkin, which she proudly dangled in front of my eyes:

---

1. And smell.

"*OED Dictionary* on audiotape." When I said no, we did not have that, she said, "Well, compact disc will have to do, then." That was my first encounter with her, and all the encounters that followed were also about audiotapes.

One night, Ms. Haskell came in loudly and spent ten minutes at the circulation desk telling a helpless library clerk what she thought of each of the seven audio books she was returning. When the clerk explained that the library was closed and she would have to leave, Ms. Haskell turned toward the audiobooks to make that night's selection. I saw where she was going and intercepted her.

"The library is closed, Ms. Haskell, you'll have to come back tomorrow."

She kept on coming, and said, "Out of my way, honey." She then shoved me out of her way. "I'll be just a second," she said. I think I was more surprised by her strength than the fact that she pushed me.

"Did she just push you?" Roland quietly asked.

"I think she did," I admitted.

"What are you going to do?"

I didn't reply. I stared at Ms. Haskell, who had made her selection.

"See, honey, that didn't take but a second."

I could have forced her to come back and check out the next day, but she would have argued that idea longer than I cared to listen. In a public place like a library, you have to choose your battles wisely. Plus, I was kind of afraid she might push me again and I'd have to fill out an incident report saying a seventy-year-old woman physically assaulted me.

～

At some point in a person's life, you stop growing; your world sort of stops and you get frustrated when the rest of the world doesn't stop with you. This period in a person's life is called be-coming a senior citizen. Senior citizens bring you cookies, smiles, and wisdom; but they also bring you a boatload of bitterness and complaints. The complaints would get louder and more bitter during twice-weekly story times, when kids and their parents rule the library.

Henry was a regular library patron and proud senior. He was also a bitter old man.

"Kids today! They have no respect," Henry said to me almost on a daily basis. He sounded like Rodney Dangerfield. "None whatsoever!" He paused and looked at a mother. "Who can blame them when you look at that! These parents just don't know how to raise their kids! They have no control! No discipline!"

"I don't know. At least they're bringing them into a library and teaching their kids about literacy."

"Is that what they're doing?! Their kids are running around like little monkeys. And I don't see any books. If literacy's so im-portant, then where are their books?"

I had, in fact, never seen Henry reading in the library, either,[2] but I decided not to bring up this fact. "They're going to story time, and then they'll get them."

"I'm sure they will. They'll get them and destroy them and pee all over the pages."

Do you know how hard it is not to laugh about a statement like that? Very hard. That's why I think anyone would understand the fact that I did start laughing. Henry, of course, became insulted.

"There's nothing funny about a bunch of kids peeing all over a book like little monkeys."

---

2. He would stay in the library for hours doing nothing but watching people and complaining. He'd ask for books, but he'd never read them in the library.

"No. No, of course not. I'm sorry. And I assure you that does not happen."

"I'd like to smack a few of those parents around is what I'd like to do. Hit them upside the head and tell them a thing or two about raising their kids."[3]

I often found it hard to reply to Henry's comments, and I would simply say, "Okay."

"And you know what'd I tell them?"

"What?"

"I'd tell them they were horrible parents. I'd tell them they need to smack their kid's mouth and wash it out with soap. And take away their toys. Toys are something kids get when they're good kids. And they'd have no video games—tearing up their mind is what those are doing."

"Sounds like you have it all worked out."

When Henry wasn't complaining or watching people, he was doing something of even greater annoyance—talking on his cell phone. Almost daily, I would hear someone loudly saying, "I can barely hear you. I'm at the library." I'd always look up to see who it was, but there was no point because it would always be Henry.

I wouldn't say anything at first, because I always believed he would quiet down. He never did. "So what you going to be wearing?" would be the next thing he would say. As I thought about how odd it was that this old bitter man was having the same conversation as some horny college frat boy, Henry would make things even odder by saying "That sounds real nice. I'll be on new medication by then." It was my job to tell him to quiet down, but I never did. I let him continue as I eavesdropped into the bizarre happenings of an eighty-year-old sugar daddy. I'd let him continue

---

3. I think he was just crazy enough to do it.

until someone complained[4] about him making too much noise, at which point I would say I hadn't noticed and I would definitely ask him to quiet down.

Henry also had a fetish for Dave Barry. "You have anything by Dave Barry?" he asked nearly every day. "That guy sure is funny. I really like him."

Every day I'd do a search to make him happy, and always tell him the same thing. "Nope. Nothing new today."

"That's too bad. He sure is funny. You have any humor books?"

"All kinds. Let me show you," I'd say, like he had never asked me this before. Then I'd point out the same books I pointed out every day. There was only one other person he liked. Larry the Cable Guy. There were two types of humor—David Sedaris humor and Dave Barry humor—and this man was a Barry man.

Henry read the same book over and over. Every day he'd bring it back, hold it in front of me, and say, "Hey, that Dave Barry is pretty funny. You should check him out. You ever read him?"

"I have. He's pretty good."

"Yeah, he's funny."

It was hard not to like Henry, but equally hard not to wish he'd just go away. This was the case with most of the library's elderly patrons. I loved them to death, but sometimes I really wished they would go away.

Most of the seniors just wanted to talk. I couldn't blame them. They were retired, lonely, and just wanted to come somewhere where there was a familiar face that never turned them away. This is how Woody[5] was. He would come in the library literally

4. They always did.
5. Ernest's replacement.

every day and say, "How's it going?" I'd tell him fine, and then he would look awkwardly around trying to think of something else to say. Usually he couldn't, and he'd simply say, "Well, it's been really nice seeing you. I'm so glad you're doing fine."

One week I was out sick for two days. Woody was thoroughly concerned when I returned to work later in the week.

"Boy, I sure was worried about you," he told me as soon as he saw me that day. "They said you were sick. How you feeling now?"

"I'm feeling pretty good. Be myself in another day or two."

That was my mistake. I showed weakness. The next day I was fine. I felt like nothing was wrong with me. I felt good and I looked good. Still, Woody asked, "So you feeling okay? You look like you're getting better. Being sick is no fun thing."

"I'm good now. One hundred percent better. Got no complaints."

"Well that's good. You take care of yourself. Get yourself better."

Three weeks later[6] he was still asking how I was feeling and telling me how bad it was to be sick. He finally stopped asking, but at least once a month he will come in and say, "Hey, you remember that time you were really sick? You were pretty sick, huh?"

I'd smile and nod. That's about all you could do to make him happy. It was nice that someone cared; but sometimes it made me sick. The thing about it, however, was, as insane as I could get from this, I knew that they were the group of people who actually cared about me. Other people came and did their thing in the library, but it was the seniors who actually paused to tell me a story.

People would come into the library every day—literally every day—but I would never learn their name. They were racing

---

6. I kid you not, three weeks later.

through their life—had jobs, kids, and meetings—and were too busy to pause and say hi. This was not the case with the elderly. They had all the time in the world. I wished they had a little less time sometimes, but it was nice knowing every day there would be at least one patron who came in and made sure you were doing okay.

$\sim$

Robert was a Vietnam vet. He was in his fifties, so he couldn't really be classified as a senior, but I called him that anyway. He was retired, hung out with World War II vets, and talked like a seventy-year-old man.

He seemed normal. He'd tell me stories about the war, so I liked him because I liked war stories. There was really nothing about him that raised any flags to say he was a little off.

Nothing until the day Hon was working while he was in the building and he expressed to me his love for her: "You got to get me that dame's number."

"Who?"

"That gal shelving books."

"Hon?"

"Is that her name? She's so pretty. Come on, get me her number. I'll owe you big."

I looked at Hon and was convinced that there had to be someone else he was referring to. Hon was older than him and not exactly something I'd call pretty.

"You're serious?"

"Absolutely!" He admired her for several seconds and finally said, "I'd like to wrap my body around her."

It was, by far, one of the most disgusting images I could imagine.

"I can't give out phone numbers. Just go talk to her."

He nodded and went to her.

I knew that once he talked to her that would be the end of that; she'd mumble something to him, and he'd know instantly that it would never work. I was wrong.

"She's playing hard to get!" he explained to me. "But mark my words: *I will get her number.*"

"So, why don't you like Robert?" I asked Hon after he left the building.

"He too young for me," she explained. "He funny to look, too, okay?"

I nodded.

Robert persisted to hit on Hon in coming weeks. First it was strange, then it was weird, then it was outright scary. He observed her shifts and started leaving only when she left.

"I think it's time you give up, Robert," I finally told him.

He didn't say anything at first, and then he admitted, "There was a girl who looked just like her in Nam; she was only a little thing. I was stationed near her house, and her family took me in. I'd go to their house every day and they fed me and treated me like a king. I loved that girl. I wanted to take her home and make her my wife."

There's not a lot you can say when a man basically admits to having pedophile thoughts. So I didn't say anything at all.

"I was relocated and given a new assignment. By the time I got back to her several weeks later the home was gone. Completely burned to the ground. And the little girl was gone—dead."

"Well, I guarantee you Hon won't be that little girl. You need to just move on, yeah?"

He nodded. Weeks later he showed me pictures of his last two wives. Both had been Vietnamese, and both looked a little like Hon. He told me about how they were both no good—he divorced them within weeks because they were crazy. The longer he came in the more I knew it wasn't because they were crazy, it was because they didn't fulfill his fantasy of marrying that little girl from Vietnam.

Hon went away on vacation for two weeks. When the man asked where she went I said she went to marry the man her family had arranged for her to marry. It was a lie—to my knowledge Vietnamese don't even arrange marriages—but it was all I could do to get him to go away. It worked. He stopped coming after that.

FOR SHELVING

For every Martin Luther King there is a Jim Lawson,[7] for every Albert Einstein there is a Joseph Rotblat,[8] for every Jimmy Doolittle[9] there is someone like Norm.

Norm used books as his guise for coming to the library, but the real reason, I quickly learned, was that he was lonely. He came in one day, sat in front of me at the reference desk, and said, "Fiction is true or false?" I said false, which made him happy. He then began a long discourse on why science was his favorite subject in high school; to make a long story short, he concluded at the end of his discourse on why science was his favorite subject that, in fact, science was not his favorite subject.[10]

---

7. A Methodist minister during the civil rights movement who used the same Gandhian nonviolent tactics as King.

8. Was part of the Manhattan Project, but quit before the bombs were dropped. Went on to become a strong opponent of nuclear weapons and won the Nobel Peace Prize.

9. Okay, so unless you're a history buff or movie buff there's a chance you might not know who Doolittle is. Long story short: after the Japanese bombed Pearl Harbor the United States sent Doolittle and a squad of bombers to retaliate. The mission, though some Americans lost their lives, was deemed successful, and Doolittle became a national hero.

10. History was, in fact, his favorite subject.

(Continues)

(Continued)

One day Norm came into the library looking sad. He sat in front of me and gloomily said, "You're sitting there today because of me." I didn't know what to say to that so I just stared, oddly curious, and waited for him to continue. "I killed Japs. Must have killed over 20,000 during the war. I flew a bomber over Japan. We'd fly nearly every day. Bomb the hell out of them, fly back, then do it all over again."

I tried to think of something to say to Norm, but in the end I could think of nothing at all. Norm didn't wait for me to speak, but paused briefly, then continued remorsefully. "Don't think a day doesn't go by that I don't think about how horrible it was what I did. I'm ashamed. But what can you do? That's war, right? That's what you do, you commit horrible deeds in the name of war. They tell you that you do it so your kids will have a safe place to live and that the thought of that is going to erase it all. But it doesn't."

"Well, there's not a single person in this country who isn't thankful for what you did."

He nodded, turned around looking at the books, then asked, "Fiction is true or false?" I said false and he stood and left.

Why did Norm tell me all this? Why not? There are thousands of seniors like Norm. Seniors who have these incredible stories to tell, but no one to tell them to. Norm had flown B-29s in World War II. He had met Jimmy Doolittle. He flew in Operation Matterhorn.[11] Now he was just this lonely old man with stories to tell but no one but a librarian to tell them to. And I was eager to hear them.

---

11. One of the notable air battles of World War II. It resulted in the loss of several strategic Japanese posts.

The elderly who wanted to use the computer were the worst because they didn't want to use the computer. They wanted *you* to use the computer for them, as if they would somehow learn by watching you do it. They never did.

There was a time when I thought that it was nice. At least they wanted to learn. But they were too worried for learning the computer. They wanted to know everything but new things.

When the library went completely electronic with its book catalog, some stopped coming to the library altogether. It was just too confusing. It was sad when this happened, but in some ways you had to sort of not care. As sad and cruel and insensitive as it was to say, they would be dead soon, anyway. No one would admit this, but I knew that's what went through the minds of people who made decisions about technology. You need to appease seniors, but you need to appease others more.

Elderly patrons are very sweet people who very frequently bring me food, tell me how much they appreciate the library's presence in the neighborhood, and small-talk about their favorite mysteries and true-crime books. They're pleasant to be around—unless they want to use a computer. I am convinced that grandkids are inherently evil people who tell their grandparents to "just go to the library and open up an e-mail account—it's free and so simple."

Of course, the free part gets them to the library in swarms, and, of course, they don't want to take part in the library's free Internet classes, because—well, in the words of one elderly patron, "I don't need a class, because my grandkid said it was simple, and you can just show me the basics." One such elderly patron came to the library not too long ago with such ideals. Strangely, his trouble was not so much opening an e-mail account as it was using the print card.

Print cards are pesky little things librarians institute for the sake of harassing patrons and discouraging them from printing anything.

Often, it works, but this little old man was persistent. I showed him step by step what to do to print, and he was doing pretty well. He seemed to be paying careful attention. He hit the print button like a pro, and walked to the print station like a king. Then he screwed up—big time. At the print station, another patron told me some teenagers had just said the f-word to her five-year-old son and then ran off to the boys' room, where she was pretty sure they were up to no good. I told the elderly gentleman to hang tight and I'd be right back to help him. I learned in just a short time that expecting him to hang tight was a mistake. When I returned to the man, he looked hopelessly confused.

"It didn't work," he explained, frustrated. "And it won't give me my print card back."

I walked to the print station and stared for several seconds at the card reader. I studied it from several angles but did not see his card. "You're sure it didn't come out?" I asked. He nodded, but then pointed at his computer. "It's in there."

I looked at the computer, confused. He pointed at the floppy-disk drive and said, "I tried pushing the button, but it still won't come out."

I kneeled down and immediately saw the print card wedged deep inside the floppy-disk drive. I had seen paper clips, scrap paper, and pencils inside the floppy-disk drive, but this was the first print card. I went to the workroom to get out some tweezers and when I returned the man was gone. I never saw him again.

～

The funny thing about old people was how much they liked Brenda. It's odd how well bitter people, by and large, get along with equally bitter people. An old person came in and argued with me for over ten minutes about the library not supplying pencils.[12]

When Brenda saw the man arguing, she simply went up to him and said, "It's really a shame. I'd be angry, too."

The patron nodded, left me, and went with Brenda, who argued with the man for thirty minutes. In the end she convinced him to write a formal letter of complaint and stick it in the suggestion box, where it was read, acknowledged, and ignored.

When the elderly came in, they were always excited to see Brenda; they would complain about the library, their life, or the way of the nation. Whatever they complained about, they always appeared better after talking to Brenda.

Brenda had a bad attitude, but a bad attitude was just what older patrons wanted.

"You just won't find a better employee than that Brenda," a senior told me one day.

"Why's that?"

"She understands. And she's always so eager to help."

"Well, that's kind of you to say. I'll be sure and let her know."

When they left, Brenda would always rush to the desk and say, "What was that patron saying to you?"

"Said you were nice."

She'd blush and then ask, "Did you tell them to put a note in the suggestion box that said what a good employee I was?"

I shook my head.

---

12. It was a fair argument. The little half-size golf pencils would cost the library less than ten bucks a month and would make people happy. The official policy is that the library can't afford to supply the building with pencils, but it's less than ten bucks! We made that much in thirty minutes on food sales.

"I really wish you would have. I want everyone to know."

Brenda was Brenda. As hard as she could be to work with, she showed me that it really took all kinds for the library to run. Without her, who would make the seniors happy? You can't just forget about them. Libraries needed to cater to teens and children, but they can't forget the ones who helped build the library—they may be bitter, but they have wisdom. Libraries needed people like Brenda exactly for people like that. She was bad at her job, but she had good people skills with seniors, and you had to just admire that. Some people were good with kids, others teens, and still others adults. Brenda was good with seniors, a group most people simply forgot, or at least wanted to forget.

～

Wheelchairs don't have to be unfriendly things, unless they are automated. Then they are machines. If a man is deaf, blind, and feisty as hell, then don't give him a piece of hardcore machinery that can do serious damage. This argument was proven during one of the library's free computer workshops.

The classroom that the computer class was taught in was nearly empty when a man came into the room in an automated wheelchair with his wife. There was a perfect handicapped spot in the back of the room. It was completely accessible for the man in the wheelchair, and I pointed it out to him. He was, of course, deaf or pretending to be deaf, and ignored everything that I said. He put his chair into speed mode and sped toward the front of the room.

Most people would run forward and help the man clear objects out of the way. But I'm not a normal person. I like to observe the handicapped, and study their moves. I'm pretty inconsiderate that way.

I watched him as his chair bumped against the tables; and I watched as two of his wheels lifted off the ground.

The other librarian saw insanity in the man's eyes and pulled back the cord to the projector so his chair wouldn't run over it. Somehow, I have no idea how, he still managed to run over the cable. The projector was knocked completely off the track on the ceiling. The man in the automated wheelchair kept going.

I grabbed the projector before it fell completely to the ground and looked at the man to wait for an apology. None came. He just kept going. Why he needed to go the route he chose, I do not know.

I ended up having to bring out the secondary projector, because the primary was knocked so far off its track it could not be fixed easily. As I struggled to make adjustments on the second projector, the man looked away, not even knowing what he had done. I think he just didn't care.

It took another twenty minutes after the class to actually get the primary projector fixed and operational. The way I see it, we spent over $40 in library work pay to fix the problem caused by some stupid old man in a wheelchair.

⌇

I hated assisting in computer classes with seniors. When I learned I was going to teach it, I decided I was going to be a good sport; I was going to give them a chance. The first thing the teacher said was, "If you have any questions just raise your hands."

A woman in the front of the room raised her hand. The librarian nodded at the woman.

"I was just getting my hand ready! I'm going to have a lot of questions."

She thought she was being cute and charming. She was neither of these things. She was annoying.

"Oh! Ha! Ha!" The teacher said.

I gave it a chance. A fair chance. But it was official: I respected the elderly, but I just wasn't cut out to teach them. It required patience I had yet to acquire. As much as I couldn't stand the idea of teaching them, I also could not wish they'd be gone; as much as they complained, as bitter as they were, as loud as they could be, they had a wisdom that could only be learned from life.

A few years ago the library decided to discard auto repair manuals; they were old, stained with grease and oil, and falling apart. They could have been replaced, but it was decided that it was more practical to order a subscription to an online database that had auto repair manuals. It was expensive, but cheaper in the long run.

John, a regular elderly patron, came into the library not long after the databases had been added to the computers. He needed a repair manual for his Buick.

"We don't carry those anymore," I explained. "The library decided it would be easier and more beneficial to put them all on the computers."

"Beneficial for who?"

I didn't reply. There wasn't anything I could say; the library had taken away books and added something that an entire group of people didn't know how to use. It wasn't fair, and I couldn't argue with him. Instead I took him to the computer and helped him get the information he needed. The funny thing was, I did four times the work helping him use the computer than I would have if the library had just kept the book.

It took ten minutes to help John, and when I finished, he asked, "So what happens when they get rid of the databases? It would be one thing to keep the books, and use this to complement them."

"They won't get rid of them."

Less than a year later, the databases were gone, the books were gone, and the library had nothing. When a person needed to fix his car, we had to refer him somewhere else. I thought John was just a bitter old man who wanted to complain about something new, but as it turned out his words were prophetic.

History repeats. John had seen history and could easily predict what would happen. Unfortunately these opinions were too often passed off as complaints and not wisdom. The more I saw this the more patient I tried to be.

Chapter 305.23	Being How
-USED-	I Came to Hate Teens
I Used to Like You,	(Well, Most of Them,
But Now	Anyway—
I Just Wish	But a Few Are Okay)
You'd Go Away:	

A teen walked out of the library with his girlfriend, looked straight at me, and said, "Faggot." I had never seen the kid before. That, in a nutshell, sums up what I think of teens. There was a time when I thought teens were alright, that they were bright and the world's future. Now? If that's the future, I'm just glad I'll be dead or almost dead before it's their turn to screw things up. I hate them. Well, most of them, but I'll get to that later.

As much as I hated them, teens were now a part of my job. The old library was surrounded by two elementary schools; the new library was surrounded by a high school and a junior high, which meant a vast majority of the patrons were teens—lots and lots of teens.

I had made kids cry before. They were easy. You get a sensitive one and read him the wrong story, and he'll start bawling his eyes out. It was a completely new thing to make a perfectly sane teen start to bust up. That's what I did.[1] Making a teen cry was one of my first clues that I wasn't quite cut out for working with teens.

The teen who cried was an Asian boy named Tony. He was an annoying teen, but, for the most part, a good kid. He was also a tattletale. He'd pick on kids and then complain when they smacked him upside the head.

For several weeks teens had been hacking into the computers to disable the library's time-out software, so they could have un-limited hours on the Internet. We had never been able to catch any of the kids, but finally one day I caught Tony. I approached Tony with Jonathan, who, for reasons I don't know, had be-friended Tony. We played good cop, bad cop. I was the bad cop. Jonathan was the good cop.

"Look, Tony, we know you hacked into this computer," I told him. "You need to tell us how."

"I didn't do it!" he whined. "Someone did it for me."

"Who?"

"They left."[2]

"Tony, I saw you do it. You were the only one at this computer."

---

1. In fact, the only time I had ever seen a teen cry about anything was when I was in sixth grade. I was at camp on a nighttime hike. The counselor decided it would be fun to play a game, so he told us he thought he heard something and said he was running ahead to check it out. He didn't come back. The boy twice my size began to cry like a little girl (actually like a newborn baby), and I had to hold his hand and tell him it would be okay. It turned out the counselor was only hiding in the tree, and he seemed to feel bad about the whole thing (even though there was a pretty big smirk on his face).

2. They always left.

"I can't tell you. The kid who showed me will know."

"Tony, you hacked into the library's computer. That's vandalism. You need to tell what you did. If you don't, then you'll never be able to use the computer again."

"Fine, I won't use it."

"Just tell him, Tony," Jonathan pleaded.

"I can't." Tony looked up at Jonathan sadly, like he had been betrayed by a trusted friend.

"Then you'll have to leave the library," I said.

"But my friends are here."

"When you come back with one of your parents so we can talk you'll be able to come back in the library."

Tony started to cry. Other kids laughed. Tony cried more when they did. Finally he left. Jonathan looked at me, equally devastated. "I never expected he'd do that."

Tony had an older, angrier brother.[3] I hated the brother more than I hated Tony. He argued pointlessly about everything. "Why'd you kick out my little brother?" he demanded I tell him thirty minutes after Tony left. "He's at home crying. He said he didn't do anything."

"He hacked into one of our computers."

"So? All the kids do that! Ha, ha! Your computers are jacked!"

"Well, when they do they get kicked out."

"That's not fair. You can't kick him out of the building for that! He didn't do anything wrong."

"He tampered with computer software. That's vandalism."

"That's not vandalism! The computers aren't broke."

---

3. Kids who cried always had older, angrier brothers.

"I'm not going to argue. Like I told Tony, he's allowed in here when one of your parents comes to talk to us."

"They'll be here, alright. My dad's a cop! He'll take you down!"

Tony's dad came an hour later.[4] So did his brother. Tony stayed home.

"My son's really upset."

"I'm really sorry for that. I know we hurt his feelings. The thing is we're having a big problem with teens tampering and altering our computers' software, and we need to know exactly what Tony did so we can tell our system administrators and they can correct the loophole."

"He's lying, Dad! Tony doesn't even know how to do it. He's stupid!"

"He confessed to knowing how to do it, and we saw him doing it. But he says he can't tell us how because then the kid that showed him will know he told."

The dad nodded. "I'll talk to him."

"That's it?" his brother said angrily. "They made him cry! He's been crying all day!"

"Well, he needs to know there are consequences."

"He didn't do anything wrong! They're liars! They're always lying about stuff."

"We'll talk about this later."

Tony came in the next day. He showed me how it was done. Then he started to cry again. I didn't want to make him cry. Maybe I was too hard. But I'm not good with teens.

"I feel like such a jerk," Jonathan told me after Tony had showed me how the hack was done. "He trusted me."

---

4. I never imagined this would escalate into this big of a deal.

"You can't be a friend to these kids. Look around. They have plenty of friends. They need role models." From that moment on, as much as I didn't like teens, that's what I tried to be—a role model.

~

You tell yourself that you've seen it all, but at least once a month one thing happens that makes you realize there was a wealth of things you had never seen.

One Friday night I had kicked out a teen for refusing to lower his voice and quit cussing. He went outside and waited for his parents. When they came, I saw them drive off,[5] and there were his butt cheeks pressed against the car window. The little bastard mooned me. And his father was in the front seat laughing. When you see a father laughing at his son who's mooning you, you really have serious doubts about why this world hasn't just completely been destroyed by now, and how it's always the dumbest people that have the most babies.

I believe I've seen it all until a person comes around and makes me doubt everything.

~

When I was a kid, I feared the librarian. When the librarian told me to be quiet, I left and didn't return for weeks because I thought she might kill me if she heard my voice again. Today? There's not a lot of fear in teens. Not only do they not respect me, one even tried to hit me. Took a swing right at my face and ended up smacking his fist into the wall. When stuff like that happens you really wonder how long before it happens for real. Before some punk kid does something stupid and takes a swing that really does make contact.

---

5. The reference desk was near the front entrance where cars passed.

There were two boys who were such close friends they seemed like a couple. Wherever one was, you were bound to see the other; when one got a bad haircut, the other would soon follow with an equally bad cut. They had rage. Lots of rage. From what? I never cared to find out. I'm sort of insensitive that way.

This is what I did know about the dynamic duo of douchebags: they had called one of our sixty-year-old librarians a "cunt-sucking bitch." They had called two other female librarians whores. And they had tried (unsuccessfully) to gay-bash one of the clerks when he was in junior high.[6] But that wasn't why I didn't like them. I gave them a fair chance. "Don't mess with me and I'll be nice" had always been my policy. But they decided to mess with me.

One day they were in the teen room listening to some rapper cuss his brains out about killing someone. I told them to turn their music off. They told me to "suck their hairy cocks." I told them to leave. They told me[7] I was a "stupid cock-sucking faggot and had an ugly girlfriend."[8] Then they did the unthinkable as they finally left the building: they screamed that they were going to kill me by shooting me in the back as I left the library at night.[9] I told them it was a federal offense to threaten a city employee and if they ever stepped foot in the library again I would call the police.

---

6. The clerk was quite a lot bigger than they were, and, as the story goes, he beat both of them up and made them cry.

7. This sounds very juvenile, and it was.

8. I was nice; I did not say to them that if, in fact, I was a "faggot," then why would I have a girlfriend?

9. Lucky for me everyone decided to have a potluck in the staff lounge during the incident, so I was left alone to face them.

Brian, the librarian for the teens, wanted to know about all misbehaving teens, and I told him about the incident when he returned from lunch. He was surprised and told me to get him right away if they came in the building, and he would talk to them. I told him I didn't want them in the library again because I felt threatened; he nodded but didn't say anything in reply.

Obviously they didn't kill me, but they did return. I got Brian when they returned. He approached the teens and I went in the back. I didn't want to deal with them. Ten minutes later he came to me and said, "All taken care of."

"So they can't come back?"

"No. They're harmless," Brian said amused.

"They threatened to kill me! They're not harmless."

"They're really sorry about that."

"They're sorry?"

Brian nodded. "They confessed to it when I pressed them. They said they were just mad because you treated them unfairly. I told them not to say they'd kill you anymore. Problem fixed."

"It's not fixed. Did they tell you what else they said?"

"Let's not argue about it. We'll just see if their behavior changes."

"So they're allowed back in?"

"As long as they don't say they're going to kill you."

"Just because they say it doesn't mean they won't do it."

"Quit worrying. They're harmless little teens."

"They're eighteen and bigger than I am."

"They said they wouldn't kill you. Let's just leave it at that for now."

Brian was a defender of all things teen. He was over forty but thought because he could throw out worse obscenities than a drunken sailor he was the best librarian for teens ever. Maybe he was. He had never had a teen moon him; I had. He had never had a teen take a swing at him; I had. He never had made a fourteen-year-old boy cry; I had. Whatever the case, being told by two eighteen-year-olds that I was going to be shot in the back did things to me. I never was concerned they would actually follow through, I just couldn't imagine spending the rest of my life having to babysit mouthy teens.

That Sunday I opened the Sunday classifieds and began combing the want ads. There were jobs for nannies, accountants, sales reps, and even dogcatchers. None of the ads said they were looking for twenty-something librarians with English literature degrees. I had made myself a professional in a profession I was becoming more and more unsure of.

~

When the teen called the woman a "white-trash whore" it wasn't that I didn't agree with him. The truth was she was a white-trash whore, and theoretically he had every right to say it. I didn't hate him for saying it; I hated him for saying it and her getting mad about it. If he would have said it and she would have walked away, then I would have gone away no different. But how many white-trash whores walk away from being called white-trash whores? I can think of none.

I acted offended at the teen's tongue, of course.[10] Then she asked the teen if he wanted to take it outside, and he sort of agreed. I hated the teen, but I equally pitied him. Apparently he wasn't the brightest bean in the barrel. This was a very big woman, who may have fought in the World Wrestling Entertainment in her younger

10. Though in actuality I found the whole ordeal funny.

years, and this was a very scrawny teen. It was like David versus Goliath, only David didn't have any rocks.

Patrons started to gather around; it was like a good ol'-fashion lunchtime brawl in high school. Patrons heard there might be a fight and they surfaced from all corners of the building.[11] They stared, amused, at the scene, hoping that any moment they'd get to see it taken outside where they would be treated to a teen taking a pounding from a fifty-year-old woman.

I had to be the person that broke it up. I didn't want to. Any other day I would have been chanting, "Fight, fight, fight," betting fifty bucks on the woman. But not that day. That day I was a librarian and I had to be professional. I separated the two to different corners of the library, and then, like a cheesy B-movie actor playing the role of a New York City cop, I told patrons to sit back down, there was "nothing to see."

Dealing with teens wasn't in my job description.

~

The tall black man who stood in front of me didn't strike me as a friendly man or a nice man. So when he said "My daughter's in the bathroom refusing to get out. Get off your lazy butt and help me," it didn't really strike me as uncalled for. I expected him to say much worse.

I didn't know what he wanted me to do. "Maybe she's just having a hard time," I suggested.

"She's not constipated, if that's what you're implying."

"There's really not a whole lot I can do. I can't forcefully remove her."

---

11. When I say patrons, I don't mean young, equally immature teens; I mean patrons older than me, patrons who should have been mature enough to tell the woman to calm down because it was just a kid.

"Well, just talk to her or something. I got to get home and I just don't want to deal with this today."

I got a female clerk and entered the bathroom. A teenage girl was crying at the sink. Another girl was comforting her.

"Are you okay?" the clerk asked.

"Is he really mad?"

"He's going to be a whole lot madder if you don't go out there. Are you okay? Are you hurt?"

She shook her head. "I'm just afraid of him."

"Does he hit you?"

She thought, but finally said no.

"You sure?"

She shook her head quicker this time.

"Okay. Well, here's the thing. I can't call the police or anything unless you tell me he's hurting you. If he is, there are people who can help you. Do you need help?"

"No."

"Then you're going to have to go out there and face the music. I'm sorry."

When she left, the dad began screaming at her and making a scene. I felt bad for her, but I couldn't do anything about it. I was just doing the part of my job that I hated most: sending kids home with their idiot parents.

～

Vanessa had the makings of a troubled teen. Her dad had abandoned her mom before she was born and she never knew him. The state had taken custody of her when she was three and her mom refused to kick her cocaine addiction habit. Vanessa was fourteen now. She had spent more than most of her life living in foster care. Her current foster parents had a half dozen other foster kids. Her foster mom bought a new Escalade loaded with

GPS, an iPod docking station, and all the latest techno-car trends with the money she received from taking care of the foster kids.[12]

Everyone in the library kind of adopted Vanessa as our own. She needed to know people cared, because she definitely didn't get that at home. We eagerly waited to hear how she did on tests or book reports we had helped her with. And cringed when she brought in new boyfriends who never met our protective approval.

She was one of the few I didn't hate. How could I? She didn't bother me, she was polite, and she was genuinely excited to learn. I looked at her and saw a kid who, in spite of everything, wanted to conquer the world. She was the kind of girl who could and would achieve everything she hoped for. You could see it in her eyes. Those were the kids who made me want to keep working. They stood for everything I became a librarian for.

FOR SHELVING

How many librarians get to have their face painted on the wall? That's legendary! That's me. Granted, the face was painted on a cartoon-like bug. You have to be happy with what you can get.

I'm not sure exactly how this painting came about; details are sketchy, like many things in my life. I remember the library's graphic artist was painting a bug theme in the children's room and I suggested she make the bugs look like writers, and then I jokingly added "or librarians." She liked my latter suggestion better, apparently, and

---

12. Money, I imagine, she was supposed to use to buy the foster kids' food and school supplies, and which she never had enough of.

went to work immediately on the Scott Bug. She decided when she finished not to model another bug after a staff member. I've always had a sneaking suspicion that she was trying to say I was the only person who bugged her, so I was the only person worthy of this pesky bug-like portrait. For many years, even after I returned to my old library, the pillar stood with my face. Then one day a new manager came to town. She didn't hate the artwork, but she wanted to prove herself and her style. Instead of having a mural on the wall in the children's room that made it seem like a children's room, she wanted plain wallpaper. It was clean and made the children's room look like a professionally decorated business office. Every manager needs her style. Lisa, the artist responsible for the mural, deserves more credit for this wall than she got from the new manager. The very least I can do is mention it here.

You tell a grown man to stop masturbating while on the computer and it's gross; you pass him off as a creepy old man with issues. You don't dwell on it because it doesn't matter anyway. You tell a fifteen-year-old boy to stop doing it, and it's sort of disturbing; it leaves a deeper impression. What's worse is I didn't catch him, other kids did. They came out and told me a kid was masturbating so hard "the entire computer table was shaking." When I went in the room I caught him doing it. He was looking at older women in bathing suits.[13]

"You wanna spank your monkey, do it in the bathroom," a teen said. The preoccupied teen ignored the other teen and pretended he had been doing nothing.

---

13. By older I mean women in their fifties and sixties.

I approached him and told him to step outside. I had Jonathan stand by my side and listen to what I said. I explained awkwardly to the boy: "It's natural to want to touch yourself down there, but you need to do it outside the library where others don't have to watch."

I expected the teen to become embarrassed, but he didn't. Instead he became straighter and said, "You invaded my privacy watching me like that. I'm going to tell my dad." Then he left, and, thankfully, did not return with his father.[14] From that day on he always came with darker pants and stayed in corners where other kids didn't see him.[15]

I was beginning to realize more and more that it didn't matter if I liked teens. My job wasn't to like patrons. I didn't get to pick and choose them. My job was to help them and make sure the library was safe.

~

One day I was walking around the library and saw a TV monitor with a PlayStation 2 plugged into it. Two teens were fighting each other in some kind of death-match game. That was hardcore gaming. I imagined their parents had told them no more video games, and so they lied and said they were going to the library, because what parents say they don't want their kids at the library?[16]

~

---

14. It was hard enough having a conversation with a teen about masturbation.

15. This was not the most disturbing incident involving a teen; there was one far worse. It happened before I came to the library. A fourteen-year-old Spanish boy who spoke no English had gone in the restroom where a ten-year-old was urinating at the stall. The fourteen-year-old proceeded to fondle the ten-year-old. The ten-year-old's father came in, saw it, and nearly killed the fourteen-year-old. Police were called out and a clerk had to serve as a translator. They arrested the fourteen-year-old kid.

16. In fact, several have; I have heard them say it: "I don't want you in this place anymore—it's a bad influence." Apparently they had already promised the family they would attend technical school, and the library had the potential to distort their minds.

Giving nicknames to problem patrons is one way to provide humor on the job. It also establishes handy covert-like code names for people should problems persist. I have nicknamed many patrons over the years: the Red-Faced Man, Mumbles, the Mole, and Potty Mouth, just to name a few.

Recently, I developed a new nickname for a teen patron: Jeffica. Jeffica has a long history with the library. About four years ago, there was a teenage patron named Jeff. He fit perfectly into the she-male category of the human species.[17]

Jeff would come to the library two or three times a week and spend hours at a table poring over books. He was usually quiet, but would occasionally harass librarians over things like having only one book of poetry by John Donne. Then one day he stopped coming. I didn't realize it immediately. It was several weeks before somebody said, "Say, I haven't seen that one guy in a while." After a brief discussion on who "that one guy" was, I realized it was Jeff, and indeed it had been a while.

I didn't see Jeff for four years, but then, without warning, he started coming in again. There are some patrons you never forget. Jeff is one of them. He had the same routine: he would pore over books for hours at a time, and at one point he complained to me that we didn't have a single book by Ben Jonson.

Toward the end of the week, he applied for a new library card because his old one had expired due to lack of use. I was surprised when I read the application—under "Name" he wrote "Jessica." It was odd; he had the chest of Jeff, the voice of Jeff, even the same dress shoes that Jeff used to wear. But there was no mistaking it: Jeff was now Jessica.

---

17. Which is the category for a person whose appearance could easily be passed off as either male or female; it was, of course, made popular by SNL's "It's Pat" skit.

~

Kids are suckers for online role-playing games. When one got popular in the library the kids would eventually play it. This would suck up the library's Internet connection, and eventually we would have to ban it because the computers were running way too slowly.

One month a game got popular and one of the mothers started playing it. She was a middle-aged mother of three kids who all seemed kind of dumb. At first she just messed around with it to see why her kids wanted to play it. After two days she became addicted. She started playing it for several hours at a time. One day she started coming without her kids because she didn't want them bugging her as she played.

The more she played the longer she stayed. The longer she stayed the more comfortable she got. Soon she began bringing food into the library.[18] Then she started bringing microwave dishes and asking us to warm them in the back. The more she came the lazier she got. Two months into her game binge, she started coming in an electric wheelchair because she was having trouble walking. She would try to charge it in the library.

One day she was hostile with Brian because she didn't want to get off the computer. When the argument was over, Brian came to me and asked, "What is the deal with that woman? What has she been doing all day?"

"Playing a computer game."

"A computer game?"

I nodded.

"I do not like that woman," he said bluntly.

---

18. I felt weird telling people they couldn't bring food, since we ourselves sold it.

I had been complaining about her and her attitude for weeks. Brian didn't take any of my complaints seriously until he himself had an encounter with her.

"All she does is play a game?" Brian asked in disbelief.

I nodded.

"Here's what I want you to do. Find out what game this is and make me a list of why we should ban it. I want to get rid of that lady. If all she is doing is playing a video game then she doesn't need to be in the library."

"Her kids come, too; some of them read."

"Well she can bring them in, get their books, and leave. This isn't some place to lounge all day."[19]

The next week, it was banned. I'm not sure how Brian, a librarian, was able to get something banned so quickly, but I'm sure he promised an administrator something. When the woman saw it was blocked she came immediately to the desk.

"Is something wrong with the Internet?"

"I'm sorry," I said, trying to sound sincere. "The site is banned."

"Banned! For what reason?"

"It was slowing down the Internet speed."

"Who is responsible for this? Was it that man?"

"I'm not sure." That was the last we saw of her. Her kids didn't get books anymore after that. I never thought my job was so much about sacrifice, but it was. What was more important? Peace in the library without this woman, or a whole group of kids who were being given the chance to read and maybe not end up

---

19. It, in fact, was for some people.

like their mother? It turned out it was peace in the library without this woman.

⌒

I went into the teen room once and saw a fifteen-year-old boy terrorizing a library chair. The room was empty except for the teen. He was making semi-loud grunting noises and ramming his head into the chair; he'd knock the chair over with his head, pick it up, and then repeat it again.

I couldn't help but watch him for a few seconds. I imagined I could film it, post it on YouTube, and get thousands of views in a day from teens who thought this teen was the greatest comedian since the Marx brothers.[20]

After several seconds, I approached the boy and said, "What are you doing?"

He shrugged his shoulders and simply said, "I don't know."

"Well, as fun as ramming a chair with your head is, let's keep to doing it in your home, okay? We can't afford to replace chairs."

"Okay." He picked up his backpack and left the library. I never saw him again.

As ridiculous as his act was, he was the model candidate for teen angst and what I dealt with daily. I hated teens, but sometimes they really made me laugh at their stupidity. There was something in how he rammed the chair that made me see how I, too, had been like that. I never rammed chairs with my head, but I had expressed myself in equally foolish ways. That's what teens do at his age. I didn't have to like them, but I did have to serve them. Seeing myself in that teen made it easier for me to identify with them.

⌒

20. Yes, I indeed know that there are hardly any teens who have heard of or seen a Marx film.

I had heard of kids knifing each other, shooting each other, beating the crap out of each other. But when a kid came to the desk and said a bully had just threatened him in the men's room with a TASER, I knew that at last teens had arrived at the digital age.

I feel old to say this, but when I was a boy we didn't threaten other kids with TASER. Even if TASERs had been around, I'm sure we wouldn't have. We exchanged harsh words and crude mama jokes; we punched them in the groin and said their girl-friends were whores. But it was all in good taste. But TASERs? What was the world coming to?

And the dumbest part of the story was that the kid was on probation and had already been busted three times. There comes a point in a man's life when he must say, "I should stop acting like I'm two years old now." But this kid had not reached it. I wondered if he ever would. I wondered if any teen ever would.[21]

~

Hearing your name on the intercom is no big deal; hearing it on the intercom with the words "Come to the information desk *right now, ASAP*" was a little more major; still, I didn't take it as such. I took it as Jonathan wanting to have his break, and he was just messing around. Turns out he wasn't messing around. Turns out a thirteen-year-old boy was tripping out at the reference desk and Jonathan had just called 911 for help. The teen was shaking and pacing and crying.

---

21. Less then four months later another teen told me he was arrested again, this time for selling heroin. (He had told me once that he would never do a "needle drug" because those were dangerous. I had a feeling he still had never tried it, he just sold it because he could get more money.)

"I don't want to die," he cried to anyone that would listen.

"You're not going to die." I then went on to ask him any question that would just keep his mind active and alert, everything from what his name was to what his favorite TV show was.

"Tell me what you took?"

"I didn't take anything!" he cried.

"You're not going to get in trouble, but you're going to get really sick if you don't let the doctors know. They have to know how to help you."

"I don't know. They said it was pot. I don't know."

"Have you ever tried it?"

"No."

"You're going to be okay. Tell me what it looked like. Did you smoke it, swallow it, or inject it?"

"It was in a pipe. And it smelt funny."

"It's fine. When the firemen get here they're going to help you get it out of you. You'll feel weird, but tomorrow it will be okay."

He shook his head. "I'm going to die—I just know it."

When the firemen got there and took the teen away, Jonathan and I laughed it off. "Looks like someone won't be doing drugs for a while."

I reviewed the video camera footage[22] before I went home for the night. The teen had come into the library about one hour before tripping out with two other teens. He looked normal at first, but then he was clearly shaken. His friends laughed at his behavior. The next day one of the teens who was with him came back to the library.

---

22. Libraries have become so dangerous that they need security cameras.

"Your friend could have died," I told him seriously.

He started laughing.

"You think that's funny?"

"No. He wasn't going to die."

"He could have." I paused. "So what'd he take?"

"I don't know. I wasn't with him."

"I checked the tapes. You walked right up to the library with him. There's cameras outside."

"We met him in the park."

I rolled my eyes.

"Honest."

"So tell me this, when he started tripping out, why were you laughing at him?"

"We thought he was messing around."

"I could see that. But after thirty minutes of it you had to start thinking something was up."

"He took some bad weed."

"Why didn't you get him help?"

"I knew he'd be fine once it wore off."

"So when he came sobbing to the desk, then why did you run off? I saw that on tape, too."

"I didn't want to get in trouble. I got a record. I stole a PSP a few months ago."

"A PSP?"

He nodded. "It's a portable game system."

"I know what it is. I also know they're like two hundred bucks. You could have got a job and had it in less than a month."

"Man, you know how hard jobs are to come by?"

I nodded. "Do you know how hard they are to come by when you got a record?"

Teens were stupid that way. And yet these stupid teens found a home in the library for some reason. It got them off the streets, and as much as I didn't want to admit it I was glad they were at the library and not somewhere worse.

I felt sorry for the teen. When he came into the library, I tried to help him. I even helped him apply for a job. I believed that he could make it. A year before he graduated high school he decided to steal a car. He didn't make it. I felt bad for him, of course, but this was just another part of my job that I didn't like. Seeing kids who didn't make it.

❧

I felt sorry for the teens. They cussed so freely and casually that I wondered how they'd ever make it in the world and how'd they'd ever make it through a job interview. I have images of some of the boys quoting what they do on *Grand Theft Auto* when asked how to handle conflict.

When I was in high school, I failed the high school reading test. The only time I ever went in the library that semester of school was to retake the reading test. The truth was I had failed because I hadn't tried. It was hard not to at least kind of feel for them because I had been one myself. I had done my share of dumb things; I was an unmotivated teen. So unmotivated that a teacher had told my mom in a parent-teacher conference that a boy with my mind is best suited for trade school, not college. The truth was IQ didn't measure creativity. No test they could give me or any other kid would be able to say that I was smart or dumb.

There was a small percentage of kids who could be rated based on those tests. The majority of high school kids? They were just trying to fit in, trying to find their place in the world. As much as I hated them, I couldn't help but feel a little sorry for them and, at least every now and then, try to give them direction.

As hard as it was for me to see and believe, the kids who came into the library acting like total morons would grow up and somehow be productive members of society. Maybe somehow I would play a part in that.

There weren't many teen programs, which was sad. The librarian in charge of these things didn't seem to notice because he was too overworked. I'm no saint. I'm a jerk. But maybe if more people tried to point at least one teen in the right direction, there'd be a few more who would go just a little bit further ahead.

There are many problems with this world, but just a few might be solved if a couple of those kids who ended up not going to college because some test told them they weren't smart enough were able to go anyway. The trouble with so many things is there aren't enough visionaries in the world, because the visionaries got stuck going to trade school.

What they hadn't told me in library school was that being a public librarian meant you were a librarian for all people. Sure, public libraries had their specialties, but that didn't mean in any way that they didn't have to assist as needed with other specialties. I didn't like teens, but if I wanted to stay a public librarian then I had to learn to work with them. Some would never make it, and when they didn't I would just move on to the next teen and hope things would be different.

Chapter 796.815	Being the People
-HELL-	Who Believe That
Hello,	Librarians Should Die, and
I'm Going	Why/How Our Hero Tries
to Kill You:	to Stay Away from Them

Maybe if it were only teens who wanted to kill me, I would have been okay and secure with my job, but the fact was, it was starting to seem like everyone wanted me dead. Early one morning, before the library opened to the public, a man waited by the back door of the building. When I opened the door, it was clear from his fidgeting that he was high on something.

I think the first clue that the man was going to be a problem was when he said to me "I want to know who took my generator. Was it you?" This was actually the first thing he said to me. It wasn't just what he said or even the hostile way that he said it that made me know that this was going to be one of the conversations they didn't teach you how to handle in library school—it was everything about him. The way he moved—fidgeted, rather—told me right away that he had had the sort of breakfast that destroys brain cells.

I had never seen the man, but I knew right away who he was. The previous night we'd discovered that some people had been stashing their belongings behind the air-conditioning unit in back of the library. A polite note was left saying that if they didn't remove the items, the library would have to remove them for them. It was nothing personal. For liability reasons, people just can't do this.

I checked the back of the library before closing to make sure everything was gone—it was—so I figured the problem had been solved.

It wasn't.

"It isn't right. That generator cost me three hundred bucks, and someone is going to pay."

I apologized to the man and explained. "The library can't be responsible for belongings left behind."

The man became more agitated. "Then you know—you know where it was hidden. It was you. You took my generator."

I shook my head no and explained further. "I saw it last night, and know a note was left for its owner to remove it from the property."

The man's eyes got bigger. He crossed his arms and nodded a bit psychotically. "I know your kind—don't think I don't. You think just because you have a job you can take from me." He paused and continued in a threatening way. "You're either going to give me back my generator or pay me. Otherwise, I'll call the police."

Even if the man had not appeared to be on drugs, I think I still would have been a little nervous. He wasn't bigger than me, but his appearance suggested the sort of man who liked to keep a knife in his pocket. Still, I did my best to hide any fear and calmly said, "Sir, I assure you that I did not take your generator. Maybe you should call the police and report it as stolen." I knew that he wouldn't call them, but I could always hope.

"Oh, don't think that I won't." He paused, and then asked, insanely curious, "Where is your car parked?"

Plenty of patrons had asked me strange things, but this was the first who asked me where my car was parked. It was almost comical to look at the man, because he actually thought I was going to tell him. I struggled to come up with a reply, but the best I could muster was, "That's personal." What I meant to say was "Sir, the fact that I work in a public library doesn't make me stupid, it just makes me poor. There's no way I'm going to tell you—a psychotic person who could very well have a knife in his pocket—where I have parked my car."

The man stood straighter, and, actually, in his straightness, began to look even crazier. "It's in the parking lot, isn't it?"

So now the man thinks he's Sherlock Holmes, I thought, amused. *A car parked in a parking lot—who would have ever guessed?*

I didn't answer his question, which apparently was the answer the man was looking for. "I knew it. I'll find it. Don't think that I won't. And I bet that generator's in the trunk."

As the man continued to yell at me for taking his generator, Murd, the library's IT guy, pulled up a van to the back of the library and started bringing in new computer monitors. Murd must have noticed the man's strange behavior but he didn't ask if I needed help. Murd actually turned, looked at the man, smiled, and then continued to ignore us.

When Murd walked by us my eyes pleaded with him to help. He didn't.

The man turned to Murd as he walked by and said, "This cocksucker stole my generator."

Murd smiled and said, "Well, there's no need to be vulgar!" He shook his head like it was a joke and then walked in the library with a computer monitor.

Are you kidding me? I wanted to scream. *The guy's nuts! Help me!*

When Murd came back out the door, I was blunt. "Hey, Murd, could you go get Faren?"

He nodded. "Next time I'm in the building. I'm in a hurry to get these dropped off."

"This is an emergency, Murd. Tell her I'm having difficulty with a patron and I need her assistance."

He looked at the generator man, then at me. He seemed disgusted but finally obeyed.

Minutes later, Faren appeared and cheerfully asked, "What seems to be the problem?"

"This man," the generator man loudly said, pointing at me, "stole my generator, and he's refusing to give it back."

Faren looked at me, as if to question if it were true.

"Last night Jonathan and I found a bunch of stuff in the back. It appeared some people were living in the garden area. We left a note to pick up their belongings. I guess one of them was a generator, and he thinks I stole it."

"Oh. Well, you aren't allowed to keep things overnight on city property," Faren diplomatically said.

"I know the law, lady! I know the law says a person cannot steal."

"Well, that's a mighty large accusation. I can assure you none of my staff stole anything. Now if that's it, I need to ask you to leave."

"That's not *it,* bitch! That's a four hundred dollar generator. It will be *it* when I get it back."

"If you don't want to leave, then I'll have to call the police."

"I will not."

"Okay. Then we'll see what the police say about you trespassing on city property."

He stepped back, but added loudly, "That generator was all I had. You'll pay! Both of you."

He left the library but didn't leave the premises. I sent a coworker out a few minutes later, who told me he was riding a bike in circles around the parking lot.

"Why didn't you just give him back his generator?" Roland asked me when I recounted the story to him.

"What would I even do with one?"

"Sell it on eBay!"

I rolled my eyes and then asked, "So if the guy comes back in, you got my back, right?"

"You're the one who took the generator," Roland laughed.

"At least call 911 or something, tell them I'm going to die."

About two hours later, he found his generator. It was in a bush a hundred feet from the library just where he left it. It seemed to confuse him.

I usually liked crazy people as they made my day go that much quicker, but not when they threatened to do things to me or my car. Shortly after the incident, I Googled "deaths in library" to see how afraid I should be.

I was disappointed. Nobody had been killed. A librarian had claimed she had been assaulted because she refused to tell another librarian if she was wearing perfume; a school librarian was under investigation for assaulting two students, and then later she claimed she herself was sexually assaulted by the person investigating the claim. So far, it was librarians doing the assaulting.

Then I got to the good stuff! The patron-abusers! A Transylvania librarian was blindfolded and tied up by students robbing the library of rare books. The students were caught when they tried to sell the books to Christie's auction house, and the assaulted librarian sued for pain and suffering inflicted during the robbery. Apparently, shows like *Antiques Roadshow* and online auction houses like eBay have made the Internet a prime resource for people stealing old library stuff.

The stories got better. A librarian in Hoboken, New Jersey, was bitten in the face and finger by a homeless man in the children's section of the library. The man was later caught and charged with assault as well as pirating audio and video media.[1] Another homeless man attacked a librarian outside after being thrown out. Apparently, he had stayed outside and watched for her, and then charged her from behind.

The closest I could find to any librarian dying was in Dublin; a thirty-six-year-old librarian was attacked so brutally that he was left for two weeks in a coma. I couldn't find any librarians who had been killed by their patrons, but I found plenty of sites for librarians with tattoos. I considered getting a tattoo, because tattooed librarians didn't look like the kind of people you'd want to mess with.

FOR SHELVING

Work-related violence is a lot less prevalent in places like the United Kingdom. One reason: people don't own guns. It makes sense. The United Kingdom imposes some of the strictest laws on the books when it comes to guns, and people don't really complain. They understand there are still people out there who like to hunt, and it's still possible to get a gun for this purpose, but many steps must first be taken; if you have spent more than three years in prison, then consider yourself out when it comes to obtaining one. What happens if you are caught

(Continues)

1. His duffel bag contained eighty-eight pirated DVDs and ten CDs.

(Continued)

possessing one and you don't own it? At the very least, you get five years in prison in addition to fines.

The United Kingdom, like the United States, has had its fair share of violent shootings that resulted in mass deaths; unlike the United States, the United Kingdom didn't just mourn and say "Isn't that a shame." They mourned and then did something about it. The gun reform has become so extreme that members of its Olympic shooting team have to go to other countries to practice their event because the guns they use are banned.

Is it worth it? You are about four times more likely to be murdered in the United States than in the United Kingdom. But then again, isn't owning a gun our God-given right?

A week after the generator man incident,[2] a man came in to use the Internet. He was middle-aged, tired, but seemingly friendly at first. I assigned him a computer on the other side of the library.

Saturdays are usually slow and quiet, and usually I passed time by studying the palm of my hand from different angles. About the only noise was me talking to pages who were equally bored.

Things got a little loud, however, when the man I had assigned to the Internet began yelling into his cell phone.[3] I approached the man and explained that it was library policy that cell phones remain off in the library and if he wanted to continue his conversation he'd have to use the phone outside. The man, clearly upset that I had so rudely interrupted his phone call, said, "If you don't mind, I'm having a

---

2. It was on a Saturday (this is not relevant, but I bet it distracted you).

3. If anyone has ever been asked to turn off his cell phone in the library, it is because many people, while normally quiet in regular conversation, get quite loud when on the phone.

very important conversation with my cell phone carrier regarding my bill and I need the Internet to explain to them my problem."

Before I could respond, the man turned and went back to his phone conversation, explaining to the customer service agent that he was sorry but an "idiot librarian" had tried to end his call.[4] Now no librarian likes to have his or her authority as librarian undermined. It's not a power issue; rather, it's a simple fact that policy has been disturbed and you don't mess with library policy and get away with it. Nonetheless, I was in a good mood, so I walked around the man[5] and said, "I understand the call is important to you, but I do have to ask that you respect others and talk in a more quiet fashion, and finish the call quickly."

He turned to me, irritated, and said, "I'll finish the call when I'm done talking and not a second sooner."

I turned off his computer and asked him to leave. That's when he stood[6] and screamed "You want to see loud?!" in a fashion that made everyone in the library turn around and look at the man a little frightened. I didn't think he meant it as a question, so I decided not to answer him, which only made him louder as he asked, "Who do you think you are?"

I knew at this point that the situation was quickly getting complicated, and to make matters worse the man really did not have very good breath. I told the man he was being disruptive and he needed to leave the library. I knew he wasn't going to go out without further fuss but I still hoped. I returned to the reference desk,

---

4. Seriously, I am a firm believer in a law that prohibits people from getting a cell phone until they pass a two-week class on cell phone etiquette. There are waiting period for guns, why not cell phones? Both, when put into the wrong hands, can do very bad things.

5. So as to face him.

6. And also when I realized he was quite tall.

and the man of course followed. He asked for my name, and when I gave it he said he was going to go see the mayor and have my job.

He started to leave but turned back around after only a few steps. "I'm going to come back for you after work! And you're going to be sorry that you ever messed with me."

He then walked up to Brenda, who actually seemed to be enjoying the scene.[7] He talked with her several seconds and seemed a little calmer. Finally he left, at which point one of the library volunteers[8] approached me and said, "Can I just say that I thought that was awesome. I totally thought he was going to jack you up right in the library!"

I ignored the volunteer and went up to Brenda. "What did he say to you?"

She laughed. "He was angry! I told him you were just having a bad day and maybe he should go complain to the main library if he felt you had handled the whole thing unprofessionally."

"Thanks for being on my side!"

"Well, he was obviously crazy! What'd you want me to say? I didn't want him to be waiting for me after work, too." She chuckled at this. I got the feeling that she was hoping he actually would return; she probably even got his name and would make a little sign to cheer for him during the fight.

Later that day I received a call from another librarian at the city's main library asking if I had had any problems that day with a patron. I said yes and asked the librarian why. He said the man had come into the main library and filed a complaint against me. I

---

7. I kid you not, if we had been serving popcorn that Saturday, Brenda would have taken a bag and watched the scene play out like it was a movie.

8. A high school kid.

asked if he mentioned coming back after I got off work to beat me up. He had forgotten to mention that.

After work, I approached the parking lot with a bit of caution, but the man was not there, nor have I seen him since.

～

Not long before people started trying to kill me[9] a man came in who was a traveling tattoo artist. I had heard of traveling everything, but a traveling tattoo artist? Something about that job seemed like a bad combination. Still, I looked with interest at all the designs he showed me. I suppose he was good, but I'm not exactly one to judge what is good and bad in that profession. I thought back to that man as I thought about tattoos. I tried to think about what tattoos might look good on me and where. I thought maybe a book on the inside of my elbow; that way when I move my arm up and down it would look like the book was opening and closing.

I got depressed. I couldn't even think of a tattoo that would make me look tough. A book! That was the dumbest idea ever. And I'd probably make it worse by picking some wimpy title like *Little Women*. The librarians on the Internet had picked tattoos of swords, falcons eating animals, and world globes being destroyed by atomic bombs. Me? I picked a book. Why was I such a geek? Why were librarians such geeks? I did a search for some of the famous ones: John Cotton Dana,[10] John J. Beckley,[11] Melvil Dewey,[12]

---

9. Or at least claiming they were going to kill me.

10. Organized the first ever children's library room, but opposed the concept of story time.

11. First librarian of the Library of Congress. He set the standards of the First Party System, and, in 1796, accused George Washington of stealing public funds. The town of Beckley, West Virginia, is named after him.

12. Hater of women, lover of libraries, starter of a nifty cataloging system.

Charles Ammi Cutter.[13] They all had the same thing in common: they were all elitist wimps. No notable, or even somewhat notable, librarian was hip or tough. There was no hope for me.

I continued to browse the online job sites and even went on an interview at a community college library. I found nothing.

Jonathan noticed my search and said, "Job got you down?"

"I'm too young to have people telling me that they're going to kill me," I sadly explained.

"I hear that. I just want to keep this job till I graduate."

"Really?"

Jonathan nodded. "I've been thinking of joining the army."

I laughed.

"What?" he said.

"You're joking, right?"

"Nope. I just want a job that's rewarding—you know? Something with more meaning."

I shrugged. "At least you'll be the one with the gun."

~

Occasionally, someone stumbles into the library with the sole intent of telling me about Jesus.

Usually our conversations go something like this:

"Do you know Jesus?"

I tell them yes.

Then they say, "Personally?"

And then I nod and say something like "He cleans my toilet," which always confuses them, so they proceed to tell me why I need to know Jesus. I hate to be rude, so usually I just listen, and they leave unconvinced that they can convert me. One man was more

---

13. Where would Dewey be without Cutter? Dewey made the subject numbers, but Cutter made the classification of organizing within those subject numbers. Plus he had a pretty cool last name.

persistent than the others. He's into codes and symbols. His name is Norm. Norm is convinced that the library is holy and everything in the library points to God's presence, from the shadows on the ground to the way certain books lean to the right side. The same week I had spent fighting off people who might return to kill me, Norm, the Jesus man, came in. How can you not wonder if God has a sense of humor when some crazy guy comes in to tell you about Jesus the same week two other guys say they are going to get you?

Norm saw a sign advertising the Friends of the Library book sale and became excited. "Do you know about the Friends?"

I nodded.

"Have you met them?"

I nodded and explained. "Most of them."

He seemed surprised and asked, "And have they explained their roots?"

I shrugged. "Not really."

He then said proudly, "They're all over the country, you know."

I nodded. "Yes, most libraries have them."

He smiled. "It's so nice for public places to include churches."

I looked at him, confused. "I'm pretty sure most don't."

Norm smiled again. "Then I guess you don't know about the Friends."

I finally caught on to what he was getting at and explained. "The friends have no affiliation with Quakers."

He seemed disappointed. "Oh, well, I guess I just assumed."

After that, Norm would frequently watch me as he wandered around the library; he'd make a point of staring at me, as if he were examining me. When I'd pass by him, Norm would say, "Jesus knows" and then look down really quickly, pretending it wasn't him who said it. At first I'd just smile at Norm and acknowledge that I knew he had said it, but then he'd just shrug and say, "Did you hear something? I didn't hear anything." When I'd walk away he'd say again, "Jesus knows."

This continued for several weeks. Whenever Norm appeared in the library, he'd find a little corner in the back, and whenever I'd pass he'd play his little juvenile game. Only to me; he bothered no one else in the library. One day I walked by Norm and he said, "Jesus knows, and you'll burn in hell!" And then he hissed.

I had gotten to the point where I didn't even make eye contact with the man. I just pretended he didn't exist and hoped he'd give it a rest, but the hissing really got to me.

"I didn't know Jesus hissed?" I said.

He shrugged. "I didn't hear anything. Did you hear something? Maybe you need to get it right with Jesus?"

I nodded. "I do hear something. I hear the tongue of Satan. It's really weird. I only hear that sound when I walk by you, but only Satan can make a sound like that."

The man seemed shaken at first, but then he stood, pulled a small, pocket-sized bible from his back pocket, and began saying, "Satan away from this man! Satan away from this man!"

I turned and walked away.

Apparently Jesus had it in for me, too.

⁓

I could take the tall man, the drug addict, the teen, but when even the bible-thumpers have it out for you, enough is enough. It was time to start working out. I wasn't going to take things sitting down. I bought an exercise bike,[14] a pedometer, and an iPod. I put the exercise bike in front of TV and the pedometer on my hip and

---

14. Fine, I would in fact be taking things sitting down.

loaded the sixty-gig iPod with exactly one song—"Eye of the Tiger" by Survivor. I was ready to go.

As it turned out, the pedometer worked only for walking and the song got quite old five minutes into my workout.[15] Afterward I looked at myself in the mirror. I didn't look any bigger. I still looked like a scrawny librarian. And I didn't even feel like I had worked out.

I told my woes to a friend. He suggested joining a gym and using more intensive equipment. I had tried a gym before; they had a rowing machine with a monitor attached so it gave the impression that you were actually rowing. The monitor reminded me of TV, which in turn made the workout go by quicker. The next time I went to the gym the rowing machine was out of order, and I never went back to the gym again. I didn't want intensive exercise equipment, I just wanted muscle.

---

15. It turned out the song I really wanted was "Another One Bites the Dust" by Queen.

Chapter 362.70869 -SMEL- You Smell Like Piss and I'm Pretty Sure It's Because You Pissed Your Pants:	Being the Homeless Who Put the People with Homes to Shame

A homeless man who had been in the library all day walked past Matt and me at closing and Matt said, "Man, that guy smells like piss all over!"[1]

I nodded.

"He was in here all day. I didn't see him move once. I bet he pissed all over himself."

When I said nothing, he walked to Brian, who was closing the door. They both watched the homeless man walk down the sidewalk. Matt said when the library was locked up, "Don't you ever wish the homeless would find another home?"

---

1. You will kindly recall that Matt was the library page first introduced several chapters ago and not seen since; he, it should be noted, constantly reeked of either alcohol or pot (sometimes both).

I answered the question myself on the inside, saying in my mind what I figured everyone was thinking but would never say because it was politically incorrect. Brian's answer surprised me, surprised all of us. "When you started working for the library you became a public servant. Don't ever put yourself above someone else. You are a slave to them as long as you're on the clock."

It made me think. Think about how often, if that was true, I really didn't live up to my job. About how often I had put the public below me. This was the reality: no one wanted to be at work all of the time—everyone could probably think of at least one place they'd rather be—but when you're a public servant you can't let the public know this. You have to be flawless for them.

Matt didn't exactly see my passion. He laughed and said, "I ain't no one's servant!"

"Being a public servant doesn't mean you're a servant in the traditional sense," Brian clarified. "It merely means you'll serve the people."

"Whatever."

Brian saw me looking at him. "What? You don't agree either?"

"No, it's true. I guess I just have to be reminded of that every now and then. It's a pretty wise thing to say for someone who's still in grad school."

"You know the patrons I remember most?"

"Who?"

"The patrons I serve the most. When I show someone where the classics are or answer a quick computer question—I don't re-member those people. I didn't really serve them. But the ones that I really spent time with—those are the ones I remembered. The ones that can honestly go out of here and say they were served."

Brian was right and, not only that, he made me feel like my job was admirable again. Maybe I would one day be killed by a psychotic patron with a knife, but at least I'd go down in style and would have helped a few people in the process. But just to be safe, I decided it might be a good idea to start working out so I would stand a better chance at living when the psychotic patron comes.

I bought a Pilates ball and an exercise DVD to go with it. This was more of a stretching exercise, but the idea of bouncing around on a big ball seemed more interesting than some muscle-toning machine. Half the exercises made me fart; the other half I could not do. By the end of the exercise DVD, I had done exactly three solid exercises.

The next day my muscles did not feel ripped or worked out the way they did in high school when I actually did work out. I ignored this. I continued working out.

I stopped after three days. I concluded that librarians just weren't made to be tough. They were made to shelve books, and you don't need a lot of muscle for that.

~

One patron was nicknamed the Red-Faced Man because years of alcoholism and living under the sun had made him appear to have one constant sunburn. He looked eighty but was probably closer to forty. He was always quiet, never argued, and rarely even spoke.

One night he had decided to make a home in the back ally. Everyone noticed but no one said anything. Technically it's city property and cannot be the home of a homeless man, but no one had the heart to say it. He was, after all, polite, quiet, and never left a mess.

No one had the heart, that is, until Brian, the librarian for teens, closed. Upon seeing the man, he said, "You can't be out here! This is city property! I'm really sorry, but you'll have to leave." Brian was always calm, but with this man there was rage in his voice.[2]

---

2. I think it was because his new home was near his car.

The homeless man looked at him like a hopeless deer staring at an oncoming truck.

"Go on! You heard me! Shoo!"[3]

The man ran off, leaving behind a six-pack of beer. "Who wants his beer?"

"I'll take it!" Matt said excitedly.

"Just get it out of here. I don't want to know anything about it."

It seemed so wrong. Brian had taken away his dignity by treating him like a dog, and then, to rub it in, he took away his beer. I'm not one to support letting the homeless indulge in alcoholic tendencies, but the man was obviously crazy and, unless someone wanted to pay for him to get help, that beer was the only treatment he had. It probably took him an entire day of begging to earn enough money for it. And Matt took it, stole from a homeless man. There are so many things wrong with that sentence.

It took one thing that Brian said to make me think he was perhaps the wisest librarian I knew, and then one action of his for me to completely question everything.

～

There are many people who stink. It's a public place and that's where stinky people go. But one day a man started coming who stunk more than most. Urine was bad but could be handled once you got used to it.[4] But sometimes it gets out of hand. One day a homeless man started visiting with a smell that could not be acquired. It was bad. It was like crap, rotten eggs, asphalt, and diesel

---

3. I am aware that this sounded like he was shooing off a dog. I'm pretty sure he was not aware of this fact.

4. I suppose you could say it's an acquired taste.

fuel all rolled into one—only worse. In reality, the smell really could not be described. It was just bad. And worse, the smell stayed. The man would leave but his smell would remain. Not for minutes or hours. It would not go away ever.

There's really no policy on stinking. When a patron complains, I usually tell them this and add, "Why don't you just move to another section of the library?"[5]

After days of my telling people this, someone finally had the nerve to do something about it. Brian, who normally didn't interact at all with adults who didn't have teen children, smelled the man and declared ten feet from him, "Ugh! That smell is horrible."[6]

"Sir," he said walking to the man, "you are more than welcome to visit this library, but not without being clean."

"I just took a shower," the man said, offended.

"I don't know with what! You stink! I'm sorry but it's true. Get some clean clothes. Get something." Brian then walked toward me and said, "That smell is horrible! I feel like I want to throw up now."

When the man was in earshot of us, walking toward the door, Brian said, "I don't even feel like I can eat now. That smell just makes me want to throw everything up."

The man, oddly, did not look humiliated or embarrassed.

"If he comes back," Brian said, "come get me. I don't want him stinking up the place. It already smells bad enough with all the junior high kids who haven't discovered deodorant."

---

5. In truth, they would have to move to another area and still cover their nose—it became that bad.

6. So much for being a servant.

I nodded. I wondered why so many of my conversations with Brian became so quickly awkward.

One patron lived in his car. You'd walk by it and all you'd see were clothes and newspapers stacked everywhere. There was just the slightest amount of room on the driver's side for actual driving but if someone five pounds bigger got in they would not fit.

The man was anal. Every day he'd come in and argue about something; usually it was the way the newspapers were arranged or why we needed to have better security for them. On a few occasions we'd even give him the change to buy his own paper. The strange thing was, he didn't want it, because he had his own subscription. He read it in the library, then copied the articles he liked, then bought his own copy, then circled the articles he liked, and then returned the xeroxed article to the library to be used as scratch paper.

One night a group of coworkers went bowling near the library. A few of us met up for dinner at the bowling ally diner before the friendly match. As we ate dinner, the man walked in.

"I know you!" he said, excited.

None of us had ever heard him so happy. "Come for some bowling?" I asked, doing my best to sound polite.

"Oh, no," he said cheerfully, "just dinner. The food's good and cheap here."

It was like a different person was talking. I looked at the food and admitted, "It's not too bad."[7]

"Sure is good seeing you guys here."

---

7. It was, in fact, bad.

"Yep."

"Really funny!"

"Yeah."

"So you're bowling, then?"

It was getting awkward. "Yeah."

"With people from the library?" he asked, looking at the rest of the people at the table. Everyone was looking awkwardly down.

"Yep."

"That's funny! You're bowling with people from the library."

I failed to see the humor, but I nodded to amuse him.

"Well, I'll let you get back to eating."

"Thanks."

"Have fun bowling."

"Thanks."

"Sure was good seeing you here."

"Good seeing you."

As awkward as that conversation was, things changed after that. Every time he came in for the next several weeks, he would mention that one night at the bowling ally. It was like seeing us had made it his best night ever. It was a little bit creepy.

The more comfortable he got, however, the more he started to open up. He lived in his car now, but before then he had actually had an interesting life. He told me about all the surveying work he did in South America for government contractors, about how the cities had emerged and why, about the revolution.

It was hard to look at him without wondering what had happened. It was hard to do that with most of the homeless patrons. Was there a moment in their life when they just stop functioning normally? Did something happen?

I had made a connection but it didn't stay. Slowly he just stopped talking to me again. It was as if we had never had anything.

∼

Matt had never seen or heard of a hernia, so when the fat man stretched and his shirt rose a little, Matt, somewhat appropriately but pretty unprofessionally, said, "Yuck! What the hell is that thing?! It's like an alien growing out of his stomach!"[8] Luckily the man did not hear and I later told Matt what it was.

At first I felt bad for the guy. He wore huge sweatpants that were held up with suspenders because the elastic had given out. He always wore the same sweaty and stained pants. And he lived in his compact-sized car, which is a situation made even worse when you have to literally squeeze into your car on account of your huge weight. I felt bad for him until he made me have to leave late. That's about the only thing that ever really ticks me off. When the clock hits closing, I want to do just that—close the building. I'm tired and I don't want to stay in the library for another second.

The man did not understand how important closing was to me. He refused to start packing up his things until one minute before closing time. This is not really a bad thing for a normal person, but not for a large person who takes five minutes to reach the front door. And when he finally reached the front door, he'd always try to sneak into the bathroom. On many occasions he did, which made us leave not only late but really late. For whatever reason, the man had a thing for bathrooms. They were his sanctuary.

Many days the janitor did not have time to clean the bathrooms until midday, which meant they were still dirty from the day before, which, the man said, "was completely unacceptable." When *his* bathroom was not clean he complained to everyone—staff, patrons—and when he ran out of people to complain to he

---

8. Matt had a way of saying what we were all thinking but were too afraid to say.

complained to himself, mumbling for several minutes about how bad it was to have a bathroom out of order.

We always suggested he use the bathrooms in the park if it were an emergency, but he didn't like this because they were not up to his standards. I always wanted to laugh when he said this and point at all the dirt on his shirt and ask if he should really have such high standards. I didn't think he would like that.

When the cleaning lady came up to me one day and said "There's a man who's been in the bathroom for two hours—I really need to clean it out," I had a good idea who it was.

I didn't really know what to do. There was no policy on bathroom use. Theoretically, with no policy, a person could use it as long as he wanted, all day if his tush could hold onto the hard plastic for that long.

Matt went in the bathroom with me.[9] I'm not sure why, but Matt decided to take charge. "Sir, you okay?"

"I'm crapping."

"Well, you've been crapping for two hours. You need us to call for help?"

"This is harassment. A man should get to crap on his own." We decided to leave to reorganize, plus the smell was pretty bad.

I called Faren. She was at a management meeting downtown. I decided this was important enough to interrupt. "He won't come out," I explained to her.

"What do you mean he won't come out?" ⟨

---

9. I was afraid to enter by myself. I had dreams that one day I would go into the bathroom and he would attack me, smother me with his fat, and proceed to rape me, though I also envisioned that his stomach hung so far on top of his penis that he would not be able to get his penis out and he'd probably just end up rubbing against me several minutes, then killing and eating me.

"Well, I mean just that—he won't come out. Been in there for two hours."

"Well, make him come out."

"What am I supposed to do? Break the door down and drag him out?" I was kind of afraid she'd say yes.

"Call the park rangers. Let them deal with it."

So that's what I did. But what could they do? "Nothing," the ranger explained when he entered the building. "There are no rules about such things."

Nearly three hours later the man left the restroom. He proceeded out the library to his car, where he ate a can of beans and then took a nap.

FOR SHELVING

Before you run off and call a vagabond a hobo or a bum a mendicant, get informed! Below are four main types of homelessness, and a description of each, so you know if you have classified them right:

VAGABOND: This is a homeless person who wanders around with no home. Vagabonds are more likely to beg for food than work for it, and they usually wander a large centralized area, not around the whole country.

BUM: A bum doesn't have a home in the sense that most people know it, but doesn't tend to wander around. A bum finds a box under a freeway and sticks to it as long as he can. Bums don't usually work.

HOBO: A hobo is sort of a lost trade in the homeless subculture. In the 1930s, they were the classy version of bums because they actually worked. Most hobos were more like traveling merchants than anything else; they didn't have homes, but only because they didn't

(Continues)

(Continued)

stick to one place. Rather, they were always traveling to different parts of the country looking for work. Many notable writers hoboed at some point in their lives.[10]

MENDICANT: Not very common in America, but this is a religious-type person who has devoted himself to God and therefore must resort to begging as a way of income.

---

10. Like Eugene O'Neil, Woody Guthrie, and Jack London.

The homeless I felt bad for were the families. There was a name for them: motel families. The thing about them is you don't always know who they are; they dress in a way that you can't tell. They're ashamed of it, so they dress and act like everything is okay. I know by their address or how they have to dial extensions to call home for a ride that they are not okay.

One night a family came to the desk looking for books about the state of Iowa. I showed them the books, and then the mom asked where the copy machine was so they could make a few copies of the important pages.

"You can check it out for free."

She nodded. "We have a few fines."

"It's fine. You can just pay whatever you were going to pay for the copies and that will be enough this time."

Brenda was working at the desk when the family checked out. "I'm sorry," she said, "but you'll have to pay off all the fines first."

The mother looked worried. "The librarian said it would be okay."

I started walking toward the desk.

"The librarian is wrong!"

"Librarians are never wrong, Brenda. Everyone knows that." I paused and smiled politely at the mom. "They are just going to pay a few dollars tonight. I said that would be okay. Her son needs the books for school."

"Well, I can't do that."

"Why?"

"They have $20 in fines. It's too high."

"Were the books brought back?"

She nodded.

"Then I don't see what the problem is."

"We're not supposed to unless they pay half."

"I'm making an exception tonight."

"Can I see you in the back?" Brenda said, irritated

I followed her to the back, where she proceeded to say, "I know you want to be Mr. Nice Librarian, but rules are rules, and I don't feel comfortable with this, especially you verbally insulting me at the desk in front of people."

"I insulted you?"

"Yes."

"How?"

"Well, you embarrassed me."

"Brenda, that's not an insult. But I do apologize if I hurt your feelings." I paused. "This family needs the book. They're homeless and they don't have enough money to pay the fine. Just let them have it."

"Well, seeing that they're homeless should be even more reason why not to let them check out; they won't be responsible."

"That's a pretty bad stereotype!"

"It's true. If you want to do this, then you do it. I wipe my hands clean of the whole thing."

I went back to the desk, took 50¢ for their $20 fine and then waived the rest of the money so they wouldn't have to be harassed the next time. Brenda stayed in the back and pretended to ignore the whole situation.

When she came back to the desk after the family had left, she pulled up their record right away and asked, "Did they pay their whole fine?"

"They paid what they needed to pay."

"You can't go around waiving people's fines. They are there for a reason."

"Brenda, part of my job means I get to decide when the rules don't apply to someone. Tonight I decided that the rules don't apply."

"And tomorrow I'm going to turn you in for what you did. The rules are there for a reason."

"Your heart's there for a reason, too. Use it before it's too late."

~

Sometimes a person gets comfortable at the library. Sometimes it's okay; usually it gets out of hand. The crazy stick man started innocently enough. He came in the library one day with his walking stick. He was obviously homeless. He just wanted a comfortable place to hang out.

Slowly he started getting more comfortable. First he moved into a dark corner near the dumpster at night; then he started stealing our newspapers in the morning before we opened; and finally he took over his own table in the library. He claimed it. No one sat at it except for him and he gave evil stares to anyone who came too close. One day he screamed at Matt for picking up a book he had left on the table when he went to the restroom. It had now gotten out of hand.

The good thing about not actually being the manager of a building is you don't have to deal with the things you don't want to. I decided to let Faren take the lead on this one.

"Sir, there's been a few reports of your conduct being inappropriate. I just want to go over the library rules of conduct with you."

"I know the rules—you don't need to go over anything with me. You're just picking on me because I'm homeless. I know my rights. I know I can be in here."

Faren nodded. "You can be in here as long as your conduct is appropriate."

"Is this about that black man stealing my book?"[11]

"Well, patrons have complained about you being hostile with them."

"They need to just leave me alone."

"Sir, you have a right to be in here, as do they. We all need to respect each other."

"I don't got to do anything."

"That's your right, but you can't be in here if you don't start improving your behavior."

He laughed. "What you going to do?"

"Well, if you don't want to respect others, then I'll have to ask you to leave."

"I'm not leaving, you damn ho."

Faren forced an uncomfortable smile and then said, "Sir, I think it's time for you to leave."

"And I said I wasn't leaving, ho!" He laughed loudly, an evil laugh.

"Then I'll have to call the police."

"Of course. All you white women are the same—haters of the homeless. Just put us somewhere where you don't have to see us."

---

11. He himself was blacker than Matt.

He stood and started waving his walking stick at her. At first I thought he was just waving it to be dramatic; then I realized he might be crazy enough to take a swing at her.

Faren left the man and called the police. "I need help immediately. I am the manager of a public library and a huge black man is threatening to beat me with a stick. I am white."[12]

The man left quickly after he heard her say this. Four police cars arrived at the library quickly and went in pursuit of the homeless man who tried to hurt a white woman. We never saw him again.

~

Because I was working at a small branch library with only a dozen or so Internet terminals (all of which are very close to where I sit), it has become a habit to do my best to ignore what patrons are viewing, so as to ensure their privacy. One week, however, I noticed a homeless woman sit down at a computer and pull from her small handbag a video camera. She logged into her e-mail account, turned on her recorder, and proceeded to record messages that had been sent to her in-box. Using a video camera in a city building without prior consent from the city is not allowed, but I let her do it for a few minutes, more for the sake of personal amusement and curiosity than anything else. Finally, after about five minutes, I became bored watching the woman, so I approached her and explained that she would have to get city approval if she wanted to use her video camera in the library.

She rolled her eyes and said, "Well, I was finished anyway." She stuffed her camera back into her bag, looked suspiciously around, and left in a hurry.

~

---

12. I kid you not, she said, "I am white."

There are different types of Internet users who visit the library. There's the casual user, who uses the library's Internet service perhaps once a month; the regular user, who uses it every day; the college user, who comes to the library only when the school's computer lab is full; and many other types, which I'll leave out for no real reason.

One day a man whom I would describe as a regular user came in. I rarely saw him doing anything on the computer except sending and reading e-mail. He was quiet, and never asked for help on the Internet. He was also homeless. As I was helping a younger patron find a book for his state-report assignment, the man came to me seeking help with printing.

When I got to his computer, I saw a picture of an overweight, fully nude Caucasian woman holding a jar of peanut butter. I told the man that this kind of material went against the library's Internet usage policy. I have had to explain this policy to several patrons who have used the Internet terminals to view pornographic images and, every time, the patron does one of three things: acts embarrassed and apologizes for his actions, or nods and quickly leaves, or tries to defend his actions by saying that he is a taxpayer and can look at whatever he wants to on the computer.

This man, however, explained quite seriously, "I didn't know you weren't allowed to look at pornography on the Internet."

I nodded and pointed at the large sign above the computers, which stated clearly the library's stance on this issue. The man nodded and asked if he could still print the picture. I said no and added that, because he'd abused the library's policy (a major no-no), he would now be banned from using the Internet. He nodded. Then, to my surprise, he flipped over a computer printout of a nude woman and left with no further comment.

I did not bother asking how he was able to print the other picture without help.

~

Hon came to me before the library opened one morning. I was processing books and she had just gone outside to get the newspaper.

"Missing is a paper?" Hon said.

"I don't know, Hon." I answer most questions from her in this way.

"Oh. Well, missing is a paper."

"Okay."

Usually, saying okay would get her to leave; today she just stood there. That meant she wanted me to do something. I stood and she started walking away in a way that meant I was to follow her. She led me outside.

"Missing is a paper?" she said then, pointing.

"They probably just didn't deliver it. Or someone stole it. It's fine."

"It's not here?"

"Doesn't appear to be."

"Oh. It's missing?"

"Yeah."

We were about to go in when a homeless man came toward us with the newspaper under his arms and said, "I seem to be having trouble finding the classifieds today. Have you seen it?"

I shook my head. "We've been looking everywhere for that! If you want to read it, you need to read it in the library."

"I was going to bring it back."

"That's really not the point. It's library property and it's stealing even if you do bring it back."

"Well, I don't see what difference it makes where and when I read it if I bring it back."

"Well, it's just library policy."

"So do you have the classified section or not?"

～

Some people are justifiably crazy. They do something stupid, but they have a reason, no matter how stupid that reason is. Some people are just plain crazy. They have no reason for their insanity.

Early one Saturday morning a man came in whistling the theme to *Popeye*. He was one of those types who were just plain crazy. He had no excuse for it. I watched the man curiously. Sometimes I don't do anything about something until someone complains. That's what I did that morning.

"There's a man who won't stop whistling," a patron complained.

"Oh?" I said, surprised.

"I'm trying to study."

I silently cursed the person. Why can't we all just get along? If someone is talking too loudly do you really need to tattle on him? Can't you just ask him nicely to settle down? Apparently not. Apparently you need a librarian to do your dirty work. So that's what I did.

The man was pacing and whistling loudly around the back of the library.[13]

I approached the man and said, "Sir, I have to ask that you keep your whistling down. There are people trying to study."

"Oh, there's people, are there?"

I nodded.

"Well, I'm a people. I'm a people! Ha, ha! I'm people! I'm people, bitch! And I like to whistle." He paused. "Should I get a library card?"

---

13. Crazy people pace a lot.

"I think you really need to settle down or you'll have to leave."

"Screw it." And then he walked out of the building. As he walked out, I laughed to myself. Just another day at the library.

That same Saturday, I was minding my own business when a library clerk came to me and said there were complaints about a patron sleeping in the restroom.

"Sleeping in the restroom?" I questioned, believing that somewhere in this short statement there had surely been a misunderstanding.

"Sleeping in the restroom," he assured me.

I hate being informed of such things, because this means I have to do something about it. I could handle the time I had to tell a man he needed to pull his pants up a little higher because he was exposing himself in such a way that it was offensive to patrons; I could handle telling patrons that they're not allowed to look for pornography on the library computers; I could even keep a straight face when someone asked if we had *The Complete Idiot's Guide to Sex*. But sleeping in the restroom—there was something sacred about the restroom that I hated to disturb.

I approached the restroom with a bit of weary caution. One man was using the urinal; another man was sleeping on the floor of stall one[14] with his head resting against the toilet. I left the restroom and told the clerk that, yes, there was indeed a man sleeping on the restroom floor. I knew what his follow-up question would be. "What should we do?" I shrugged, waited for the man using the urinal to leave the restroom, then entered the restroom once more and said, "Sir, are you okay?" It had not escaped me that the man might have had some sort of freak restroom accident and was thus unconscious.

---

14. The only stall.

"Yes," came his reply.

I was really hoping he was unconscious and there was thus a reason for his odd behavior that was justifiable, and a reason that would mean I could call the fire department and have it deal with the problem. Instead I had to reason that the man was just plain nutty, and I hated having to reason such thoughts about patrons. I thought quickly for what I could say: "There's no sleeping allowed on the bathroom floors." There was nothing original about this but it was fast thinking.

"Okay," came his reply.

I had expected some resistance and when none came a part of me was a little disappointed. I left the restroom with that feeling of accomplishment you get when you kick a man out of the restroom for sleeping on the floor, then I ran to the front of the library to get a good view of the man when he left the library.[15] When the man left, I was surprised to see that this was a regular patron, granted one that was sometimes a little off but not exactly the type of person I'd take for sleeping on restroom floors.[16]

There was one final incident in the bathroom that Saturday.[17] This bathroom incident involved a man who sang romantic Spanish tunes. I was sitting at the information desk looking intently at a blank computer screen and dwelling on why a man would sleep on a restroom floor when Matt came to me and said, "There's a man in the bathroom who's been in there a really long time."

---

15. He had been behind the stall with the door shut and I could make out only his backside.

16. The same patron I overheard one day conspiring with another crazy patron about how to create a small business that would attract women, who would in turn want to be their girlfriends. (I'm pretty sure the small business never happened.)

17. It was not entirely unlikely for so many odd things to happen in one day; odd things have a tendency to come in pairs of two or three.

I shrugged and thought to myself that it was a little weird for Matt to be keeping track of how long patrons used the restroom. I said the patron was probably just having a rough go at it and to let me know if he was still there in thirty minutes.

Matt nodded and continued. "That's not all. He's singing in Spanish. He keeps flushing the toilet and then singing a new song every time he flushes it. He's flushed the toilet at least ten times since he went in."

I asked what songs he was singing. I don't know why I asked that—I don't think I would have treated the situation differently if he were singing disco or grunge. I suppose I was just curious.

Matt shrugged. "I don't know, it's in Spanish. But they sound romantic."

I nodded. "Follow me." (It's always a good idea to approach a strange situation in the library with another person who can act as a witness should anything happen that requires police attention.) I stood with Matt at the restroom door for several minutes, listening to the man sing in Spanish. He had a nice voice, although he sang high notes a little off key.

"What are you going to do?" Matt finally asked me.

I shrugged. I was preparing the encounter with the singing restroom man in my head. First I'd ask if everything was okay, then I'd tell him to wrap it up because we were closing the restroom in five minutes. I hated restroom encounters with patrons—there was no way to make them less awkward.

I started for the restroom door, but it opened before I went in. A tall Latino man with a large sombrero on his head exited. He was wearing a Disneyland T-shirt and faded jeans and he carried a ceramic cactus (the ones street vendors sell for haggled prices in Tijuana).

"Everything okay?"

The man smiled and nodded. "Sí." Then he left the library.

I went back to the desk and thought about the bathroom, about all the things that had happened there that day. I was a servant—even to people who sang in the bathroom or slept on the floor. I was a servant to people who had absolutely no money and did things that were flat-out bizarre. It was humbling and rewarding.

Serving the homeless made me love my job just a little more.

Chapter 306.7 -LOVE- For Love or Library:	Romances in Unlikely, Sometimes Compromising, Places

Every office needs a good office romance. I can't stress that enough: *every office needs a good office romance*. It provides a healthy dose of gossip, which in turn boosts morale. Libraries are no different. All of the problems at my library could be summed up quite simply: no one in the library was dating within. They were all outsourcing, either to other libraries or to other business sectors.

I developed a strategy. Someone needed to date. It didn't matter if it were real. But there was a rule: they couldn't say they were dating. The most vital part of this strategy was that no one would ever know if it was for real. That's how good gossip is started. People needed to get caught alone looking like something was about to happen, but then acting like it was no big deal and nothing was going on, taking the "we're just friends approach."

I decided, further, that it would be even better by mixing old with young. Having a twenty-year-old woman caught with a fifty-year-old man. Then go even further by having the girl fake morning sickness. That kind of healthy gossip could keep a library running for years.

The trouble with my strategy was not so much my idea as simply no one wanting to try it out.

You can tell a lot from a man by his taste in women.[1] I'm not sure what it says about a man, but I'm certain it says something. Male librarians tended to have taste that varied from librarian to librarian. Roland liked the weird ones.[2]

"Did you see that girl?" Roland asked me one night.

I turned around and saw no woman, and then Roland pointed, and sure enough there was a woman. It rarely happened that Roland would point out his attraction for a woman who actually looked like a woman. "I like them bulky and in charge," Roland would say whenever I commented to him about his taste.

A group of library employees went to New York one year. Roland was one of those who went. We visited the UN building. A large blonde Swedish woman was our guide. She was a good guide, but she sort of scared me. She spoke in commands. Everything was a command. "You take picture *now*"; "To left you see painting that man Norman Rockwell did do"; "You pause now to study big room for leaders."

Toward the end of the tour I commented quietly to Roland, "Bet she likes to keep it rough."

---

1. Female librarians are different; no one can read their minds.

2. Freaky weird, not weird weird.

"She could spank me around any day."

I thought he was joking. He was not. I stared at the woman's large biceps, listened to her deep commanding voice, and began to see that indeed she was his type. Then I heard her laugh for the first time. It was the sound of a drunk angry man, but a laugh nonetheless. I saw a big grin on Roland's face and knew exactly what Roland was thinking. He wanted her to take him back to her place and throw him on her Ikea bed, where she'd spend the entire night beating him senseless. They wouldn't make love, but somehow the pain for Roland would be just the intimacy he was looking for.

Jonathan was the opposite. He liked them classy. Girls without college degrees need not apply. Jonathan didn't have a degree, so this seemed odd, but whatever worked. As much as he wanted a girl like this, all he got were moms. I told him that if he wanted a girl like that, then he needed to go to an academic library, but for some reason he didn't believe me. He thought by chance the woman of his dreams would walk in any minute to do serious research at a library whose most scholarly work was a companion guide to *Harry Potter*.

And me? What library patron did I find most attractive? None. There was something unprofessional about the whole thing.

~

One day I was sitting at the desk staring blankly at the phone.

"Waiting for some hot mama to call you?" Melissa asked. Melissa always had a sincere concern that everybody had somebody in their life.[3] She was a children's librarian, so, naturally, upbeat was in her nature.

---

3. That certain somebody in Melissa's life was pretty complicated; she had many somebodies, depending on what night of the week it was. (Librarians can be sluttier than they sometimes let on [myself excluded]).

"I wish. Just bored."

"When was the last time you went out? Had a little fun?"

"Too long."

"Don't you think it's time? You come to work every day, and then you go home. That's no way to live your life."

"Don't you have a story time to get ready for or something?"

"That's no way to live your life!"

"I live it."

"How long have you been out of school?"

I really wished a patron would come to the desk so I could avoid answering any more of her questions. They didn't come. "Two years."

"And on average how many nights a week do you go out?"

"I think it's more like how many nights a month, and I'm lucky if I go out once."

"And what do you do with all your time?"

"I'm too tired to do anything after work."

"Come on! You're not even thirty. You still have a little life in you."

I didn't say anything.

"You know, you have a lot to offer any girl. You have a good job, a graduate degree, and you're well-read. So what's the problem?"

"What's your deal today? Can't you pick on someone else?"

"Start living a little! Start asking girls out!"

"I wouldn't know where to look."

"Girls are all around—you just got to start asking them out. They're not just going to fall out of the sky, you have to make an effort. Make a goal. Every week ask at least twenty girls out."

"Twenty?"

"Sure, why not?"

"Who does that?"

"A guy that wants to live it up! Enjoy life! Not live for his job!"

"I don't live for my job."

"Then it's settled! Twenty girls!"

I'm pretty sure she was smoking weed when she told me that.[4] I had no intention of asking out twenty girls, but she made a good point. Who was I kidding? Half of my unhappiness at work was based on the fact that work was all I had. When I wasn't working, I was writing. They were both good things, but too much of it and I was going to wind up a bitter old man at the age of thirty-five, regretful that I had worked hard and had no one to share it with.[5]

There's a void in the soul of every person that can be filled only with companionship. Humans aren't meant to be alone. It's only when we find someone to really share our lives with that we finally begin to discover ourselves.

But I was a lost cause, and I had told myself I was a lost cause for so long that I had convinced myself of the fact. I was okay with this.

～

When the wart-faced man walked into the library, I had a feeling he would be trouble. He looked around the library with an odd glare in his eyes. He smiled at more than one teenage girl. He sat at a computer and pretended to be using it, but his eyes were wandering constantly on the teen room. Aside from his odd behavior,

---

4. Seriously, she reeked of the stuff.

5. I already kind of acted like an old man, but at thirty-five I would have the grey hair to convince people of the fact.

he also looked crazy. He wore baggy, ratty clothing; he had a wart the size of a quarter on his nose; and his hair appeared like it had not been washed in a week.[6]

I kept a close watch on him. When he went to Hon and appeared to be talking to her, I got nervous. Why would he want to mess with a helpless older Vietnamese woman who couldn't speak English? I went toward Hon, and got close enough to hear what was being said.

"Where do you want me to take you for dinner?" the wart-faced man asked.

Hon giggled but said nothing.

"It's our anniversary."

Again Hon giggled.

Then it hit me. This crazy wart man wasn't just crazy, he was Hon's boyfriend. Someone had told me a few months ago that she was dating a scary looking Irishman, but I didn't believe them. I didn't believe she was capable of it. As I watched her giggling and him rambling, I wondered what their conversations could possibly sound like.

I found out when he left the library how she met him: in the parking lot of the library. I wondered who possibly could have met their boyfriend in a parking lot. Then I looked at Hon. As bad as it looked, at least she had someone. Then there was me. It sort of was a major defeat to know even Hon had someone in her life, weird as he may be.

It was the ultimate insult to the pathetic life I was leading—the final wake-up call. I needed someone, too.

---

6. He also had red Irish hair and a short stature and at first I thought perhaps he was a leprechaun.

CORNY LIBRARY PICKUP LINES AND HOW LIBRARIANS EFFEC-
TIVELY SHOOT THEM DOWN:

Pardon me, could you please tell me what kind of card I need to
check you out?
Visa, MasterCard, or American Express.

You must have been burning books, because you're looking hot.
*My apologies. The new "Harry Potter" is coming out and I was
in the back burning the Newbery winners to make room for it.*

Can you tell me where I can find books on overcoming a deeply passionate love I have for a librarian?
636.45 MICH.

Libraries should allow food in the building, because right now I could
just eat you up.
*Policy is policy, but if you'd really like to change that, the
appropriate forms are behind you. Just drop it in the suggestion box when you're done and in due time it will be pulled out
and set in the loser pile.*

I know what I need to access the Internet, but what do I need to access your heart?
A life.

What book would you recommend to help me sweep you off your feet?
"How to Divorce a Jealous Mad Person."

Can you tell me how to spell love? I'm writing a letter to you.

Do you mean the agape love or the love you have for someone you don't have a chance of ever getting?

Can you settle a bet? My friend says librarians have no life but I say they're wild beasts. Can I take you out to dinner and prove my friend wrong?

Tell your friend he's right.

As I work near Disneyland, I see a lot of people walk into the library from out of town, people visiting the city for the conventions, the amusement parks, or[7] the motels with hourly rates. Most of these patrons never come in long enough for me to remember their names, but there are exceptions. One such exception was Zelenka, a homely Czech, and Veronica, her much more attractive[8] friend, who were both working for a hotel for the summer.

Veronica never once came into the library unnoticed. Whenever she entered the building, it was like seeing a model do her thing on the fashion runway, putting on a little show for every person in the library.[9] It was fun watching all the desperate old men[10] trying their best to communicate with the Czechoslovakian vixen, who knew little English and really just wanted to check her e-mail. There were even one or two requests for books on learning the

---

7. Though they certainly won't admit it.

8. Also Czech.

9. Male, female, and even small children.

10. Who normally were occupied in Internet chat rooms and posting personal ads on dating sites.

Czech language. Library pages, in their own attempts to get to know the wondrous lady better, would accidentally tap their book carts against the back of her chair, then apologize and engage in small talk, not seeming to notice that she probably understood only 10 percent, at best, of what they were saying. Sometimes the pages would say something she understood and she would smile and joyfully repeat whatever word she had picked up: "Ah, yes, *pancake!*" Then, believing they had established a common connection, they would use the word in every sentence that followed.

I, of course, kept it professional.[11] I felt a little sorry for Zelenka, who got no attention, but it was her own fault for this; there was no dazzle in her step or charm in her smile, and she had a horrid sense of fashion. To be quite honest, her name only comes to mind when thinking of Veronica, but that's beside the point. As their stay progressed and it became certain that they would soon leave for their homeland, patrons and workers alike made mad attempts to have just one date.

Ultimately, however, it was I—the librarian—who had the last waltz, though not literally, of course. The library was closing one night and Veronica was the sole patron in the building; I had not seen her companion, Zelenka, all day. As best I could tell, Veronica was supposed to have a ride home, but something happened. How anyone could have left such a beauty abandoned at a library in the night is beyond me but someone did, and I knew it would be up to me to protect the damsel in distress from the dangers of Southern California.

I used gestures and slow speech to try to tell her that if she stayed outside the library alone she would surely die and that she

---

11. A hazard of the job being that all librarians must pretend to be boring while working, except children's librarians, who, I'm pretty sure, take pills to maintain their abnormal amount of energy and perkiness.

should let me give her a ride home. And she did. I tried to make her feel safe as we drove; I told her about my country and asked her about hers. It was the same corny small talk I observed patrons using on her in the library, the same corny small talk that she never seemed to understand.

She smiled mostly and stared at me in confusion. Once, she said "I am Veronica" and another time "The bus stop is near, no?" But mostly she smiled and said yes to things that didn't exactly warrant an answer.

Before taking her home, I had never had any sort of conversation with her. The only thing I'd ever asked her was "How are you today?" and "Would you like to use the Internet?" Now that I had her in my car and I was asking her less generic questions, she seemed less attractive. Seeing her stare at me, confused, as I did my best to make her feel comfortable, made her seem a little dumb. I realize this feeling was caused mostly by the language barrier but, nonetheless, I couldn't help but feel as though I'd violated something a little sacred and had stolen forever that beauty she had once given to me. She was like a store mannequin meant to be adorned but never touched.

When I pulled into the parking space in front of her motel room, I thought of all of the patrons who had dreamed of such a moment—to be here, in front of her room, in the right seat to make a move. They probably would have had pickup lines that she would not have understood, or perhaps tried to charm her with their looks or incoherent ramblings that passed as humor in English, but there was only one thing I had in mind to say to her. I told her good night. She told me, "I go. The bus stop is near, no?" And then she waved and ran to her room. From that moment on, I did not view her with the same admiration that I had when she first came into the library. All I saw when she came into the building was the friendly woman who had said "I am Veronica" when I asked her

"Do you like California?" I learned an important lesson with Veronica. I realized that some patrons were special and should never be touched. They were given to the library to be mysterious figures who walked through the doors and were never meant to be known, people who were meant to be recounted through the ages in break rooms as legends and myths of the library.

The next day, Melissa found out about what happened and said, "So?" She sounded like a guy hitting up for information about some girl he left the bar with.

"So, what?"

"Don't so what me!" She giggled. "I heard you went home last night with the Czech girl!"

"I didn't go home with her, I took her home."

"Whatever! So tell me what happened?!"

"Well, I put her in my car and I took her home. Then I went home."

"Are you kidding me?"

"No."

"You're hopeless! This was your chance to make a move."

"A move on what?"

"Come on! She was pretty!"

"Yeah. Pretty in a way that I'm not interested in."

"So what are you interested in?"

"Let's just say if all I was interested in was beauty, I would be all over Virginia Woolf."

"Who's Virginia Woolf?"[12]

I rolled my eyes. "Never mind."

"Come on! Be serious! Tell me what your type is!"

I shrugged. It had been so long I honestly didn't know anymore.

---

12. She only worked in a library—why on earth would she know who that was?

"It's time to figure it out," Melissa said. "Just go on a couple dates. Have some fun. Live a little."

I couldn't argue with her. I really couldn't. But where could I go? I went to the only place I knew to meet women: the Internet.

In my younger, more curious years, I had dabbled in online romance. I had exchanged e-mails and IMs with girls. It was fun, but it was always too hard for me to create a real person electronically. What ultimately happened in every case was that we just stopped e-mailing. It didn't really hurt, because as much as we knew each other through e-mails, a certain part of that person wasn't real because we had never had human contact.[13] Nonetheless, I decided to give it another chance.

I opened up my account. I created a profile that was honest about the good things, and, curiously enough, failed to mention the bad. Immediately I started browsing profiles and e-mailing random strangers about their interest. For two months it was the same. They were boring, generic e-mails, about hobbies, that were fun at first, but quickly faded into the mundane. Eventually I didn't bother replying to the e-mails[14] because it just didn't go anywhere. The only people who really made an effort were older women.[15] They were fun to talk to and we had a lot in common, but they were old and we both knew it would never go anywhere.

---

13. E-mail's sort of funny that way. (As a parenthetical note to the footnote, a few years back a neighbor who had never been lucky with women [on account of his bad looks] spent six months chatting online with a woman; he was serious about her [he even printed out every single e-mail they exchanged and filed them for future use—yeah, it was creepy] and decided after six months that they should meet. Before he left on his romantic outing he showed me a picture of the woman. There were three people in the photo [two average-looking women and one ugly-looking guy]. I asked who she was, and he said he'd find out on the date. The next day I asked how it went. He shrugged and said it had been okay. I then asked which one she was in the picture. He sadly looked down and said softly, "The guy.")

14. Or they didn't bother replying to mine.

15. Two, to be exact.

One day, out of the blue, when hope was almost lost, I saw a profile from a girl who said she wanted to be a librarian. That sentence alone made her instantly attractive. I wrote her immediately and checked every thirty minutes to see if she wrote back. She did—nearly a day later.

Her name was Diana. The first few e-mails, we both saw that we had a lot in common; the next few proved that we had a lot not in common. As much as we liked the same music and movies and practiced the same faith, our lives were completely different. We had different life experiences and different lifestyles. She stayed up late, I went to bed early. She was just starting school again, I was regretting ever going. She liked to go to downtown Los Angeles on the weekends, I liked to go home on the weekends. She wanted to see the world, I had already seen it. She had tattoos, I had birthmarks.

It was like I could make a list of a million things that made our lives different. But it didn't matter how many things were different about her, because there was one thing that was right—I couldn't stop thinking about her. From that very first e-mail she was always on my mind; every time I went online to check my mail I hoped there was a message from her and when there was it made my day.

We talked for a month. With other girls, e-mails would die down after a week. With Diana, they increased. And they got longer. The more she wrote the more we both had to say. I wanted to meet her, but I was no good at asking girls out. I kept thinking of how I could do it. Then finally the answer came by way of a holiday Christmas party. I didn't want to go and I needed a reason not to. I told her about the situation and asked if she'd be my excuse not to.

She said yes.

A part of why I wanted to meet her so badly was because I needed a reason not to like her. I found something wrong with every girl I had ever met, but so far, as different as we were, I found her to be flawless. In one of the e-mails, we had talked about paper airplanes and spotted dick. Not in the same sentence, of course. So we decided we would go to a British pub that was known for spotted dick[16] and then fly paper airplanes off a parking structure when we were done. If nothing else it would make a good story: I had dick with a girl I met off the Internet!

The day of the meeting, I talked a librarian into covering for me so I could sneak off a little early. I was a nervous wreck but I didn't know why. I wanted to find a reason not to like her but I would be devastated if she didn't like me back. I had to be perfect for this girl I was afraid of liking for a reason that I couldn't understand. Random fears went through my head as I fearfully waited in front of the pub. What if I got the dick all over my face? What if she was crazy and she tried to kill me with her fork? What if she poisoned my drink? Then she arrived and, as awkward as it was at first, all those fears went away. She was exactly what she said she would look like and more.

During dick I wiped my face every five seconds to make sure no dick remained on my face. I don't remember what we talked about. I just remembered liking it, and not knowing why. We said nothing, we said everything. When we finished dick, we went and had tea; when we finished tea, we flew airplanes; when we finished airplanes, we sat on a bench until midnight and

---

16. Among other things.

laughed at all the drunks walking to and from the bars. We bet on which guys would win their drunken fights and what slutty girl they would end up with.[17]

We talked about family, politics, religion, school, everything you shouldn't talk about with someone you want to see again. Neither of us wanted the night to end; we were so desperate to stay together that when it got too cold and windy to stay on the bench we went to an In-N-Out Burger until it closed at two.

We ended the night with a hug and a promise to meet again.

We began constantly texting. She was in school and I was at work; texting was our only form of communication.

There was only one problem: the first hang-out was not a date. I considered it a date,[18] but she did not.[19] So I had to officially ask her out, which I dreaded. And worse, if it was a date then I had to make it a meaningful one.

We looked at Christmas lights and drank warm tea and cocoa on our first real date. Then we stayed at a bookstore until closing. Then we went to a twenty-four-hour Denny's, and stayed until after two.

It was wonderful. Every date we didn't want to part. There was one further problem: we weren't technically dating. We were only going on dates. Apparently there was a difference.[20] If I wanted it to be real dating of the exclusive nature, I had to ask her.

---

17. This was in downtown Fullerton (a nice small city that contained two colleges and lots of frat boys) on Saturday night where every girl (minus the one I was with) played the role of skanky whore and every guy (minus me) played the role of man with dick and wanting to use it on whomever will lower her pants.

18. It was easier that way.

19. She liked to make things complicated on me that way.

20. I honestly didn't know there were so many rules and names for seeing a girl.

On Christmas I made her a scarf, which I learned to do from working at the library,[21] and got her one of my favorite books,[22] and we went to church. Afterward we drove around Orange County until nearly five in the morning. Later that night I asked if we could call it dating and she said yes.

Dating continued for a month. Then one day her friends went to New York for a week and I knew she would be lonely. I knew I couldn't take her to New York on that day, so I decided to do the next best thing. I brought New York to her. I got documentaries to watch on New York, movies that featured New York, a Broadway play on DVD, a concert on DVD, and I cooked a New York style breakfast, lunch, dinner, and desert. At night, during the play, I asked her to be my girlfriend. She said yes.

After another month, she had been my inspiration and I asked her to be a little more. I asked her to be my muse and even gave her a muse ring.[23] We had fun together, but we weren't anything alike personality-wise. They say opposites attract. Maybe they do. I needed her and she needed me and together we needed each other. That's what ultimately made it work.

All through college my priorities had been focused on college; after college it was on work and writing. Suddenly my world got taken on a wild ride. From the instant I met Diana, work didn't matter, writing didn't matter, only she mattered. I did the other things. I didn't hate them, but whenever I did them my mind was on her.

I think there's a hopeless romantic in all of us. We all want someone to impress—and someone to impress us back. There are

---

21. I learn lots of things at the library.

22. *Wise Blood.*

23. I spent $10 on it to prove how serious I was.

so many clichés to describe how and why I liked Diana, and yet it's all summed up in one: she made me feel good.

For the first time in my adult life I realized I didn't need to focus on finding a job or a book publisher or anything like that. I needed to focus on finding someone to share my life with. What good is a job when you have no one to complain to about how bad it is sometimes?

All this time I had wondered if I was doing the right thing, becoming a librarian, when in reality it didn't really matter. It doesn't matter if you're a librarian or a firefighter. In the end, people rarely remember what you did. They remember who you are. How can you really become someone without another person constantly there to tell you who you aren't and how to become better?

At last, I had a romance of my own.

Chapter 643.7	Being the Reasons
-LIBR-	Our Hero Believes
This Library Is	His Job Just Might
Falling Apart:	Kill Him After All

Everyone needs a vacation, managers included. I just wish they wouldn't take it on my watch. The library powers that be somehow figured it would be cheaper for me to be in charge of the building during my manager's absence rather than having an actual manager. It was correct, because they didn't have to pay me a manager's salary; it was incorrect because I am not management material.

Faren said two important things before she left. To me she said, "Make sure things don't fall apart." To Brenda she said, "Make sure to keep the other clerks on track." And then she left. It seemed like a harmless way to leave things.

It wasn't. Brenda read the manager's comment as "You are in charge of all the clerks and you can boss them around."[1] Not to get all Rodney King[2] on the reader, but why can't we just get along? Why is that so hard?

Not even a day had passed when Brenda said to several of the clerks, "I'm in charge of you and you're going to do what I say. Is that understood?"

This of course ultimately led Brenda into getting into an argument with every single clerk. In less than three hours' time, nobody was talking to anyone.

I hated to reprimand employees, but something had to be done. The next day I told Brenda that we needed to talk.

"Yes, we do," she answered. "I was just about to come get you. Follow me."

I hadn't expected her to be so commanding but I followed.

She led me to the back of the library, took me into Faren's office, and she sat behind the manager's desk. "Sit down," she commanded, pointing at the chair on the other side of the desk.

It wasn't going as I had planned it.

"You need to be more supportive of me. Everyone's picking on me. We're both in charge and we need to act like a team."

"Actually, I'm in charge."

---

1. In fact, she would be in charge of no clerk, but because the senior clerk also happened to take her vacation that week she decided she deserved to fill her role. (She did not deserve it.)

2. The now famous police assault of Rodney King, of course, sparked the 1992 Los Angeles riots. But what became of the man who just wanted us to get along? He won nearly 4 million dollars in a civil case, tried to start a rap label, was arrested again for spousal assault, went to rehab, left rehab, and got arrested again for pretty much the same thing he got arrested for in 1992. All his money is now gone. His beating led to a riot that caused over 1 billion dollars in damage, fifty-plus deaths, 2,000-plus injuries, with over 3,000 businesses damaged, and he ended up just repeating his crime. It's stories like that that make you believe in America.

"Don't you pick on me, too. I'm documenting everything that happens this week. I'm going to make sure everyone gets reprimanded by the manager."

"I think the problem here is you're acting like you're the boss and no one wants to hear it."

"The problem is you're not doing what Faren told you to do."

I sighed. The woman was nuts. "Let's stop right here. I want you to tell me exactly what you think the problem is. Don't get hostile. Let's just communicate. I want to know what you think the problem is."

"I don't know," Brenda whined. "I didn't do anything wrong. All I did was tell all the clerks that I would be in charge of them this week and they had to do what I said."

"I think that might be the problem. Faren left me in charge of the building, but I haven't gone around and thrown it in everyone's face."

"Maybe you should. People need to know who the boss is."

"How about this? How about you let me talk to each of the clerks, and from here on out you don't talk to them about who's boss."

Brenda shook her head, then asked, "How about you do whatever you want because you're going to do that anyway, and I document what I don't like and I report all of it?"

"Fine."[3]

"You have been warned. You should have played ball on my team."

I was beginning to feel like I was involved in a fight with a four-year-old. I left the office and passed Roland, who was processing books at a desk by Faren's office.

---

3. I really wanted to go back to being a plain old librarian with no responsibilities.

"Looks like you really blew this one," Roland said

"You heard that?"

He nodded and joked, "Could have been a contender. Now Faren's going to get back and know never to put you in charge of anything. Hon will be in charge of things before you."

"Thanks for the support."

"Well, I'm sorry. You just really screwed it all up. What do you want me to say?"

"Why don't you try saying nothing?"

"No."

"No? What do you mean no? You're the yes man, you can't say no."

"I just did." He reclined in his chair and laughed. "Looks like you're having a bad day."

I left Roland and nearly tripped over Hon. Hon didn't say anything to me, she just stared. It was an evil stare. Brenda and Hon were friends. I had insulted her friend, so I had insulted her.

For the rest of the week, no one talked. Everyone felt isolated. The only people who did talk talked about what had happened and what they thought of Brenda. No one liked anyone else.

Toward the end of the week a patron came in complaining that he had returned a book and that we were charging it to his account. He asked to see a supervisor and someone brought out Brenda. Brenda did her best to help the man, but when she did not take the book off his account, the man became hostile. He took a seat on the floor and said he wouldn't move until we took care of the problem.

"You're in charge! You deal with him," Brenda said of the man.

Ultimately Brenda didn't want to handle problems; she just wanted to stand up in front of everyone and tell them what to do.

I could tell the man had returned the book. No one would sit on the library's pee-stained carpet with his kind of conviction and be telling a lie. And if he was telling a lie—if he was that good an actor—then I didn't care anyway. I didn't lose anything by taking the book off his account.

As the week went on, some of the temperatures cooled. The gossip had died down but there were still hard feelings on all sides. To top it off, the teen patrons had been loud all week and the staff was at their wits' end with them. I decided until the teens were ready to behave they would not get Internet access unless they had homework to do.

"I don't agree with that," Matt, the page who wanted to get high with me at the company picnic, told me.

"Why is that?"

"Just because a few are acting up, you can't take away the privileges of all. If adults were misbehaving you wouldn't take their Internet away."

"Adults are also adults. Until teens reach the age of eighteen then they'll be treated unfairly. That's just the way it goes."

"It's censorship."

I hated when people use that word in the library, especially when they used it falsely. "There's a big difference between censorship and punishment."

"Well, I don't agree."

"I respect your viewpoint, but I believe it's better this way."

The page left and I thought that would be the end of things. Teens were acting better because they couldn't get on the Internet and get into trouble, and when teens weren't loud, the staff seemed happier.

But that was not the end of it.

Thirty minutes after Matt left, I received a phone call from Faren. "Is it true that you aren't letting any teens on the computer?"

"No."

"Well, I just received a text message from Matt saying that you weren't allowing teens on the computer."

He texted her? I thought to myself. *How did he even have her number?* "Not all teens," I clarified. "The teens have really been misbehaving all this week. So for the rest of the week I said the only teens who get on a computer are the ones who need to do homework."

"Well, that ends now."

"Okay," I said, still dumbfounded that a page had gone above me to Faren.

Ten minutes later she called again to make sure the teens were using the computer again. She called two more times after that to tell me why I wasn't to do that again.

I found Matt in the back of the building doing no work.

"Hey, you think next time you have a problem you could do me a favor and not text the manager? That was my call and if you have a problem with it I'm sorry, but I'm in charge right now, not you."

"Whatever."

It was insubordination. Blatant insubordination. It was a word I had never really considered before. It made me feel old.

Part of what had happened the entire week is that the employees had played free-for-all, not as a team. Faren wasn't there, so everyone wanted to do as they pleased. Make their own rules. Be in charge. I felt like I was the only person who didn't want to be in charge. I just wanted to sit at the reference desk and answer questions; that's all I ever wanted.

When Faren returned, she lectured me on how I hadn't been harsh enough and how I needed to be more assertive with employees. I nodded and agreed. That's what she wanted to hear.

One thing I had learned was it didn't matter if you were right or wrong—sometimes it's better just to take the fall. At the end of the day no one wants to, but someone has to. Leadership isn't about showing presence and saying you're in charge, it's about taking the blame so no one else has to. I was in charge that week. It didn't matter if Brenda had started a hundred catfights, I was still in charge and I was to blame.

FOR SHELVING

Every riot has its riot photo or video. LA had Rodney King, the Toledo Riot had its images of neo-Nazis, and Tiananmen Square had its Tank Man. The photo of the Tank Man is enduring; few people remember what the protest was all about but millions know that photo.[4] *Time* magazine even named him one of the 100 most influential people of the twentieth century. So what became of the man who was nearly run over by tanks? Who knows!

The thing about Tank Man is that no one actually knows who he was. A British newspaper said it was a student by the name of Wang Weilin, but this claim is, for the most part, no longer believed. Some say he is in hiding; others say he was arrested right after he was pulled into the crowd by watchers; several reports say the man was executed weeks later.

One thing not always shown[5] is the tanks trying to avoid hitting the man, or the man jumping on the tanks where he allegedly provoked the driver.

---

4. In a nutshell the protest was about reform, but that's not the point of this commercial break.

5. How great would the emotional outcry be if they did?

You work at the same place long enough, you inevitably see the theory of "It's not personal, it's business." You tell yourself that it can be different at your job, that you can get close to the people you work with. Then one day something happens that makes you reconsider all of this.

One day I arrived at work and discovered Brenda had disappeared. She was there in the morning but gone by lunch. There were many awkward silences when her name was uttered. Locks and passwords were changed. Most of the employees felt a bit endangered for their lives; they were afraid that she would appear again one day and in a fit of rage kill us all. When you work at the library you sort of sign your life away.

I didn't like Brenda, but you work with someone long enough and she becomes like family. There are brothers and sisters you get along better with but everyone's family and when something happens to one of them you can't help but care.

For weeks people wondered about her, e-mailed her, and tried to call her, but there was never a reply. Rumors spread about what had happened. They ranged from her killing someone to her saying something she wasn't supposed to. None of the rumors came from confirmable sources.

A month later, when it became official that she would never come back, I finally received an e-mail from her saying that she could talk if I wanted to call. Always in the mood for a bit of good gossip I of course took her up on the offer.[6]

"So what do you want to know?" Brenda asked immediately; there was no small talk.

---

6. It might seem that I was the last person Brenda would call, but in reality Brenda and I did, for the most part, get along. She had worked with me longer than anyone else, and thus knew I would be the one she trusted the most to spread the gossip tactfully.

"Are you okay?"

"I am."

"That's what we've worried most about."

"Where did everyone say I went?"

"Some said medical leave. Some said you finally went crazy and tried to kill Faren. Everyone said something."

"And you? What did you say?"

"I didn't know what to think. I just wanted you to be okay."

"So you want to know?"

"Of course I do."

"It was about having too many late fees on my card and not returning or paying to rent videos. That's the excuse, anyway. You know they've had it in for me for a long time. They finally got their chance."[7]

"That really sucks."

"You work for somewhere for so long and you feel like no one can touch you. Don't ever believe that. They can always touch you."

"Yeah."

"It's not so bad. They gave me a month's pay if I promised never to sue. I took it, because what could I do?"[8]

We talked a little about what was going on with other workers and then we said good-bye. I knew when I hung up the phone that that would be it. We'd occasionally e-mail and send greetings on holidays, but our relationship would change because we would no longer work together. What kind of relationship was that? It

---

7. They indeed had had it in for her; people didn't get fired for what she did. There were other reasons, but I won't write them here.

8. She was all about getting money. She once told me about a cop hitting a car and how if that happened to her she'd sue for everything she could even if it were minor and she had not been hurt. That was just the kind of person she was.

only can survive if you work together? Suddenly you no longer have anything in common?

People speculated about what had happened. I told them it was just a hundred little things that had added up to one big thing. I understood why they would want to get rid of someone like her, but I didn't understand why they had waited so long. There were dozens of other people like Brenda who worked throughout the library—some were even worse. Why was she the example? And why did they even have to make anyone the example? The decision to fire Brenda was solely business and not personal, and yet it changed the entire workplace, environment, and tone of the library. People walked with their heads lower. She was a casualty of workplace warfare, but her symbolic death had made us all victims to the war's brutality.

The only people who seemed able to work as if nothing had happened were the very people who knew exactly what had happened, the people who had decided to let her go. To them it was business, but only because they had distanced themselves to make it such. They didn't get involved in the lives of staff. Work was work and home was home and the two never came together. Is that how it was supposed to work? Was I supposed to come to work and say it was dog-eat-dog, we were all out to keep our jobs, and it was best not to get to know each other? Perhaps, but what kind of environment is that? The more I thought about it, the more I saw that might have been what management wanted. But that wasn't what the public wanted. We were there to serve them and put on a nice show. You can't do that without working with people you know well, not just professionally but also personally. But that just wasn't how it always was. In the end, it's true: no one is indestructible. No one's job is safe. We can all be replaced.

Epilogue

Two years had gone by since I left my old little library. I had grown. The old library had finally been rebuilt, and I would be returning to it.

It didn't seem the same when I went in. It was a new library, a changed library. Just like me, it too had changed. Things would never be the same. Two years. People had moved, got new jobs, been fired, been transferred, or retired. I stayed. I had my reasons. Of the many people who were there when I started, only three remained.

I went into the building before all the books came. I stood in the middle and just surveyed it. It was empty, just how I had left it, void of all books. But it was different than how I had left it, because, as I looked around this time, I could see where the books would go, where the children would roam, where I would sit. I could see the potential of something great. I could also see the potential of something big.

It would never be the little neighborhood library. This new library was more than three times its size. You can't have the same sense of community when you have something large. People who would be regular faces at a smaller library are mere background images at a place like this.

This is my life, my passion. I look ahead and see the road is long, but the road is bright.

~

The grand opening was grand, as it should have been. Everyone from the mayor to the governor was invited.[1]

We listened to the council members talk about how much they cared, but they didn't. They didn't care for us; they didn't care for the library; they cared only about looking good. They used their minutes to talk about the city's safety record, other things they've approved to build, and, of course, Disneyland and the two professional sports teams that call Anaheim home. There were over 100 Anaheim residents present, so you couldn't really blame the council members for campaigning, but it would have been nice to hear them sort of talk about what the library meant to them. But I'm not bitter.[2]

The truth was they wouldn't have known what to say, because libraries aren't for them. Libraries are for the community. When politicians go home, they order their books on Amazon; they don't come to the library.[3]

~

---

1. Of course, the governor didn't come.

2. I am, in fact, bitter.

3. I'm sure some do, but I have never known any to.

I feel old sometimes. I tell stories like a seasoned vet to young idealist rookies whose names I don't bother to remember. I'm only twenty-eight but I have battle wounds, which makes me older and wiser.

I used to go to staff functions and retirement parties and think about how they were just a bunch of old-timers and I couldn't relate. Now I not only relate, I have my own stories to tell.

～

The new library is like a new house; every day I see something new. It's sparse, but every day it grows with furniture, new books, and new computers. It's not like the old library; it has a personality all to itself. I miss the old library sometimes but I'm happy where I am.

In the end, it is a different library with different people and even a different attitude, but it's still a library. Ultimately, a library is a library.

FOR SHELVING

Some libraries are big, others small; some have food, others don't; some are quiet, some loud. But they're all libraries.

The success of Disneyland put Anaheim on the map. Families poured into the city. There was only one problem with the fledging city: how to get people to stay. Disneyland, at this point, was still a seasonal attraction. Hotels weren't eager to spend large amounts of money when their rooms would be filled for only part of the year.

In 1960 sixty-one business leaders came together and formed the Anaheim Visitor and Convention Bureau, with their main goal being how to capitalize on the success of Disneyland year-round. Their solution was simple: build a convention center. After the convention

(Continues)

(Continued)

center was built, Anaheim was ready for large-city status, complete with a baseball team, a hockey team, and, for a short time, a football team. It's grown from 15,000 people in the 1950s to 350,000 today.

I've heard awkward stories about people who've seen their patrons in an uncomfortable setting. It's never happened to me until quite recently. I was at a funeral. Can you see the writing on the wall? No? Let me elaborate just a bit more.

The church where the funeral was being held was only a few blocks from the library where I worked. The church's elementary school had visited the library a handful of times, and I was usually the one that read them stories.

After the funeral, as I walked through the parking lot with other mourners, I heard a kid yell from the playground on the opposite side of the parking lot: "Hey, it's the library guy." I've always wondered what it would be like to be a celebrity and not be able to go anywhere without someone shouting your name. I sort of felt like a celebrity at the funeral, and now I know how it feels, awkward—incredibly awkward.

I looked at the handful of kids who had gathered together after they heard the child's announcement. They stared at me with curious eyes and seemed excited that I had stumbled into their territory. I smiled, waved, and then bowed my head and pretended to be mournful. I hoped the wave would have been mighty enough to silence them. It wasn't.

Another child yelled across the parking lot: "What are you doing here, anyway?"

I looked around, hoping by chance no one else had noticed the scene. Unfortunately, people had. I wasn't about to yell out to the kids, "I'm at a funeral," so I pretended I hadn't heard them and walked quickly to my car.

That really sums up my life. I'm a celebrity to the community but to no one else—a librarian. Maybe I won't be remembered as a remarkable person. Chances are I won't be remembered at all, but for a small number of kids and adults I had made a difference. They might not remember me, but I played a part in what they have eventually become. That's who I was, and would be, and would always be: a librarian.

~

It seemed fitting to end this book someplace; at a library I didn't know with people I had never seen seemed as good a place as any. I picked quite randomly a library in the richly funded Orange County city of Brea.[4] The library was next to one of the nicest malls in the county, so I had high expectations.

I arrived five minutes before the library opened to observe. There was only a handful of people at the entrance but they looked like they could have just as easily be put in front of my library. There was a man dressed decently but carrying enough plastic bags to surely be homeless. There was an anxious Asian woman who stood inches from the front door just so she could be the first one in. There were elderly ladies who talked about how wonderful their little library was.

I could see the librarians inside and they could see me. They were in no hurry to open the doors, and I felt for them. I, too, had looked at those doors and dreaded the beginning of real work. They opened

---

4. A city known for taking the homeless and transporting them to a poorer city because it made the place looked run-down.

the library five minutes late because they were in no hurry to get their day started.

It was different standing on the outside looking in. I felt like a patron. I was angry when they opened late. I felt like they were wasting my time, even if it was only five minutes.

I surveyed the library when I first walked in. It looked old, like a library waiting for an update. I wanted to plug in my laptop but there were no outlets. I went to the information desk. The librarian was the typical stereotypical librarian—ugly, clunky glasses, hair in a tight bun, and clothing that could just as easily have been put on a man. She looked irritated when I asked her where I could plug in my laptop: "You have to use your own power supply." Then she turned away, like that was the only question I was allowed to ask. She was intimidating, just like all librarians could be.

The library was everything that was wrong with the modern library. It was not equipped for computers, there was no room for study groups, and no food or drinks were allowed. Fifty years ago libraries had no competitors. There were bookstores here and there but people went there to buy books; they did not go there for group study. Now people use bookstores the same way they used to use libraries. I've often asked fellow librarians how long before libraries start to realize that the modern library isn't a monopoly, that competition is fierce, and that they have to run the building as such?

There are few libraries that serve food and drink and I can't figure out why. It's not because they're worried about spills. That's what they say, but in reality the profit from selling books fully accommodates the cost of any spills. The real reason is because "that's the way it's always been done." I was at a library in Riverside and they had a vendor on the second floor selling drinks and pastries. He made at least a $1,000 a day and the library was sharing in that profit.

Libraries need to change, just like everything else does. They need to serve drinks, but the needs go deeper than that. What about the Dewey Decimal system? It's old school! You don't see that in bookstores. Sure, it's great in the large reference libraries, but those only account for a small percentage of all public libraries. Modern libraries need to go beyond Dewey and bank off the bookstore model. Create sections of subjects with large signs that clearly say these are religion books and these are craft books. If a person walks up to me and says "Where are the religion books?" and I say "In the 220s" they'll look puzzled, but if I point and say "Over there in the religion section," they'll get it. It's so simple.

And please! Please! Can we get a place to plug in the laptops, the iPods, the USB drives, and the cell phones? Get with the times, people! Almost every college student has a USB storage device, but few libraries will let you save to them. We don't have to destroy the library of the past. We just need to give it a face-lift.

~

When I was in college, I had one pair of nice pants and two button-up shirts; the rest of my closet was T-shirts and jeans. Now? There're jeans somewhere in there but I never wear them—perhaps I never will again. I keep them there more as a memory of who I was and where I've come. I wouldn't consider wearing them. Even when I go to the grocery store, I wear slacks. That's how sad I've become.

I became a librarian in some ways because that's just the path I was on at the time. I don't think anyone ever really knows what they'll be when they're grown up. They have things they enjoy, sure, but these things change as quickly as the day. I believe we are guided by destiny and chance. We stay with it not because it's what we always wanted to do but because we are happy. In the end, we all just want to be happy at what we do.

There are good days and bad days, but in the end I really can't complain.

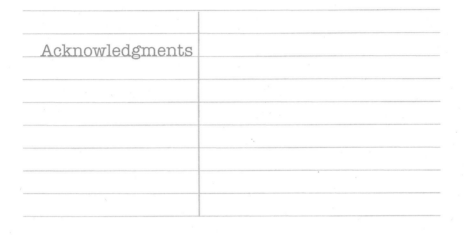

Acknowledgments

It is unfortunate that there must be heroes and villains to every true story. Ultimately, it is the writer who often comes across as the hero of the quest, but I would be nowhere without these villains, and I thank them. But this really isn't an acknowledgment so much as a statement.[1]

The first thing many people ask these days about a memoir is if it's true. It's appropriate for me to acknowledge this. Of course it is—kind of. Many things in the memoir have been exaggerated to protect the identities of a great many people, and to make this book more entertaining for you, my dear reader. Many characters are more compilations of several librarians and library support staffs that I have worked with than one person, though some are not. Everything in this book happened.[2] When, how, and with whom it happened does not really matter, does it? If you have a problem with such exaggerations, then I recommend you stay away from the humor

---

1. Unfortunately, a statement page could not be provided in this edition of the book.

2. Though some in less exaggerated forms.

section of your local library or bookstore. I also recommend you stay away from such classic true accounts as Mark Twain's *Roughing It*.[3]

I'd also like to clear up the fact that I believe Kurt Cobain did not commit suicide and in fact was murdered. Yes, it is indeed possible he somehow managed to pull the trigger of his shotgun with his toes,[4] but isn't it more fun to believe in conspiracies? And with that note, I think it is entirely likely that Marilyn Monroe did not commit suicide but was killed off by someone that Kennedy hired. Jim Morrison is also living in Spain under the name Jorge Ortez.

While some may not believe that it's appropriate to acknowledge, I disagree and will therefore acknowledge:

"A lot" should be one word. No one over the age of twenty-one can use it correctly anyway. "Whom" and "who" should be replaced with simply "who." Whenever possible, graphics should replace words.

It is true that in eleventh grade I failed the high school reading test and legally could not read. I eventually passed it, but I acknowledge it quite loudly because it's an example of how ridiculous public education can be. But how could I not equally acknowledge that, if I had passed it, it is entirely likely that I would not have majored in English or been inspired to write a book.

There are a number of other things that I should acknowledge since I'm acknowledging other embarrassing things like having the state of California say you couldn't read. They are, but are not limited to: listening to Bo Bice on several occasions and considering seeing him live; wearing boxers with Scooby-Doo on them (though I in no way endorse the show); having a huge man-crush on Mark Twain, Thomas Pynchon, and David Foster Wallace; reading an occasional book by John Grisham or Tom Clancy; nearly crying at the end of every *Princess Diaries* movie; peeing in the swimming pool when I was a kid; eating paste; having a huge crush on Flannery O'Connor; Screech being my favorite *Saved by the Bell* character. And finally, and most shamefully, not being a fan of the number twenty-two.

Wikipedia is *not* a good source for all your information; I acknowledge this. But I still occasionally use it,[5] and I also still encourage people to create false information about me on Wikipedia whenever possible.

---

3. Or really anything that Mark Twain wrote and said was true.

4. Even though he had shoes on.

5. By occasionally, I mean a lot, and by a lot I mean a lot.

I also acknowledge that I am not the Scott Douglas who sang in the Christian rock band White Heart and was later sent to prison on sex-related crimes. I have also never listened to the Christian rock group White Heart and do not understand how anyone's heart can be white. It makes no sense.

I have read every *Harry Potter*.[6]

I would like to acknowledge some of the best advice anyone ever gave me:[7] The lazy man works twice as hard.

I endorse the following companies/corporations and ask in return that they provide me with gift certificates and/or samples of their products:

- Microsoft
- Sony
- Samsung
- Toshiba
- Apple Corporation

The following bands/musicians (listed in alphabetical order) provided the white noise to my writing:

AC/DC; Aerosmith; The Album Leaf; Alter Bridge; Bad Company; The Beach Boys; The Beastie Boys; The Beatles; Beethoven; Big Tent Revival; Billy Joel; Bo Bice; Bob Dylan; Bobby Goldsboro; Bon Jovi; Boston; Bruce Springsteen; Buddy Holly; Chicago; Coldplay; Cold War Kids; Collective Soul; Creed; Danney Alkana; dc Talk; Deadboy and the Elephantmen; Dixie Chicks; Elton John; The Doors; The Eagles; Elvis; Eric Clapton; Evanescence; Everclear; Faith Hill; Fleetwood Mac; Garth Brooks; Ginny Owens; Goo Goo Dolls; Green Day; Guns N'Roses; The Hollow; Incubus; Jars of Clay; Jennifer Knapp; Jewel; John Denver; John Williams (the classical guitarist one); John Williams (the movie one); Johnny Cash; Journey; June Carter Cash; Kendall Payne; The Kry; Led Zepplin; Lenny Kravitz; Lifehouse; Linkin Park; Louis Armstrong; Lynyrd Skynyrd; The Mamas and the Papas; Matchbox Twenty; Metallica; Michael W. Smith; Michelle Branch; Nickelback; Nirvana; No Doubt;

---

6. A comment better suited for a statement page, but what can you do?

7. Even though the advice was not directed at me and I only heard it because I was eavesdropping.

Norah Jones; Patti Smith; Paul McCartney; Pearl Jam; PFR; Phil Collins; Pink Floyd; P.O.D.; Queen; Ray Charles; R.E.M.; Resurrection Band; Rich Mullins; Rolling Stones; Roy Orbison; Santana; Sarah McLachlan; Sevendust; Shakira; Sheryl Crow; The Shins; Simon & Garfunkel; Sixpence None the Richer; Smalltown Poets; Steppenwolf; Steven Curtis Chapman; Sting; Susan Tedeschi; Switchfoot; Third Day; Trans-Siberian Orchestra; U2; Vertical Horizon; The Village People; The Wallflowers; Weird Al Yankovic; The White Stripes; The Who; and Woody Guthrie.

I hereby acknowledge the following locations, which offered me excellent places to write this book:[8]

Brea Public Library, Brea, California; Biola University Library, La Mirada, California; Coffee Bean, Brea, California; Elva Haskett Library, Anaheim, California; Euclid Branch Library, Anaheim, California; Central Library, Anaheim, California; Sunkist Library, Anaheim, California; Fullerton College Library, Fullerton, California; California State University (Fullerton), Fullerton, California; Cerritos Public Library, Cerritos, California; Bedroom, Anaheim, California; Patio, Anaheim, California; car (at following stop lights: Lincoln/ Brookhurst; Broadway/Magnolia; Broadway/Euclid; Euclid/Ball; Commonwealth/Brookhurst; Valencia/Brookhurst); Hyatt Regency Century Plaza Hotel and Spa, Los Angeles, California; plane from Minnesota to Amsterdam (somewhere over the Atlantic); plane from Amsterdam to Minnesota (somewhere over the Atlantic); plane from Los Angeles to New York (approximately between Arizona and Mississippi River); plane from New York to Los Angeles (approximately between Detroit and Kansas); Kenyon University, Gambier, Ohio; hotel, Paris, France (name is a haze).

I should acknowledge that I tried to visit the Columbia University Library in New York, but was denied admittance even after informing them I was writing a book on libraries. I'm sure it's a nice building, though.

Wardrobe was purchased at the following locations:

Amazon.com; eBay; It's a Wrap; JC Penney; Levi's Factory Outlet; Old Navy; Orange County Fairgrounds; Nordstrom Rack; Ross; Target; Van Heusen.

---

8. And by excellent I mean they had chairs, lighting, and tables. I in no way mean that they were actually nice places, though some were.

Some say Sears is a nice place to buy clothing, but it's appropriate to acknowledge here that Sears is up to no good. When I was seventeen and had just gotten out of the hospital after spinal surgery a month before, I was tackled to the ground by Sears security, who accused me of stealing a $2 phone cord.[9] Apparently, on camera it had appeared that I had taken it, but when they later found the $2 phone cord, they apologized for the mistake.[10] I acknowledge that I have since avoided shopping at the store and it would perhaps be a good idea for you to as well.

There are a couple people I think it would be well to acknowledge and thank: My mom and first editor; my dad, who will try to read this book but will also be hoping for a condensed audio version and/or movie; my brother and his wife, Dorothy; John Warner, my editor at McSweeney's Internet Tendencies, who first told me I should write some of my library adventures down and then was kind enough to give me an avenue to publish them; Andrea Somberg, my patient literary agent, who was wise enough to believe a book about libraries could be sold to a publisher and who was good enough to actually sell it; Shaun Dillon, the fine editor at Da Capo, for believing in this book early on; all the other people at Da Capo I have failed to mention; Anaheim Public Library, for giving me the money to pay my bills; my dog, Shadow, who provided me companionship on several walks; Cornel Bonca, the first writing teacher who encouraged me to pursue writing; CSUF, for giving me a good education despite being a state school; Fullerton College, for giving me a good education despite being a community college; the cast and crew of *The Golden Girls*—they just don't make TV shows like that anymore; all the family and friends that I'm just too lazy to mention.

Obviously, this being a memoir, there are many people who appeared in this book that I should acknowledge; but, honestly, haven't I already acknowledged them? So what if I changed their names and identifying characteristics? They would know it was them if I pointed it out and said "That's you." I could acknowledge them—each and every one—but I'm not going to because (1) I just don't feel like it and (2) some would get mad and only a few would be flattered. If you want to be acknowledged and I have not acknowledged you here, then just come up to me sometime and say

9. I kid you not, he tackled me for a $2 phone cord.

10. Actually it was a store manager who apologized, and only after my mom complained.

"Hey, why don't you acknowledge me?" And I will acknowledge you right there on the spot.

I acknowledge Roland for all you have told me about French pop and also acknowledge that to this day I still have not listened to any of it. But I still, nonetheless, acknowledge you and wish you well.

I also encourage you, dear reader, to pick up the phone book, randomly select a name, and know that I am grateful to that person you have randomly found.

All of us have had muses in our lives—people who inspire us to do better and support us greatly when we endeavor to be creative and artistic. This book has had but one and her name is Diana. I acknowledge her.

In the spirit world, I would like to acknowledge God (not the secular one that people tend to throw out when they're trying to sound spiritual; or the Christian one that people say to sound righteous and better than you; rather the God I believe in—the one who has three parts: Father, Son, and Holy Spirit; the one who forgives me when I do something dumb; the one who does not condemn me when I break a promise or give food to a sinner—and on that note the one who doesn't praise me when I give food to a saint; the one who doesn't say I must vote Democratic or Republican. Yeah, that one. He's sort of been forgotten by postmoderns and Christians alike, but he's still around and I'm thankful for what he's done in my life and all the promises he kept with me. None of this would be possible without his presence in my life).

Finally I would like to acknowledge a certain writing instructor at Fullerton Community College who told me my writing was no good and that one day I would be serving him coffee at Starbucks. I will not say his name, but he knows who he is and he will be getting a copy of this book as proof that I am indeed not now, nor ever will be, serving him coffee at Starbucks. I acknowledge him because we all need people in our lives that we have to prove wrong.

NO ANIMALS WERE HARMED DURING THE MAKING OF THIS BOOK (ALTHOUGH MANY TREES DIED AND I'M SORRY FOR THIS, BUT UNTIL YOU PEOPLE GO DIGITAL AND BUY E-BOOKS I REALLY CAN'T DO ANYTHING ABOUT IT.)[11]

---

11. Bill Gates did not pay me to say the above, but I wish he had. He is very rich. I am not.